Insensible of Boundaries

Black Print and Organizing in the Long Nineteenth Century
offers new and innovative studies of Black print culture, social
movements, and Black organizing collectives to tell fuller stories
about the actors, ideas, and actions influencing practices of
Black freedom and their dissemination across generations.

Series editors:
P. Gabrielle Foreman
Department of English and African American Studies
Pennsylvania State University

Shirley Moody Turner
Department of English and African American Studies
Pennsylvania State University

Derrick Spires
Department of English
University of Delaware

The series is affiliated with the Center for Black Digital
Research (#DigBlk) at Pennsylvania State University.

Insensible of Boundaries

Studies in Mary Ann Shadd Cary

Edited by Kristin Moriah

PENN

UNIVERSITY OF PENNSYLVANIA PRESS

PHILADELPHIA

Published by
University of Pennsylvania Press
Philadelphia, Pennsylvania 19104-4112
www.pennpress.org

Printed in the United States of America on acid-free paper
10 9 8 7 6 5 4 3 2 1

A Cataloging-in-Publication record is
available from the Library of Congress

Hardback ISBN 978-1-5128-2661-6
eBook ISBN 978-1-5128-2662-3

maryann shadd

long before other women
you ran a newspaper started schools
let your voice ripple across the 49th and 51st line

neither home here or south of the border
staggered by brandings and whiplash
struck by bondsmen and shackles

at words with churches and abolitionists
who wanted nothing more than separate spaces
to house black bodies on their own

(in elgin dawn buxton winchester sandwich
haiti jamaica and sierra leone)

you used a man's name in print
but not amongst suffragettes
who had other ways to keep their distance

yet with both you cut a syntax
fierce and uncensored
and what those children you taught
learned became the call to all you left
across southern fields and eastern coasts
and within mid-western farms—

this was the space you balanced
and it was all that mattered
what your body told you
because of breasts buttocks blackness

what your words spelled inside the *provincial freeman*
when you crossed these lines
with everything you ever held precious
riding like lightning through this northern air

you were driven then across boundaries
in ways only a few could understand
so built your work like a well out of the earth

in chatham and windsor where you set down
into an endless resistance
                                        —charles c. smith

CONTENTS

BIOGRAPHICAL NOTE

Mary Ann Shadd Cary was born to Abraham Doras Shadd (1801–82) and Harriet Burton Parnell (1806–83) in Wilmington, Delaware, in 1823. She was the eldest of their thirteen children. The Shadds traced their roots to both Africa and Europe and were part of the free Black community in Delaware, although increasingly racist restrictions on education in the state prompted the family to move to Pennsylvania when Mary Ann was still a child. She completed her education and became a teacher at the age of sixteen, working in a number of states across the Northeast. Like her parents, she was also an active abolitionist.

In 1851, after attending the first North American Convention of Colored Freemen at St. Lawrence Hall in Toronto and at the invitation of Henry and Mary Bibb, prominent Black newspaper publishers and activists living in Sandwich, Canada West (now Windsor, Ontario), she moved to Canada and opened a school for refugees from American slavery.

In 1852 she published *A Plea for Emigration; or, Notes of Canada West*, a political pamphlet in support of Canadian immigration for those seeking to escape the effect of the Fugitive Slave Act of 1850. In 1853, she published the first issue of the *Provincial Freeman*, with the help of Samuel Ringgold Ward and Rev. Alexander McArthur. For a time, Shadd (later Shadd Cary) shielded her role in the paper's publication and editorship in order to evade criticism due to her gender. In fact, she published work anonymously and pseudonymously throughout her life, in addition to spelling her name using various combinations of her given name, Shadd, and her married name, Cary. Her newspaper was culturally and politically important, but it folded in 1860 due to financial concerns.

Thanks to the *Provincial Freeman*, Mary Ann Shadd Cary is now most widely known as the first Black woman to publish and edit a newspaper in North America. Shadd Cary's prolific editorial work during her time in Canada includes Osborne P. Anderson's *A Voice from Harper's Ferry* (1861), an account of the raid on Harpers Ferry written by the only surviving Black member of John Brown's party. However, throughout her life she held many roles and was also known for her accomplishments as an educator, abolitionist, suffragist, and lawyer.

She married entrepreneur Thomas F. Cary in 1856. They had two children together, Sarah and Linton, before Thomas F. Cary's untimely death in 1860. Shadd Cary remained in Chatham, Ontario, for the first few years of the Civil War, and in the wake of her husband's death. But in 1864, at the encouragement of her friend and colleague Martin R. Delany, she joined the effort to recruit Black soldiers for the Civil War at a recruiting base in New Albany, Indiana.

She returned to the United States permanently after the Civil War, in 1865. She and her children eventually settled in Washington, D.C. There, she taught and pursued a law degree at Howard University. She also became active in the women's suffrage movement and the temperance movement. Toward the end of her life, she ran a legal practice from her home and continued to write for the Black press. She died of stomach cancer in her seventieth year.

ACKNOWLEDGMENTS

This volume is the product of luck, determination, and vision on the part of many. As a newly minted assistant professor, my conversations with Gabrielle Foreman about how to bring the Colored Conventions Project into the classroom evolved into envisioning new research collaborations. Our shared drive to make Mary Ann Shadd Cary's voice more resonant in scholarly discourse informs this volume. This project is emblematic of the dynamic research possibilities that emerged from workflows of the Center for Black Digital Research, where Jim Casey, Lauren Cooper, and Gabrielle Foreman have fostered a culture of innovation in a new generation of Black scholars and students of the Black diaspora. My partnership with the Center for Black Digital Research has allowed me to meet incredible colleagues like Nneka Dennie, whose dedication to the publication of the collected works of Mary Ann Shadd Cary is so crucial right now.

The Social Sciences and Humanities Research Council provided critical financial support in the form an Insight Development Grant that has funded this work. The Center for Black Digital Research, the Penn State Humanities Institute, and the Just Transformations Fellowship at Penn State eased the pressure of the tenure track just enough to help me focus on editing, writing, and organizing.

I had the good fortune to be able to share the very early, quite rough draft of the introduction to this volume during talks at the Rare Book School, panels at the Association for Documentary Editing conference, the Delaware Historical Society, and the 2022 Emancipation Day Celebration hosted by the Ontario Black Historical Society. The generosity of my hosts and the organizers for those events have all contributed to the success of this project. My work with Sean Smith at Archives Ontario to digitize the Mary Ann Shadd Cary fonds and make them publicly accessible has introduced me to new ways to think about her public-facing legacy. At the University of Pennsylvania Press, Walter Biggins has been a strong supporter and clear adviser. This work could not have been done without them.

Of course, this project would not be possible without the path carved by trailblazing scholars like Jane Rhodes, Carla Peterson, and Adrienne Shadd whose attention to the life of Mary Ann Shadd Cary has informed generations of Black feminist scholars and remains an important touchstone for so many others. But my work has also brought me into conversation with women like Shannon Prince and Melissa Nelson, whose work within Canadian institutions builds on the stunning legacy of Mary Ann Shadd Cary. Scholars like Natasha Henry and Channon Oyeniran exemplify the drive to organize and educate Black communities in Ontario about their history, and it has been an honor to get to know them over the course of this project.

At Queen's University, I have benefited immensely from the support, friendship, and mentorship of Katherine McKittrick, a generous reader of drafts and proposals and a source of general encouragement. The work that Katherine has put into building a strong Black Studies program at Queen's University is an example of the Black feminist organizing principles that characterize the work of women like Mary Ann Shadd Cary. Katherine has long understood the value and relevance of Mary Ann Shadd Cary scholarship and the future possibilities it opens, and I am grateful for it.

Under the leadership of my colleague Sam McKegney, the Department of English and Creative Writing generously provided subvention funding to support the publication of images in this volume and helped to administrate my research leave at the Pennsylvania State University in 2022. I am grateful for my department's unwavering support of this work and his advocacy.

I have worked closely with Rachel Fernandes as a research assistant on this project for several years. Her dedication to the work of the Center for Black Digital Research and Mary Ann Shadd Cary has been a boon. In a similar way, the enthusiasm of graduate and undergraduate students who have taken courses on Black archival practices and nineteenth-century Black literature has revealed anew the ongoing appeal of Mary Ann Shadd Cary. Muna Dahir, Milka Njoroge, Marcus Harwood Jones, Melissa Noventa, Sydney Searchwell-Simpson, Makaila Atsonglo, and Tianna Edwards bring an electricity into our shared learning spaces that has been inspiring.

Friends near and far helped to ground me during this work. Conversations about editing and writing with Kate Broad, Karen Dubinsky, Susan Belyea, Kandice Chuh, and Ashwini Vasanthakumar kept me clear-eyed and buoyant.

The First Book writing group formed by my former classmates at the CUNY Graduate Center, Sharon Tran, Frances Tran, Kristina Huang, Chris

Eng, and Jesse Schwartz, read early drafts of my chapter on Mary Ann Shadd Cary and Elizabeth Taylor Greenfield, provided valuable editorial feedback, and acted as sounding boards during conversations about academic publishing and other early career issues. Our Zoom sessions were an important outlet during the COVID-19 pandemic, as I worked on this project.

My family has always kept me grounded in crucial ways. June, Chris, Alexis, and I nurtured and protected each other before, during, and after unprecedented times. I only wish that Marjorie Owen Moriah had been here to see it, too.

I began working on this volume before the pandemic, and I asked my contributors to begin thinking about their chapters during some of the most trying months of that ordeal. *Mary Ann Shadd Cary in the Here and Now* could not exist without their support, commitment, and belief that, in the midst of it all, Mary Ann Shadd Cary and the lessons we might still learn from her matter. Their scholarship speaks to the best parts of the world we are in and what we strive to bring into the world we are building.

"Who Am I Now?"

Toward a Mary Ann Shadd Cary Renaissance

KRISTIN MORIAH

Stated plainly, the facts of her life are as follows: Mary Ann Shadd Cary was born in Wilmington, Delaware, in 1823 at a time when owning Black Americans was still legal within the state and a driving force in its economy. Her parents, Abraham Doras Shadd and Harriet Burton Parnell, were born free, but they did not take their freedom lightly. The Shadds were conductors on the Underground Railroad and active members of the abolitionist movement. Their eldest daughter, Mary Ann, "described her father, Abraham D. Shadd, as the chief brakeman on the Delaware Underground Railroad."[1] Education was a central value for the Shadd family, and they fought to ensure that each of their thirteen children had the opportunity to attend school. The Shadds left the state of Delaware when educating Black children became illegal there, settling in West Chester, Pennsylvania. Abolitionist activism and the importance of education were lessons that the Shadd children took to heart. Six years after leaving Delaware, at the age of sixteen, Mary Ann Shadd would eventually become a teacher. She taught at schools in Pennsylvania, New York, Washington, D.C., and Canada West. She began writing and participating in Black political discourse at an early age. She self-published her first pamphlet, "Hints to the Colored People of the North," in 1849 when she was only twenty-five years old. Her determination to write and participate in literary discourses was intense. In that same year, her letters to Frederick Douglass were published in the *North Star*. Like her father before her, Mary Ann Shadd Cary was an active participant in the Colored Conventions movement, a rarity for Black women in the nineteenth century.

As a young activist, she attended the first North American Convention of Colored Freemen held in Toronto at St. Lawrence Hall in 1851. Soon after, Mary Ann Shadd Cary published *A Plea for Emigration* (1852), a document that firmly established her support for the project of Black migration to Canada in the wake of the Fugitive Slave Act of 1850. Mary Ann Shadd Cary eventually immigrated to Windsor, Ontario. She founded the *Provincial Freeman* newspaper in 1853, becoming the first Black woman editor and publisher in North America. Through the *Provincial Freeman*, she fostered a critical forum for intellectual and political exchange across borders and Black communities. It remains one of the most important records of early Black life in Canada and a testament to the broad spectrum of Black politics and print in North America. It also established Shadd Cary as a counterpoint to canonical writers like Susanna Moodie, a white Canadian settler whose memoir *Roughing It in the Bush: Life in Canada* (1851) became emblematic of nineteenth-century Canadian women's writing.

As a progressive journalist, staunch abolitionist, and political activist, Mary Ann Shadd Cary pushed the boundaries of expectations for Black women in the nineteenth century. Her husband, Thomas Cary, died in 1860, only four years and eleven months after their wedding. Eventually, she and her young children, Sarah and Linton, moved back to the United States. Shadd Cary began a new chapter that included working as a recruitment officer for the Union Army. Mary Ann Shadd Cary became the only Black woman from Canada that we know of to help recruit Black Union soldiers for the war effort. After the Civil War, upon graduation from Howard University, she went on to become one of the first Black women in the United States to earn a law degree. She was the first Black woman to vote in a national election in the United States. She led a life of many firsts. Her exceptional achievements have not gone unnoticed by major North American institutions. Since 1994, she has been officially recognized as a person of historical significance by the government of Canada. In 1998 she was inducted into the National Women's Hall of Fame in the United States. An overview of Shadd Cary's legacy and life greets visitors as they enter the National Museum of African American History in Washington, D.C., one of her hometowns. Her house on W Street NW in Washington, D.C., is a national historic landmark. Recently, the Archives Ontario Mary Ann Shadd Cary fonds (a cache of her correspondence, handwritten drafts, and other ephemera) have been accepted for entry into Canada Memory of the World Register by the Canadian Commission for UNESCO.

Mary Ann Shadd Cary was a notable member of the class of Black feminist intellectuals that would become known as "race women." Brittney Cooper explains that race women "explicitly fashioned for themselves a public duty to serve their people through diligent and careful intellectual work and attention to 'proving the intellectual character' of the race."[2] Though Cooper focuses on Black women intellectuals in the post-Reconstruction United States, when we look at Mary Ann Shadd Cary, we find strong evidence that the activist tradition of Black women intellectuals in North America has long roots. Shadd Cary stands as an early model of how Black women could seize opportunities to shape public discourse while overcoming substantial barriers. As legal historian Martha Jones puts it, Shadd Cary was part of the Black vanguard.[3] And yet, during her lifetime she faced harsh public criticism and rejection for her monumental efforts. Describing her first pamphlet. "Hints to the Colored People of the North," a correspondent for the *North Star* reported that "very little money has been paid for it," and that some readers "said that had they known that the work contained some things which it does, they would not have had it as a gift."[4] Undaunted, Shadd Cary insisted on the right to be heard in person as well as in print. She was one of only three women delegates to participate in the 1855 Colored Convention in Philadelphia, a victory that was won in the face of significant opposition to women speakers.[5] As a result, she faced criticism and derision in abolitionist newspapers.[6] Critics took particular issue with her willingness to transgress gender boundaries.[7] Some of that pushback resulted in outright omission from historic records. For example, speaking of the 1855 Colored Convention, Gabrielle Foreman notes that "nowhere does the powerful emigration debate between her and fellow delegate J. J. Bias that spilled over into the postconvention coverage appear."[8] So, while Mary Ann Shadd Cary seems to have always occupied the outer limits of nationhood and gender, her positionality was a both blessing and a curse. She was not invested in the respectability politics that were so important to Black political leaders during the period and she paid a price for it.[9] In contemporary discourse, she is someone Stefano Harney and Fred Moten might describe as a subversive intellectual.[10]

Nevertheless, over the span of seven decades, Mary Ann Shadd Cary took on many professional roles including educator, abolitionist, editor, writer, cultural critic, and entrepreneur. Despite these stunning accomplishments, considerations of her legacy have often been circumscribed by gender.

W. E. B. Du Bois's description of Shadd Cary is informative here. Explaining that she was "well-educated, vivacious, with determination shining from her sharp eyes," Du Bois also takes the time to write that Shadd Cary: "was tall and slim, of that ravishing dream-born beauty,—that twilight of the races which we call mulatto."[11] Here, Du Bois's patronizing description of Shadd Cary's body and mind is significant because it points to the way that Shadd Cary's prodigious cultural contributions were often minimized by the fact of her gender. The implications of this kind of sexism have been profound—her male colleagues and interlocutors (Frederick Douglass, Martin Delany, William Still, and Henry Bibb to name a few) have long enjoyed significant critical attention. Today, a cursory search of the MLA International Bibliography reveals fewer than twenty scholarly works about Mary Ann Shadd Cary. A similar search of the Arts & Humanities Citation Index reveals even fewer hits.[12] The dearth of critical attention is especially unusual given that during her lifetime her outspokenness in writing and in public was frequently a subject of news and even gossip. Here, of course, I refer not only to early, occasionally glowing, reports about her activism in publications like the *North Star*, but to the harsh criticism she faced from foes like Henry Bibb, the publisher of the *Voice of the Fugitive*, who famously claimed that "Miss Shadd has said and written many things which we think will add nothing to her credit as a lady."[13]

In other words, Mary Ann Shadd Cary was a polarizing yet notable trailblazing nineteenth century Black feminist with radical politics who occupied multiple subject positions during her lifetime. She was adventurous, unpredictable, and prolific. She was always on the move. In material like an evocative letter written to her brother at the beginning of her sojourn in Canada, we can sense her breathless excitement for the controversial project of Canadian settlement for Black Americans seeking to escape chattel slavery.[14] In that letter, now in the Archives Ontario Mary Ann Shadd Cary fonds, find evidence that "in anything relating to our people," she was "insensible of boundaries," and we get an inkling of the strength of her political motivations and her prose.[15] Of course, what began as a short visit to a Colored Convention ended up as a major intervention into Black life and politics. A strident advocate for immigration to Canada in her early adulthood, Shadd Cary dove headfirst into early Black Canadian political debates around heated issues like segregated schooling, Black political organizing tactics, and white philanthropy when she moved north of the border. Even from a contemporary vantage point, her early life and activism can appear almost like a whirlwind. She has always been hard to pin down. Shadd Cary's commitment to the plight of Black immigrants to Canada and her Canadian citizenship notwithstanding, some Canadians understand her as a U.S. phenomenon. By contrast, in the United States, she has become increasingly recognized for her stunning professional achievements and for her role in Black political organizing before, during, and after the U.S. Civil War.

There have been several attempts to fix her in the public imagination and perhaps right past wrongs. In recent years, public works of art dedicated to Mary Ann Shadd Cary have popped up in major cities in Canada and the United States. The tributes piled up rapidly as the two hundredth anniversary of her birth approached. In 2021 a post office in Wilmington, Delaware, a city that remains closely associated with the Shadd family, was named after her. On October 9, 2020, Mary Ann Shadd Cary was featured in a Google Doodle in honor of her 197th birthday. A Google image search reveals even more contemporary art in her likeness. Significantly, in June 2018, she was the subject of an "Overlooked No More" obituary in the *New York Times*.[16] The column was meant to make amends for the paper's historic disinterest in the life stories of individuals who are not white men. It provided a comprehensive overview of Mary Ann Shadd Cary's life, but the column was slightly misleading. In Black intellectual circles in the nineteenth century and beyond Mary Ann Shadd Cary was quickly recognized as a person worth watching. But we must remember that Shadd Cary was identified as a figure of interest by journalists reporting the goings on of Colored Conventions well before the Civil War. And her name appears frequently in catalogs of notable Black women written by her contemporaries and Black scholars in the early part of the twentieth century. In the Black communities in Canada and the United States where many Shadd family descendants still live, her memory is alive and well thanks to the ongoing work of the Shadd family and its extended members, including independent historians Adrienne Shadd and Irene Moore Davis. One might argue that the Black community's interest and investment in Mary Ann Shadd Cary never died.

Her cultural and historic importance feels like an open secret. In some circles, it *almost* goes without saying that Mary Ann Shadd Cary is one of the most significant Black feminists in North American history. It is a paradox that scholars have grappled with over decades. Despite a resurgence of interest in nineteenth-century Black life and culture, it seems that Mary Ann Shadd Cary has never quite been given her due in terms of recognition as an important figure in nineteenth-century Black organizing, arts, and letters.

This volume aims to resolve some of that tension. What happens when we rectify the tendency to ignore the ways she has been remembered and center Mary Ann Shadd Cary's voice in debates about Black citizenship and belonging? What impact can she have on our understanding of Black political organizing, print culture, and public life in the nineteenth century? What does her varied and long-standing engagement in the public sphere tell us about gender, politics, and place? These are questions that continue to be worth answering when it comes to Mary Ann Shadd Cary. Along with my contributors, I argue that she provides a model for thinking about Black feminist intellectual life and Black life across the Black diaspora that has rarely been paralleled. Her impact on Black feminist intellectual history has been profound and continues to reverberate.

This volume of essays draws from the field of Black feminist studies and scholarly investigations of the lives of nineteenth-century Black women whose literary contributions were often overlooked in the same way that Mary Ann Shadd Cary has been. We owe so much to Black women like Mary Ann Shadd Cary in the here and now. To be sure, a return to Shadd Cary began in the 1970s with the republication of a 1926 biographical sketch written by Sarah Cary Evans, her daughter.[17] The 1970s marked a pivotal moment in the study of Black women's intellectual history. SaraEllen Strongman notes the significance of that era and has termed "the discovery and reclamation of Black women writers from the past" that took place during the 1970s "the archaeological impulse."[18] In the case of Mary Ann Shadd Cary, that impulse has had deep implications. Historian Jane Rhodes notes that "few nineteenth-century African American women produced a written record that has survived the passage of time. This lack of documentary sources has been a key obstacle in the writing of Black women's intellectual history"[19] This, too, is changing. With the help of my colleagues at the Center for Black Digital Research (CBDR), I have fostered conversations with Archives Ontario about the permanent acquisition the Mary Ann Shadd Cary fonds.[20] At CBDR, the work of Shirley Moody Turner and her team to create an online paper locator for Black women organizers, the Black Women Organizers Archive (BWOA), also promises to shift the field. The BWOA directs researchers to all known repositories for nineteenth-century Black women organizers like Mary Ann Shadd Cary. Changes like these will lay the groundwork for much-needed future research in this field. As it stands, Jane Rhodes's *Mary Ann Shadd Cary: The Black Press and Protest in the Nineteenth Century* (1998) remains the most comprehensive single-authored work about Mary Ann Shadd Cary nearly twenty-five years after its publication. Rhodes's scholarship situates Mary Ann Shadd Cary in a long line of Black women journalists that includes the legendary Ida B. Wells. Rhodes's biography reminds us that Mary Ann Shadd Cary is also a foremother of many contemporary Black women journalists.[21] *The Black Press and Protest* stands alongside Carla Peterson's *"Doers of the Word": African-American Women Speakers and Writers in the North (1830–1880)* (1995) as one of the most important scholarly sources about Mary Ann Shadd Cary. In *"Doers of the Word,"* Peterson traces an interdisciplinary approach to the study of early Black feminists. Peterson argues that Black women writers like Mary Ann Shadd Cary were so estranged from the nation that the interrelated questions of how to address mainstream North American society and how to make themselves at home there formed the basis for their writing.[22] This nuanced analysis of the rhetorical moves made by Shadd Cary and her contemporaries encourages close reading of a range of their writing and has informed generations of Black feminist scholars.

While *Insensible of Boundaries: Studies in Mary Ann Shadd Cary* builds on the intellectual labor of Black feminist scholars such as Jane Rhodes and Carla Peterson, it also seeks to reinvigorate and expand the field by bringing scholars on both sides of the U.S.-Canadian border into a sustained conversation. The care taken to solicit research from scholars on both sides of the Canada-U.S. border speaks to Shadd Cary's investment in both countries and her pragmatic approach to citizenship and belonging. Scholarly articles about Mary Ann Shadd Cary from the late 1990s and early 2000s by Christian Olbey and Shirley J. Yee build on the momentum created by Rhodes and Peterson.[23] More recently, scholars like Ikuko Asaka, Andrea Stone, Winfried Siemerling, and Theresa Zackodnik have included chapters in their scholarly monographs that contextualize Mary Ann Shadd Cary's broad impact.[24] A recent scholarly edition of her *Plea for Emigration*, edited by Phanuel Antwi, has made Mary Ann Shadd Cary's most famous literary work more accessible for postsecondary students.[25] Even so, a recent anthology edited by Nneka Dennie, *Mary Ann Shadd Cary: Essential Writings of a Nineteenth-Century Black Radical Feminist* (2023), has redirected attention to the depth and breadth of her intellectual contributions. Dennie's work picks up where Teresa C. Zackodnik leaves off in *"We Must Be Up and Doing": A Reader in Early African American Feminisms* (2010), an anthology that contextualizes select speeches and editorials by figures Mary Ann Shadd Cary, Sojourner Truth, and Frances Ellen Watkins Harper. And there is, thankfully, more work to come.

Clearly indebted to such innovative Black feminist scholarship, in this volume, my contributors and I aim to strengthen the argument for the significance of Mary Ann Shadd Cary's intellectual contributions and cultural criticism in its own time and ours. In the past, this task has proven difficult because of the depth, breadth, and numerous locations of Mary Ann Shadd Cary's work. And so, despite her sizable accomplishments and her impact on Black life in North America, *Insensible of Boundaires: Studies in Mary Ann Shadd Cary* is the first edited collection about this iconoclastic thinker. Though this is the first collection of scholarly essays on Shadd Cary, scholars whose work is featured here are not the first to delve into Shadd Cary's legacy. Building on ongoing conversations, with this collection, the contributors and I examine the lasting impact of Mary Ann Shadd Cary's cultural significance and intellectual contributions. Turning a critical eye toward Mary Ann Shadd Cary today provides us with insight into the very foundations of Black intellectual life in North America and across the Black diaspora. This work is crucial to our conception of Black life. Derrick Spires has argued that in analyses of the concept of citizenship in Black print culture, "overemphasizing Douglass flattens out a vibrant intellectual network of newspaper correspondents, convention goers, pamphleteers and artists, whose key texts and forms were more often than not generated collectively."[26] While Spires focuses on the articulation and enactment of Black citizenship in early Black print culture, I suggest that Mary Ann Shadd Cary life and work provide an ample addition to such studies. Winfried Siemerling argues that, "as one of the most important Black activists and writers . . . in Canada, she contributed decisively to its Black cultural development but also helped to shift, from her vantage point north of the border, the focus of emigrationist debates in the United States."[27] Today, we again find ourselves in the midst of debates around Black citizenship, immigration, and enfranchisement across North America. As such, time is right for us to take up Mary Ann Shadd Cary's mantle. In this volume, I have centered scholarly work from a broad range of interdisciplinary perspectives including but not limited to historical, literary, gender, ecological, bibliographical, visual, sound, and performance studies. On these pages, my colleagues and I work across scholarly boundaries as we reexamine the work of one of the key figures of Black feminist thought and action in North America. This methodology is deeply informed by Mary Ann Shadd Cary's thinking about the importance of boundary crossing to Black life and political organizing.

Insensible of Boundaries: Studies in Mary Ann Shadd Cary is divided into four parts. In the Prelude, or "The Struggle to Emerge: What Black (Canadian) Studies Might Mean; or, The Return of Mary Ann Shadd Cary," Rinaldo Walcott revisits the potential of Shadd Cary's symbolic role in the North American landscape and beyond. It has been over twenty years since Walcott, at the forefront of Black Canadian studies, posed the questions "who is she?" and "what is she to you?" and asked how Black studies, Canadian studies, and Black diasporic discourses might adopt this nineteenth-century figure as an intellectual guide while arguing for a sustained conversation concerning Blackness. In some ways, the answer seems simple: Mary Ann Shadd Cary was a trailblazing North American Black feminist, activist, journalist, and educator. Yet despite the groundbreaking work of Walcott and his colleagues in Black Canadian studies, public awareness of Mary Ann Shadd Cary remains minimal in North America. In this volume, Walcott revisits that earlier moment in the project of Canadian multiculturalism and finds that while Mary Ann Shadd Cary's name may have more currency today, the kinds of Black radical politics to which Shadd Cary devoted her life are often stalled by contemporary indigenization, equity, inclusion and accessibility measures. Walcott reminds us that we still have some miles to go in the ongoing project of Black liberation.

The chapters in Part I, "'To Set Forth the Advantages of Residence in a Country': Black Feminist Geographies," explore Mary Ann Shadd Cary's relationship to immigration, nationalism, land, and colonization. In "Two Mary Carys in Canada West," Jewon Woo investigates Mary Ann Shadd Cary's relationship to Mary Bibb, a fellow immigrant to Canada and the spouse of *Voice of the Fugitive* publisher Henry Bibb, Shadd Cary's very public adversary. Woo explains that the two Marys nearly collaborated on a quarterly entitled *Afric American Repository* and posits that the two women's proposed collaboration leads us to questions about Mary Ann Shadd's relationship with other Black women activists, and further about Black women's transformative friendship for shared interests, which has been rarely mentioned in the study of Shadd Cary. Woo's chapter offers an alternative understanding of Shadd Cary's relationship with Mary Bibb and other Black feminist activists like Frances Ellen Watkins Harper, Charlotte Forten, and Charlotte Ray. In "Mary Ann Shadd Cary in Mexico," Kirsten Lee expands the study of Shadd Cary as a transnational Black Canadian-American figure to enrich her analysis of Black liberation in the Global South. Linking Canadian studies, Black feminism, Indigenous studies, and nineteenth-century American literature, this essay examines the political intersection that Shadd Cary inhabits and theorizes as a Black feminist emigrationist. Lee focuses sharply on the role of Mexico and Central America in Shadd Cary's political thought, particularly in her 1852 treatise *A Plea for Emigration; or, Notes of Canada West*, which includes Mexico as a territory of note in its full title. "Mary Ann Shadd Cary's Black Soil Ecology," Eunice Toh considers the racial politics of U.S. agriculture in relation to Black emigration in the nineteenth century. Toh focuses on the way that Mary Ann Shadd Cary's *A Plea for Emigration; or, Notes of Canada West* (1852) takes up "ecological themes in its promotion of Black emigration from the United States to Canada." Toh points out that "while one might expect this pamphlet to focus on the moral, social, and political conditions of the region," the pamphlet starts "with extensive information on the quality of the region's climate and soil." This starting point leads Toh to consider "the material and symbolic possibilities of Shadd Cary's ecological mediations." Taken together, these chapters shed new light on one of Mary Ann Shadd Cary's place-based politics.

Part II, "'To Display Her Powers': Mary Ann Shadd Cary's Impact on Black Theater, Sound, and Performance," focuses on the work of nation-building and the Black creative work that Mary Ann Shadd Cary has inspired. In "Mary Ann Shadd Cary, Her Life and Legacy: A Production," Lynnette Young Overby and her students discuss the process of creating, producing, and assessing the performances of the dance production *Mary Ann Shadd Cary, Her Life and Legacy*. According to Overby and her collaborators, the production demonstrates how arts-based research can be used to illuminate African American history and develop a more dynamic understanding of Shadd Cary as a complex historical figure for artists, performers, and audiences. In "'A Greater Compass of Voice': Elizabeth Taylor Greenfield and Mary Ann Shadd Cary Navigate Black Performance" Kristin Moriah examines Mary Ann Shadd Cary's interest in America's first Black opera singer, Elizabeth Taylor Greenfield, and finds that the two shared much in common, including a position in the public eye and investment in border crossings of all sorts. These chapters affirm the significance of Shadd Cary's investment in arts and culture, as evidenced on the pages of the *Provincial Freeman*, and her role as a source of inspiration for contemporary arts and entertainment.

Part III, "'Led as by Inspiration': Black Feminist Activism," delves deeply into the feminist aspects of Shadd Cary's activism. In "Plotting New Gardens: The Black Feminist Roots of Community-Building in *A Plea for Emigration*,"

R. J. Boutelle and Marlas Yvonne Whitley examine the role of Black feminist praxis in Mary Ann Shadd Cary's writing. They argue that *A Plea for Emigration; or, Notes on Canada West* (1852) also afforded Shadd an early opportunity to cultivate her Black feminist thinking. Boutelle and Whitley's analysis lays bare the underlying Black feminist ethos of community-building that Shadd advances more explicitly in her later writings. They argue that *A Plea for Emigration* is deeply invested in Black feminist ethics of collectivity, which emphasizes community uplift and interdependence as opposed to colonialist romances of individualism. In "'They Would Agitate for the Independence of Thought and Action': Mary Ann Shadd Cary's Black Feminist Organizing in Washington, D.C., 1867–93," Brandi Locke takes a closer look at Mary Ann Shadd Cary's political activism during her time in Washington, D.C., in order to underscore Shad Cary's contributions to Black feminist political consciousness. Locke's extended view of Shadd Cary's intellectual development and political contributions shifts our attention away from Shadd Cary's pamphlets and her editorials for the *Provincial Freeman*. Locke contends that "Shadd Cary's mounting dissatisfaction with her own continued marginalization in movements and her continued precarity in society inspired a profound transformation of her political consciousness and organizing methods." The work in this part stands as a testament to Shadd Cary's deeply considered intellectual practice.

The closing part, "'Subjects Better Understood, and Within Her Sphere': Black Digital Humanities," includes chapters that incorporate methodologies like the digital humanities in Black feminist research. In "Dimensions of Scale: Invisible Labor, Editorial Work, and the Future of Quantitative Literary Studies," Lauren Klein compares the editorial work of Mary Ann Shadd Cary and Lydia Maria Child to demonstrate the way that digital humanities methods like topic modeling and statistical analysis can aid in the identification and description of their otherwise obscured editorial labor. In "Parsing the Special Characters of African American Print Culture: Mary Ann Shadd and the * Limits of Search," Jim Casey, cofounder of the Colored Conventions Project, also offers a significant example of the role of digital tools in the study of Mary Ann Shadd Cary. Reading the asterisks found on the pages of the *Provincial Freeman* as evidence of Mary Ann Shadd Cary's authorship, Casey argues for a reevaluation of the limits of search tools in digitized newspapers. Finally, in "Mapping Mary Ann Shadd Cary: Using Bibliographic Analysis to Uncover Labor," Demetra McBrayer uses descriptive bibliography to examine the *Provincial Freeman* and argues that Shadd exemplifies the intersectional sensibility and focus on collectivity that scholar Patricia Hill Collins argues are essential to Black feminist thought. With this in mind, McBrayer asks "how the methodologies of digital humanities and book history can push against the inherent aspects of those fields that obscure or overlook Black life to center and celebrate it." In the process, they add immeasurably to our understanding of the extent of Shadd Cary's editorial labor and gives us a preview of new kinds of Mary Ann Shadd Cary scholarship to come.

The title of this introduction is a nod to Rinaldo Walcott's landmark 2000 essay about Mary Ann Shadd Cary and a nod to Beyoncé's "Summer Renaissance" (2022). It is meant to signify the centrality of reinvention, renewal, playfulness, and subversiveness to Black feminist intellectual history and praxis. Mary Ann Shadd Cary is perhaps the same as she always was, but we are beginning to know her and her many facets a bit better. The title is also a gesture toward the way that the spirit of collaboration and innovation is embedded in the work. This volume was developed through my collaboration with the Center for Black Digital Research, including a symposium that was held in fall 2021. I think of this as an example of the way Mary Ann Shadd Cary has directly impacted our collective methodologies. Such collaborations hold public engagement, openness, and accessibility as central values. Our aim has always been to foster further conversations and new work. With the publication of this volume, my hope is that we will see an even greater resurgence of scholarship, art, and performance that testifies to Mary Ann Shadd Cary's deep and lasting impact on Black culture. So, in the spirit of Mary Ann Shadd Cary, my hope is that we will continue to do more *writing*, *reading*, *creating*, and *organizing*, and, if need be, talk less.

A Note on the Text

In *Insensible of Boundaries: Studies in Mary Ann Shadd Cary*, Mary Ann Shadd Cary is referred to as Shadd Cary, using both her given and married names, in recognition of nineteenth-century Black feminist emphasis on family and community ties.[28] Scholars differ as to the correct spelling of Shadd Cary's name. As with many things, her take on names is difficult to pin down. Shadd Cary signed her correspondence and published works in multiple ways throughout her life. And after her marriage to Thomas A. Cary, she was referred to in the press in a number of different ways, including Mary A. S. Cary,[29] and Mary A. Shadd Cary,[30] Mary Shadd Cary,[31] and M. A. S. Cary.[32]

From this, we can surmise that the conscious adoption of the name Cary was important to her, as was her enduring connection to the formidable Shadd family. The spelling of her name in this text acknowledges as much.

Chapters in this volume adhere to the advice in P. Gabrielle Foreman's "Writing About Slavery? This Might Help," including the practice of using the term "'enslaved' (as an adjective) rather than 'slave' (as a noun) [which] disaggregates the condition of being enslaved with the status of 'being' a slave," in recognition of the fact that "people weren't slaves; they were enslaved,"[33] and Shadd Cary's preference for the active, clear voice, over the passive anything.

Notes

1. Cheryl Janifer Laroche, "Secrets Well Kept: Colored Conventioneers and Underground Railroad Activism," in *The Colored Conventions Movement: Black Organizing in the Nineteenth Century*, ed. P. Gabrielle Foreman, Jim Casey, and Sarah Lynn Patterson (Chapel Hill: University of North Carolina Press, 2021), 253.

2. Brittney C. Cooper, *Beyond Respectability: The Intellectual Thought of Race Women* (Urbana: University of Illinois Press, 2017), 21.

3. Martha S. Jones, *Vanguard: How Black Women Broke Barriers, Won the Vote, and Insisted on Equality for All* (New York: Basic Books, 2020).

4. J.B.Y., "Miss Shadd's Pamphlet," *North Star*, April 23, 1849.

5. Derrick R. Spires, *The Practice of Citizenship: Black Politics and Print Culture in the Early United States* (Philadelphia: University of Pennsylvania Press, 2019), 108; Jane Rhodes, *Mary Ann Shadd Cary: The Black Press and Protest in the Nineteenth Century* (Bloomington: Indiana University Press, 1998), 109–10; Juliet E. K. Walker, "Promoting Black Entrepreneurship and Business Enterprise in Antebellum America: The National Negro Convention, 1830–1855," in *A Different Vision: Race and Public Policy*, ed. Thomas D. Boston, 280–318 (London: Routledge, 1997).

6. Carla L. Peterson, *"Doers of the Word": African-American Women Speakers and Writers in the North (1830–1880)* (New York: Oxford University Press, 1995).

7. Peterson, *"Doers of the Word."*

8. P. Gabrielle Foreman, "Black Organzing, Print Advocacy, and Collective Authorship: The Long History of the Colored Conventions Movement," in Foreman, Casey, and Patterson, *The Colored Conventions Movement*, 41.

9. Hazel V. Carby, *Reconstructing Womanhood: The Emergence of the Afro-American Woman Novelist* (New York: Oxford University Press, 1987).

10. See Stefano Harney and Fred Moten, *The Undercommons: Fugitive Planning & Black Study* (Wivenhoe: Minor Compositions, 2013). Here, I am thinking specifically of the opening to the chapter entitled "The University and the Undercommons" in which Harney and Moten describe the characteristics of the subversive intellectual: "the subversive intellectual came under false pretenses, with bad documents, out of love. Her labor is as necessary as it is unwelcome."

11. W. E. B. Du Bois and Shirley L. Poole, "The Damnation of Women," *The Crisis* 107, no. 6 (2000): S1–S8.

12. My methodology here is a nod to the introduction to Eric Gardner's *Unexpected Places: Relocating Nineteenth-Century African American Literature* (Jackson: University Press of Mississippi, 2009).

13. As quoted in Rodger Streitmatter, *Raising Her Voice: African-American Women Journalists Who Changed History* (Lexington: University Press of Kentucky, 1994), 28.

14. Mary Ann Shadd Cary, "Dear Brother," Toronto, Canada West, September 16, 1851. In a letter recently acquired by Archives Ontario, Shadd Cary addresses her brother and says: "I heard you were in Buffalo—I have not time to say much to you for I leave here for Sandwich Canada West today, I have been here more than a week and like Canada very much."

15. Mary Ann Shadd Cary, "Letter to Frederick Douglass," *North Star*, March 23, 1849.

16. Megan Specia, "Overlooked No More: How Mary Ann Shadd Cary Shook Up the Abolitionist Movement," *New York Times*, July 26, 2018, https://www.nytimes.com/2018/06/06/obituaries/mary-ann-shadd-cary-abolitionist-overlooked.html.

17. See Sarah Evans, "Mrs. Mary Ann Shadd Cary (1823–1893): The Foremost Colored Canadian Pioneer in 1850," in *Homespun Heroines and Other Women of Distinction*, ed. Hallie Q. Brown (New York: Oxford University Press, 1992).

18. SaraEllen Strongman, "The Archaeological Impulse, Black Feminism, and *But Some of Us Are Brave*," *Feminist Studies* 48, no. 1 (2022): 33–52, 35.

19. Rhodes, *Mary Ann Shadd Cary*, xv. Speaking of one of the oldest biographic sources about Shadd Cary, a biographical sketch written by Mary Ann Shadd Cary's daughter Sarah Evans, Rhodes also notes that "although many of Evans's recollections are not supported by the historical record, her essay has become a primary source for many interested in Shadd Cary's life" (xvi).

20. The history of that collection and the role of her descendants, particularly Ed and Maxine Robbins, in their stewardship and preservation, are the subject of Allison Margot Smith's documentary *Mary Ann Shadd Revisited: Echoes from an Old House* (YouTube Video, March 1, 2016).

21. Here, I am mindful of Nikole Hannah-Jones, a world-renowned journalist who received critical acclaim for her work on the 1619 Project, an initiative that sought to draw connections between the lived experiences of contemporary African Americans and the earliest days of the transatlantic slave trade. I am also reminded of Nana aba Duncan, an established Black Canadian journalist who has recently taken on the role of Carty Chair in Journalism, Diversity and Inclusion Studies at Carleton University's School of Journalism and Communication, Canada's oldest journalism school. She has spoken openly about the way Mary Ann Shadd Cary's legacy will help to shape her work at Carleton where she has launched the Mary Ann Shadd Cary Centre for Journalism and Belonging.

22. Peterson, *"Doers of the Word,"* 90.

23. Christian Olbey, "Unfolded Hands: Class Suicide and the Insurgent Intellectual Praxis of Mary Ann Shadd," *Canadian Review of American Studies* 30, no. 2 (2000): 151–74; and Shirley J. Yee, "Finding a Place: Mary Ann Shadd Cary and the Dilemmas of Black Migration to Canada, 1850–1870," *Frontiers* 18, no. 3 (1997): 1–16.

24. Ikuko Asaka, *Tropical Freedom: Climate, Settler Colonialism, and Black Exclusion in the Age of Emancipation* (Durham, NC: Duke University Press, 2017); Andrea Stone, *Black Well-Being: Health and Selfhood in Antebellum Black Literature* (Gainesville: University Press of Florida, 2016); and Winfried Siemerling, "Black Activism, Print Culture, and Literature in Canada,

1850–1865," in *African American Literature in Transition, 1850–1865*, ed. Teresa Zackodnik (Cambridge: Cambridge University Press, 2021), 271–306.

25. Mary Ann Shadd, *A Plea for Emigration; or, Notes of Canada West*, ed. Phanuel Antwi (Peterborough, ON: Broadview Press, 2016).

26. Spires, *The Practice of Citizenship*, 2.

27. Siemerling, "Black Activism," 280.

28. See Tera W Hunter, *Bound in Wedlock : Slave and Free Black Marriage in the Nineteenth Century*. Cambridge, MAs: Belknap Press of Harvard University Press, 2017.

29. "Anglo-African Magazine," in *Frederick Douglass' Paper* (Rochester, NY) XII, no. 9, February 11, 1859: 2; and *Readex: African American Newspapers*. Accessed 21 February 2024.

30. "Editorial Notes," in *Arkansas Weekly Mansion* (Little Rock, AR), June 23, 1883: 1; and *Readex: African American Newspapers*, accessed February 21, 2024.

31. "The Women of the Race, Their Practical and Creditable Progress. Edmonia Lewis, the Sculptor—Happy," *Cleveland Gazette* (Cleveland, OH), March 12, 1887, 1; and *Readex: African American Newspapers*, accessed February 21, 2024.

32. "Locals," *Washington Bee* (Washington, DC), July 18, 1885, 3; and *Readex: African American Newspapers*, accessed February 21, 2024.

33. P. Gabrielle Foreman et al. "Writing About Slavery/Teaching About Slavery: This Might Help," community-sourced document, February 1, 2023, https://naacpculpeper.org/resources/writing-about-slavery-this-might-help/.

PRELUDE

CHAPTER 1

The Struggle to Emerge

What Black (Canadian) Studies Might Mean; or, The Return of Mary Ann Shadd Cary

RINALDO WALCOTT

In the summer of 2021, the artist Adeyemi Adegbesan (also known as Yung Yemi) unveiled a mural of Mary Ann Shadd Cary at Mackenzie House Museum in Toronto (Figure 1.1). The mural was installed on an outside wall at the side of the museum, and it is an arresting portrait of Shadd Cary. Titled *Luminary: Mary Ann Shadd,* the work " imagines her in a contemporary light adorned in regality and symbolism representative of her bravery and visionary insight in the fight for equality and justice." In the didactic that accompanies the mural we are further told that "the building on King Street where Mary Ann published her newspaper in the 1850s no longer stands." And further, "as we recognize Black excellence and create new monuments, her portrait will be installed at Mackenzie House Museum." No time or date is provided for the installation of the portrait. Of course, I can only speculate that this interest in Shadd Cary is in part conditioned by the reckoning museums, monument commissions, and other public art entities have recently had to contend with as resistance to a landscape populated with white racist colonizers continually comes under pressure for removal and change. Mackenzie House Museum is the historic house of the first mayor of Toronto, William Lyon Mackenzie; his grandson William Lyon Mackenzie King would become Canada's tenth prime minister. King would serve three separate terms beginning in 1921 and is generally considered the architect of the modern nation as white people cemented their founding of the nation on stolen Indigenous lands.

Figure 1.1. Mary Ann Shadd Cary mural by artist Yung Yemi on the outside wall of Mackenzie House in Toronto. Photograph by Rinaldo Walcott.

I first noticed people posting pictures of Adegbesan's mural the summer of 2021 on social media, while other people were also lamenting that the racial reckoning many had felt was coming after the unprecedented protest due to the very public murder of George Floyd in May of 2020 did not seem to reap the kinds of sustained antiracist commitments that were made in the eventful first instance of the spectacular act of anti-Black racism. As I watched social media, I also witnessed two other interesting "phenomena." The first was the announcement from a number of universities of initiatives like equity, diversity, and inclusion (EDI) specialists with individual professors moving across positions inside schools or moving on to new schools to take up these positions, the announcement of cluster hires for Black professors, and other small-scale initiatives meant to convey a sense of change; and, second and related to the first, for the first time in my professional life I witnessed also a host of announcements of Black Canadian journalists revealing their recruitment to journalism schools as professors, fellows, visiting professors, and the like. Clearly, something notable of attention had been and has been happening. It is in this context then that I return to thinking with Mary Ann Shadd Cary.

This essay is located in an invitation to think with and rethink an earlier essay. The earlier essay, "'Who Is She and What Is She to You?': Mary Ann Shadd Cary and the (Im)possibility of Black/Canadian Studies," was first published in *Atlantis: Critical Studies in Gender, Culture, and Social Justice* in 2000, or more than twenty years ago, in a special issue called "Whose Canada Is It?" I described the essay then as such: "This paper addresses the relationship between Black Studies, Canadian Studies and Black diasporic discourses and incorporates the figure of Mary Ann Shadd Cary as an intellectual guide to argue for a place within Canadian Studies for a sustained conversation concerning Blackness. The paper is a conceptual exercise in working through the concern of why discourses of Blackness in Canadian Studies operate much like a special effect and why Canadian Blackness is also not sustained in Black Studies discourses." At that time, I was preoccupied with figuring out a way to make Black studies a concerted effort in the Canadian academy even if we had to smuggle it into Canadian studies. The essay was also occasioned by the founding of the Center for the Study of Black Canadian Studies, which we (myself and Prof. Leslie Sanders) decided to house at the Robarts Center for Canadian Studies at York University, Toronto, where I was then employed. Finally, the initial essay was to be enlarged as a chapter for the book I was then working on but abandoned, "Disturbing the Peace: The Impossible Dream of Black Canadian Studies." As you might tell from all the titles, we were trying to make something appear. The something was not just Black studies (because I would argue it was already in Canada) but Black Canadian studies.

The first part of the title of the essay came from the lyrics from Gladys Knight and the Pips song "Who Is She?" The last lyric in the first stanza of the song is "Daggumit, who is she and what is she to you?" I had been involved in various attempts to figure out how to sustain conversations of Blackness and Blacklife (Walcott and Abdillahi) in Canada in various multidisciplinary fields that did not only understand it as recent or through the lens of multiculturalism. Shadd Cary was and remains the kind of figure who I believe could help me make that conceptual intervention. Her life in Canada coincided with and overlapped that of Canada's Susanna Moodie, a white immigrant settler who published the important and foundational work *Roughing*

It in the Bush (1852), followed in 1853 by *Life in the Clearings Versus the Bush*, for the field of Canadian studies. There is much ink on Moodie. You can draw a through line from these works to Margaret Atwood's *Survival: A Thematic Guide to Canadian Literature* of 1972. If Moodie is the feminist proto-hero of Canadian studies, no such case could be made for the fellow traveler Shadd Cary who was barely commented on. No book existed alongside Atwood's *Survival* that might offer an intellectual intervention and foundation that would make us recall Shadd Cary in the same manner that Atwood's book worked for Moodie.

In 1853 Shadd founded the *Provincial Freeman*, an antislavery newspaper, and she traveled widely in Canada and the northern United States to seek subscriptions for it and to participate in antislavery rallies and meetings. Prior to founding the newspaper Shadd had already published her pamphlet *A Plea for Emigration to Canada West* in 1852. I am making a very simple correlation here. Canadian studies found Moodie; they did not find Shadd Cary. That difference was my initial interest, but it was also an opening for me to grapple with what Canadian studies could never contain no matter how hard it tried, and that Shadd would inhabit for the field the structure of haunting, much like the lynching in *Roughing It in the Bush* that literary scholars in Canada rarely if ever comment on. Shadd Cary's biography provided me an opening to think Canada and to think beyond Canada. She, in my view, continues to provide that for us still.

Three things came together for me to think within at this time in history (2020 and into the present): the request return to my initial essay; my noticing the announcement of university cluster hires for Black scholars and the recruitment of Black journalists to journalism schools; and Adegbesan's mural of Shadd—all of them haunted by the figure of Shadd Cary hovering over them. At the time of the initial writing of this essay I noted that there was not one journalism school named after Shadd Cary in Canada that I knew of, no endowed chairs that I knew of, no public monuments even though she is designated a Person of National Historic Significance, and definitely no Black studies departments or programs, but there is a public school named after her and the promised portrait is coming. I recount all this for one simple reason. Since the initial draft of this essay Carleton University, Ottawa, which has been remaking its journalism program with high profile Black and Indigenous journalists, in 2022 announced the Mary Ann Shadd Cary Centre for Journalism and Belonging. This is a notable change, but the center, beginning with a $15,000 fund from the university, is not well funded (Ramzy).

I needed Shadd Cary then; and if she had not existed, I would have invented her. Why? My thinking at that time was so influenced by and indebted to Paul Gilroy's *The Black Atlantic* and his chronotope of the ship. He wrote in this still stunningly important work: "The image of the ship—a living, micro-cultural, micro-political system in motion—is especially important for historical and theoretical reasons that I hope will become clearer below. Ships immediately focus attention on the middle passage, on the various projects for redemptive return to the African homeland, on the circulation of ideas and activists as well as the movement of key cultural artefacts: tracts, books, gramophone records, and choirs" (4). I was so taken by Gilroy's articulation of how Black possibility was laden with connection and practices of circulation that I needed to make connection and circulation work for what was then my sense of Canada too. Indeed, in my first book, *Black Like Who: Writing Black Canada*, in the most earnest fashion, despite the lakes that surround us, I suggested that, "if the ship is Gilroy's metaphor for the black Atlantic, the vehicle in which he travels and docks at the doorstep of African-Americans, then for overland travel, jogging might be the metaphor that best characterizes the back-and-forth movement of black Canada and its offerings to the discourse of diaspora" (18). I was invoking Martin Delany's jogging to the North for freedom and the Underground Railroad and of course on foot land travel across the Canada-U.S. border, but also more generally the empirical reality of Black movement across the U.S.-Canada borders for Black people as a central element of Black life in Canada. Of course, Shadd Cary, just like Harriet Tubman, is one of those figures who refused the border of Canada and the United States and instead utilized the border when necessary for safety and ignored it when necessary for their personal and renewed political activities that required them to be in the United States. It is, indeed, their refusal to fully settle in any one place while deploying either geography for their political projects as best they could that remains importantly fascinating for me as a story of diaspora worth noting and returning to. Indeed, the first essay was in part exercised by Jane Rhodes's otherwise excellent book *Mary Ann Shadd Cary: The Black Press and Protest in the Nineteenth Century* (1998) in which Rhodes's minimal concentration on Shadd Cary's life in Canada remains a curiosity for me, given that the newspaper was founded and published in Canada. Shadd Cary traversed the Canada-U.S. border, as already mentioned, often making trips to the U.S. northern free states to speak of the urgent need for abolition and to sell her paper the *Provincial Freeman*.

I do not come to thinking and writing about Shadd Cary as a professional historian; for me Shadd Cary is an intellectual guide and an incitement to risk thinking Black life beyond the containments of the correction of history or returning an important Black figure to the normative historical register. Therefore, while my thinking about Shadd Cary is an outcome of my reading of the historians and an acknowledgment of the need for the work of the historians, I see my work as in dialogue with her unfinished project of freedom. My reading of Shadd Cary and her importance is conditioned by and filtered through what others have achieved of her life from the archives, and given those biographical sketches and their significance for modern Black life, I continue to believe Shadd Cary's life helps us to think deeply about how diaspora might work across and within and against the containments of national spaces. In my attempts to think about Shadd Cary and to think alongside her I draw on a method of reading from Avery Gordon best understood as "often barely there." I do so to invent a language and a set of ideas that might make it apparent for asking the kinds of questions that might mobilize conversations about Black Canadians in the space of Canadian studies as a scholarly formation. Twenty years ago, the essay that provokes this new one was an attempt to intervene into Canadian studies and to do so using Shadd Cary to demonstrate that Black life in Canada did not always have to begin from scratch and/or the era of post-1960s multiculturalism. In that moment Shadd Cary was both foundational and a political guide for me (Walcott 2000).

In Avery F. Gordon's *Ghostly Matters: Haunting and the Sociological Imagination*, she argues that "haunting is a constituent element of modern social life. It is neither pre-modern superstition nor individual psychosis; it is a generalizable social phenomenon of great import" (7). Gordon proceeds to elaborate:

> If haunting describes how that which appears to be not there is often a seething presence, acting on and often meddling with taken-for-granted realities, the ghost is just the sign, or the empirical evidence if you like, that tells you a haunting is taking place. The ghost is not simply a dead or a missing person, but a social figure, and investigating it can lead to that dense site where history and subjectivity make social life. The ghost or the apparition is one form by which something lost, or barely visible, or seemingly not there to our supposedly well-trained eyes, makes itself known or apparent to us, in its own way, of course. The way of the ghost is haunting, and haunting is a very

particular way of knowing what has happened or is happening. Being haunted draws us affectively, sometimes against our will and always a bit magically, into the structure of feeling of a reality we come to experience, not as cold knowledge, but as a transformative recognition (8).

The insight and analyses of Gordon in *Ghostly Matters* on why haunting and its recognition are important to various social context have much import for Canadian studies and its synecdoche the Canadian nation-state. What is curious to me is that in our time of representation mattering, even as scholars and professionals are recruited in universities' performance of responding to anti-Black racism, in particular Shadd Cary's name and her contributions remain a ghostly presence. Who will teach her legacy in Canada's journalism schools? Do those j-schools even know of her existence? And this is particularly important both historically and pedagogically as journalism as a practice finds itself in its own crisis of legitimacy that is not only about the face of those who bring us the news, who present it to us, but also about its existential importance and survival in a world vastly reshaped by the immediacy of various social media platforms that need the news, abuse the news, and create the news. I am sure that many could find contemporary figures who could be claimed as inheritors of the Shadd Cary legacy in the United States and Canada. For example, I could imagine some naming Nana aba Duncan in Canada or Nikole Hannah-Jones in the United States as likely candidates. My point though is that the radical project of liberation for Black people that Shadd Cary concerned herself with is often stalled by EDI measures. For example, the Duncan-run center is poorly funded. And while Hannah-Jones now occupies an important role at Howard University, training a new generation of scholars, her project can be assessed as more reformist than liberatory. Shadd Cary's intellectual contributions are not easily recuperated for our EDI era.

Let me take a detour through Canadian studies so that I might return to what was once my impossible dream of Black (Canadian) studies. For me this is a story of haunting and its many ghosts, of how the shadowy figure of Blackness lurks or haunts Canadianness, understood as whiteness, and what kinds of effort must be accomplished to render this haunting unimportant, and further whether we can break through this haunting if our past remains a largely silent one. In their still groundbreaking *"We're Rooted Here and They Can't Pull Us Up": Essays in African Canadian Women's History*, coordinated by Peggy Bristow (1994), six Black Canadian feminists write in their brief preface: "Despite the increasing scope and authority of women's studies, the role of Black women in Canada's history has remained largely unwritten and unacknowledged. This silence supports the common belief that Black people have only recently arrived in Canada and that racism is a fairly recent development. This book sets the record straight." In the introduction to this sweeping six-chapter work they write: "A Black feminist historiography would begin with the writings of newspaper editor and publisher Mary Ann Shadd who, as early as 1852, wrote *A Plea for Emigration to Canada West*, a treatise informing Blacks in the United States about the benefits of emigrating to Canada West. She also wrote articles on women's rights and informed her readers through the *Provincial Freeman* newspaper of suffragist meetings in Canada West and the United States." They continue: "In our discussion of how this book was to take shape, we recognized all the omissions in Canadian history and what sustains them. We agreed that these omissions are part and parcel of the endemic racism that fuels the Canadian intellectual tradition."

What work might Black (Canadian) studies do to interrupt this tradition? What kinds of intellectual investments both in terms of personnel and money would be necessary? Do the recent announcements of Black studies programs bring us into this kind of terrain? Or are we in the era of EDI management strategies more adept at announcing each new hire, even what course might be taught as a public relations and individual ego-satisfying game, but one that is built as the childhood story goes on a foundation of sand? I do not ask these questions to be dismissive of recent "gains." I ask them to alert us to the structure within which those "gains" are achieved. I ask them in the same fashion and attitude that Shadd Cary asked of the abolitionists to stop talking and do something.

Contemporary Black life in Canada sits permanently in the structure of haunting. Much of it might be characterized as concerned with the "hauntological," following Jacques Derrida. Derrida suggests that hauntology, which is the end of a certain history, encapsulated in an event, twining the first and the last time of the event, offers us a way to read ghosts and their cultural impact (10). I am reading the events of cluster hires, j-school recruitments, and murals and promised portraits as hauntological in structure. These practices do not break out of the logic of representation to provide us avenues for new world makings. In each case the dead and even the living function to suture contradictions around exclusion and anti-Black racism inside a structure not meant for Black survival. In Derrida's case he is reading the ghosted body of Karl Marx and the ghosted and failed politics of

Marxism. In my case I am reading the ghosted insistence of Shadd Cary as what Carla Peterson described as a "doer of the word." Further, I am suggesting that much of our present moment is conditioned and haunted by what it does not yet know, what it cannot yet tell, and what it is forced to invent. Black Canadian culture is yet to fully tell its free story, to riff off of William Andrews's *To Tell a Free Story*.

It is fundamentally, a Black Canadian elsewhereness that haunts Canadian studies because of the story that Black Canadian extensions of the geobody of Canada reveal about the unfinished project of modernity in Canada, the central role of migration, and thus the contemporary failure of Canadian multiculturalism to truly liberate. My initial intervention into Canadian studies was about its inabilities to think concretely around Blackness and Black people as a starting point because I believed that as a field concerned with the nation in all its myriad ways Canadian studies as an interdisciplinary and multidisciplinary field has to date not been able to adequately address Blackness as constitutive of Canadianness. The field has instead been quite happy to use Blackness as a kind of special effect, which appears and disappears, beginning from scratch each time as though no history of other appearances existed. It was this willful attempt to always have Black people and Blackness as a surprise and never accorded as a serious and sustained presence in Canadian studies that I was endeavored to disrupt in the initial essay.

I now fully know that Canadian studies cannot be a place where Blackness in Canada lives as an intellectual exercise in the academy. The profound foundational intellectual inheritance of anti-Black racism surfaces too powerfully when the absented presence of Black people and Blackness is broached in Canadian studies. Indeed, Black studies as a multidisciplinary and interdisciplinary field holds the promise of providing better assessments of Blackness and Black people's impact on the nation and beyond than any singular disciplinary field can (with apologies to the historians I need). The promise of interdisciplinarity is one that I believe is necessary for making sense of Black diaspora people's lives globally. Interdisciplinarity allows me to draw on a number of different disciplines to make sense of the haunting qualities of Black life in Canada. But by so doing it also allows me to bring a critique to the field of Canadian studies, a field that also claims to be interdisciplinary too, demonstrating how a field that is nationally bounded and that foundationally understands the nation as white cannot produce the kinds of knowledge necessary for moving toward Black freedom. Canadian studies proper as a field can only be a liberal containment of Black intellectual desires.

It is important to note and mark that Black studies in Canada is necessarily a Black diaspora studies. By this I mean that Black studies in Canada must necessarily traverse borders while being acutely aware of the ground from which it is practiced. It is this attitude to which I am gesturing. In Shadd Cary's critique of the colonization movement, she wrote: "We go further, we want that the colored man should live in America—should 'plant his tree' deep in the soil, and whether he turns white, or his neighbors turn black by reason of the residence, is of no moment. He must have rights—must not be driven to Africa, nor obliged to stay in the States if he desires to be elsewhere" (*Provincial Freeman*, May 27, 1854). Here we get from Shadd Cary a radical articulation of Black people as worldly citizens, a sentiment that in my *The Long Emancipation: Moving Toward Black Freedom* (2021) I also share as a kind of rhetorical flourish, given that Black people are the only people who can claim world citizenship grounded in the manner of our rapturous invention.

Any Black studies program that refuses the location of its practice is one worth questioning, one that opens itself up to reinforcing national myths about the place of Black people and thereby instantiates the idea that Black people do not actually belong here. Traversing borders is not a refusal of belonging; rather it is an attempt at making connection. So, if my initial essay was attentive to the impossible dream of Black Canadian studies, I can now say that the dream is no longer so impossible but rather potentially hampered by an inattention to Canada. I would say the dream is deeply fraught and we ought to be able to notice that fraughtness. It remains important to point out that not all Black people studying Black people and Black life are doing Black studies, especially so in Canada where the dominant paradigm for thinking about nonwhite people has been the nebulous antiracism frame. This claim is not one about policing boundaries but rather one about the stakes of what Black studies should do, might do, and can do. For me Black studies is in the tradition of Shadd Cary; it is to use this contemporary articulation, abolitionist in its best possible articulations—it means to end this world as we know it and to aid in the emergence of a new and better one.

So, there is currently a small mushroom. Black studies programs are beginning to mushroom across Canada. Certificates and minors are popping up in many places, and positions in Black studies are among the Black cluster hires across Canada. Fifty years after Black studies' institutional founding in the United States, its arrival at an institutional level is now occurring in Canada. There is much we can learn from the United States on this front. Almost three decades ago I was hired at York University in a position advertised for a specialist in "Black North America or Latino/Latina North America," so Black studies has a longer institutionalized mark as I would name that hiring. But importantly, I invoke the personal because it helps to illuminate that Black studies without institutionality has existed for a long time. I have been forced to rethink my understanding of my scholarly formation. I did all my degrees in Canada. For more than seven years I taught Black studies courses in what was a department then called the Division of Humanities. These new programs in Canada do not solve the problem of Black studies' emergence; they open up new questions concerning containment.

A Black assertion will not be easily accepted as one that is valid given the repression of Blackness that sits firmly at the root of all that is Canada and haunts it; people want ghosts gone; few want to live with them as a reoccurring presence. However, if we read the work of David Austin and rosalind hampton, among others, one might acknowledge that a noninstitutional Black studies has long existed in Canada. But even more formally, Black studies existed in the university far beyond and below its recent institutionalization. I could narrate my own university education as one in Black studies without a program. Sylvia Wynter, in "On How We Mistook the Map for the Territory," in recounting the struggle for Black studies in the United States argues that in its institutionalization and thus defeat it was unable "to complete intellectually that emancipation" it had inaugurated (111). Wynter argued and pointed out how liberal humanism and partial induction into the ethno-class of the West undermined and led to confusing the territory for the map—for example, Black studies became the "reterritorialized and ethnicized 'African-American Studies'" (116). What is now called EDI works and functions to manage more radical Black demands, while leaving the map still in the hands of the Western bourgeois human—a category that the Black can never fully enter.

The kinds of intellectual formations that *Fear of a Black Nation* by Austin maps haunts Black studies in Canada now. Equally so are figures like Shadd Cary and Tubman whose binational presences provide another important route and root for Black studies here. What holds these two examples together is how the many different players cross many different borders— what I would term diaspora movements constitute what can be a foundation of radical Black studies in Canada. Austin's account of the 1960s in Montreal and the intellectual formations occurring there are important for making sense of the *longue durée* I am gesturing to. Black studies as struggle and connection then across differences is, as they say, "rooted here and they can't pull

[it] up" (Tubman via Peggy Bristow). J-schools could learn something Adrienne Shadd, a descendent of Mary Ann, wrote: "Black Canadian newspapers were an important source of communication for newly arrived fugitives who were unable to make direct contact with loved ones for lengthy periods."

She further states: "Among the many important services these newspapers provided, they enabled fugitives themselves to place notices in the advertisement sections, which could run almost indefinitely if need be."

This logic spills over for Black (Canadian) studies more generally. What or how might j-schools inhabit Mary Ann Shadd Cary? For example, in some spaces in the United States Ida B. Wells holds an important material symbolic significance for a journalism of truth-telling. How might Shadd Cary be mobilized for difficult intra-Black dialogues and conversations through and beyond journalism?

Let me finally turn to two recent events or controversies that I believe remain unresolved in the Canadian academy but that I think have much to contribute to how Black studies unfolds in Canada and what it can and will do. The first is the Black Canadian Studies Association (BCSA) and the Federation for the Humanities and Social Sciences: The Black Canadian Studies Association and its (ongoing) tensions with the Federation for the Humanities and Social Sciences threaten to open a significant and potential reordering of Black life in the Canadian academy if its rather modest demands can be heard and acted on beyond a logic of shame and protest as has been the case so far. In a recent article one of the BCSA's copresidents rosalind hampton detailed the history of the association's conversations and negotiations with the federation. The initial negotiations began when a Black student was racially profiled at the 2019 Congress of the Humanities and Social Sciences in Vancouver. Since then, the BCSA has canceled its conference twice in part because the association and the federation have not been able to agree on the conditions that would make its participation under circumstances that might be less anti-Black. In 2021 several other organizations and even one university press has withdrawn from the congress in support of the BCSA. What we are witnessing is how Black studies as an insurgent form of study destabilizes white authorizing institutions. The Federation for the Humanities and Social Sciences as a micro-presenting representation of the white nation unravels when Black assertions provide another account of what Canada might be. The struggle here is then not one of inclusion as the federation's "Equity, Diversity, Inclusion, and Decolonization" (EDID) committee suggests but rather one of the very foundational theoretical or conceptual stakes of the organization and by extension what Canada is. The Black assertion will not be easily accepted as one that is valid given the repression of Blackness that sits firmly at the root of all that is Canada. Hampton has explored this claim that I am making here in *Black Racialization and Resistance at an Elite University*, a study of McGill that demonstrates how the university retains it colonial roots while adapting in late modern Canada as a tentative multicultural organization. Noting that McGill is a founding institution of Canada even before confederation, the important point I am making here is that hampton brings to the conversation with the Federation for the Humanities and Social Sciences an understanding of the structure of white settler feeling; hampton's research helps us to understand that a seat at an unreconstructed table, as normative EDI claims would have us do, does not radically shift the terms for living better collective lives. Indeed, in this instance EDI is in opposition to Black studies no matter how it phrases its own response as one of including more of us—a response that leaves some of us to wither.

Fifty years after the founding of Black studies in the United States, Canada's most important research funding body, the Social Sciences and Humanities Research Council, does not have a Black studies subject matter category under which folks are allowed to place their applications for funding. So even in the post–George Floyd moment when momentary institutional regret has led to programs targeting Black scholars and hopefully Black subject matter, Black studies as a scholarly field still remains officially absent in all the subject matter categories available that a scholar can choose from when applying for grants. The specificity of the remedial programs haunts the ongoing anti-Black structure of the remedial program as that which targets but cannot be fully included. The special program is anything but special. Therefore, Black studies still remains fugitive, marooned, and smuggled into the Canadian academy. I am not sure cluster hires change the profound consequences of this intellectual partition, even with the mushrooming of programs.

The second is *Aimé Avolonto v. York University President and Board of Governors*. This case is particularly important because it makes front and center how EDI initiatives do and cannot transform the epistemic violence that the university represents for Black people. Avolonto was hired before the recent post–George Floyd cluster hires and other EDI initiatives, but his case demonstrates the university's intractability to change and its anxieties with Black people. Black studies can help us to understand how a case like this comes to be, how it unfolds, and how Black and other scholars position themselves in relationship to it. Black studies allows us an understanding of the institution in which just being a part of it is never enough. Black studies then requires that we make the political appear, and in this case that means that we bring to bear in our analyses not just the history of white women's deep partnership in white supremacy and its ruling regimes, but also how other nonwhite, Black, and Indigenous people can now be recruited and can become complicit with routinized banal white supremacist logics in late modern capital and therefore collaborate in rendering Black people always suspect and in the extreme have us disappear all the way to death. Black studies' insistence on not just critique but transformation and reinvention remain a difficult problem of its incorporation into the university as it is.

We are in another moment of struggle to transform the university into what the shorthand term "social justice" seeks to mark—an institution among many others that must serve the people and not capital. In North America EDI and other aliases have emerged as the dominant incorporative mode to retain the inequitable foundational life of the traditional university; the blunt force of dismissal, nonrenewal, total disregard, and flagrant hegemony has asserted itself as a way to preserve the foundation of the inequitable university that is the backbone of knowledges launched against Black personhood or the Black life form.

> Nevertheless, we cannot ignore the common practice at universities of hiring women and racialized persons—Black women in particular—to do so-called "EDI" (equity, diversity, and inclusion) work on behalf of the institution. On the one hand, these workers typically have crucial lived experiences and scholarly expertise related to the forms of oppression and inequity that such committees are meant to address. On the other hand, such positions come with the strong potential of having to defend institutions and institutional processes against racialized and other activist scholars and students demanding change. Do institutions hire EDI workers to dismantle and abolish their colonial-capitalist structures and practices? Or are EDI workers typically hired to manage issues related to equity and diversity in ways that allow the institution to continue its business with minimal interruption? (hampton, "Black Canadian")

EDI seeks to give some of us flowers as a compromise for maintaining that brutal and violent foundation of the university. I say to those of us willing to inhale the scent of those flowers that the flowers are neither the holy spirit, nor do they care.

Finally, hampton further notes regarding her own research on higher education in Canada, "examining how McGill University has managed and suppressed generations of Black student campaigns for Black/Africana Studies, through strategic bureaucratic cycles of 'consultation' and committee formation. As a Black professor in that study noted, 'When it comes to anything to do with racism it's "we're going to consult." And then they pray that you will go away'" ("Black Canadian"). The lessons here are many; Shadd Cary and Austin Clarke, both journalists, both made important and crucial contributions to Black life in Canada. Clarke was also a part of the founding of Black studies in its early days in the United States, teaching at Yale at the time of its founding there. It is not facile to say that Black studies has been in Canada longer than we might understand. It is more important to ask what kind of Black studies we will have, though. Black studies emerges in this structure of haunting. Haunted by figures like Shadd Cary, Tubman, Austin Clarke, and George Floyd, Regis Korchinski-Paquet, and, of course, Abdirahman Abdi, Andrew Loku. Adegbesan's futuristic but return to the past mural of Shadd Cary opens many questions for me, chief among them is how a Black Canadian present rather than a future is yet to fully reckon with how its past remains subtended and thwarted by a present that would rather not hear that past. In this instance Shadd Cary remains the kind of ghost we should want to travel with.

Works Cited

Andrews, William. *To Tell A Free Story: The First Century of Afro-American Autobiography, 1760–1865*. Urbana: University of Illinois Press, 1986.

Atwood, Margaret. *Survival: A Thematic Guide to Canadian Literature*. Toronto: Anansi, 1972.

Austin, David. *Fear of a Black Nation: Race, Sex, and Security in Sixties Montreal*. Toronto: Between the Lines, 2013.

Bristow, Peggy, coord. *"We're Rooted Here and They Can't Pull Us Up": Essays in African Canadian Women's History*. Toronto: University of Toronto Press, 1994.

Derrida, Jacques. *Specters of Marx: The State of the Debt, the Work of Mourning and the New International*. Trans. Peggy Kamuf. New York: Routledge, 1994.

Gilroy, Paul. *The Black Atlantic: Modernity and Double Consciousness*. Cambridge, MA: Harvard University Press, 1993.

Gordon, Avery F. *Ghostly Matters: Haunting and the Sociological Imagination*. Minneapolis: University of Minnesota Press, 1997.

hampton, rosalind. "The Black Canadian Studies Association and Changing Academia: Thoughts on Congress." *The Typescript*, March 12, 2021. Online.

———. *Black Racialization and Resistance at an Elite University*. Toronto: University of Toronto Press, 2020.

Peterson, Carla L. *"Doers of the Word": African-American Women Speakers and Writers in the North (1830–1880)*. New Brunswick, NJ: Rutgers University Press, 1998.

Ramzy, Mark. "Nana aba Duncan Announces Launch of Mary Ann Shadd Cary Centre for Journalism and Belonging." *Charlatan*, May 19, 2022. https://charlatan.ca/nana-aba-duncan-announces-launch-of-mary-ann-shadd-cary-centre-for-journalism-and-belonging/.

Rhodes, Jane. *Mary Ann Shadd Cary: The Black Press and Protest in the Nineteenth Century*. Bloomington: Indiana University Press, 1998.

Shadd, Mary Ann. *A Plea for Emigration; or, Notes of Canada West*. 1852. Edited by Phanuel Antwi. Peterborough, ON: Broadview Press, 2016.

Walcott, Rinaldo. *Black Like Who: Writing Black Canada*. Toronto: Insomniac Press, 1997.

———. *The Long Emancipation: Moving Toward Black Freedom*. Durham, NC: Duke University Press, 2021.

———. "'Who Is She and What Is She to You?': Mary Ann Shadd Cary and the (Im)possibility of Black/Canadian Studies." *Atlantis: Critical Studies in Gender, Culture and Social Justice* 24, no. 2 (2000): 137–46.

Walcott, Rinaldo, and Idil Abdillahi. *BlackLife: Post-BLM and the Struggle for Freedom*. Winnipeg: ARP Books, 2019.

Wynter, Sylvia. "On How We Mistook the Map for the Territory, and Reimprisoned Ourselves in Our Unbearable Wrongness of Being, of *Desêtre*: Black Studies Toward the Human Project." In *A Companion to African-American Studies*, ed. Lewis R. Gordon and Jane Anna Gordon, 107–18. Malden, MA: Blackwell, 2006.

PART I

"To Set Forth the Advantages
of Residence in a Country"

Black Feminist Geographies

CHAPTER 2

Two Mary Carys in Canada West

JEWON WOO

At the second National Emigration Convention, held in Cleveland, Ohio, in 1856, delegates resolved to publish a quarterly, titled *Afric American Reposi-tory*, as a collection of Black-authored literary works to showcase intellectual achievements of people of African descent.[1] The organizer Martin R. Dela-ny's attempt to publish it at the first convention two years previously went futile because he could not find enough collaborators. However, at this time, several editors were willing to take over the project. Notably, Black women figured prominently in migration conventions. At the 1854 meeting of the National Emigration Convention of Colored People, nearly one-quarter of the "executive delegates" were women, including the vice president, Mary E. Bibb.[2] Although the minutes of the 1856 meeting have not been located, we can assume that Black women's leadership would continue. The *Provincial Freeman* on November 25, 1856, reported on the decision that nine editors and publishers would issue the *Repository*. Among them were Mary Ann Shadd Cary, editor of the *Freeman*, and Mary Bibb, widow of Henry Bibb, who had published the *Voice of the Fugitive*.[3] Their proposed collaboration guides us to Shadd Cary's association with other Black women activists, and further to how their transformative relationship would shape her Black femi-nist vision and practice stretching into the postbellum years.

Shadd Cary's relationship with Mary Bibb is worth investigating for two reasons. First of all, it suggests one aspect of Black women's dynamic network in the intersections of race and gender within a Black and male-dominant community. It is well known that Henry Bibb, one of the most influen-tial abolitionists and self-emancipated people in North America, attacked

Shadd both in person and in his newspaper. In response to Bibb, Shadd
fiercely fought back, as the history of their bitter battle was well preserved in
archives. Their conflict started with "philosophical differences over what was
the best direction for building and sustaining Canada's Black communities."[4]
Shadd's gender identity, which was considered unsuitable for leadership in
the nineteenth-century context, fueled their conflict, whereas Henry Bibb's
masculine arrogance bluntly attacking her remained rarely contested. Historians like Jane Rhodes have assumed that Shadd Cary had a more hostile
relationship with Henry Bibb's wife, Mary. The well-educated woman was
presumed to operate the newspaper and the Refugee Home Society behind
her husband because he was not a sophisticated writer and was busy with
his frequent trips for fundraising and lectures. Nevertheless, the two Marys'
relationship remains murky after Henry Bibb's sudden death in 1854. Rather,
from that point on, Shadd Cary and Bibb seemed to form a sort of amicable,
if not less antagonistic, connection for their mutual work on the Black community in Canada West in the 1850s.

Second, our examination of the two Marys challenges the previous scholarship of Mary Ann Shadd Cary as a lone heroine who fought for Black
women's rights and sheds light on her place in the genealogy of Black feminist collectivity. Unfortunately, Shadd Cary has been portrayed not only as
averse to Mary Bibb but also as barely having meaningful bonds with other
Black women leaders, as if she overlooked the necessity of Black female solidarity in her social reform effort. For example, the earlier study has depicted
Shadd Cary in Canada West as alone confronted by the male leaders, as
W. E. B. Du Bois later eulogizes Shadd who "threw herself singlehanded into
the great Canadian pilgrimage when thousands of hunted black men hurried northward and crept beneath the protection of the lion's paw."[5] In this
manner, her biographers Jim Bearden and Linda Jean Butler dramatize her
struggle with other leaders by comparing her to a protagonist in a fairy tale.[6]
Based on these early portrayals of Mary Ann Shadd, Jane Rhodes argues
that Shadd was "not necessarily part of an established network of antebellum black women" and that she began to join women's associational politics only after the Civil War.[7] However, although it is true that Shadd Cary
actively engaged in feminist politics after the late 1860s, her earlier period
is significant in that she prepared a foundation for her Black feminist activism through her expansive and complicated relationship with other Black
women. Elizabeth Cali warns against the tendency to consider Shadd Cary
exceptional or unconventional because we may ignore "the recognition of

nineteenth-century African American women's political work as a genealogy and a constellation of nineteenth-century African American women who published and created public political community space for themselves and their Black women peers."[8] Shadd saw the importance of her role in building a Black community, just like many, often nameless, Black women activists who had paved the way for her and who followed her footsteps. Therefore, tracing Shadd Cary in the context of a Black women's collective can lead us to see a bigger picture of early Black feminist history despite the dearth of records about them.

This essay argues that Shadd Cary founded her feminist vision upon the ever-evolving coalitions with Black women peers, examining the dynamic relationship between her and Mary Bibb in mid-nineteenth-century Canada West. As Martha S. Jones frames, this time period is particularly important for us to understand Shadd Cary's maturation as an activist of Black feminism because it was the moment when a new generation of young women like her, who were "raised under the influence of the century's early path breakers," including Maria Stewart, Jarena Lee, and Jane Merritt, joined activism "in substance and style."[9] Similarly, R. J. Boutelle and Marlas Yvonne Whitley in this volume point out that Shadd's *A Plea for Emigration; or, Notes of Canada West* (1852) envisioned the centrality of a Black women's collective in community-building through coded references to the labor women routinely performed. At the moment of this generational shift, Shadd developed her feminist view on Black-women-led activism not only through her experience with the virulent masculine culture in the community leadership, but also through her persistent effort to ally with exemplary Black women. As many scholars have noticed, Shadd's conflict with Henry Bibb to some extent colored her perception of his wife, Mary. Because of the lack of Mary Bibb's own records, she is subject to our judgment and biased portrayal propelled by the cultural obsession with heroism in history, which is fated to end up with a single narrative about the past.[10] However, I also notice that the conflict led Shadd to witness Mary Bibb's complex position as a wife and leader within the Black community. This essay reviews them with and without Henry Bibb's mediation, so that we can understand the two women's commonalities in their background, ambition, and achievements, which must have kept them in collaboration for the tight-knit settlement of Canada West. Even if Shadd Cary could not avoid an antagonistic relationship with Mary Bibb, her activism continuously evolved centering Black women's networks in coalition with, for example, Sojourner Truth, Elizabeth Taylor Greenfield, and

Frances Ellen Watkins Harper in the 1850s. In this way, she could emerge as a feminist leader in postbellum politics, epitomizing the dialectic relationship between oppression and activism, which Patricia Hill Collins considers critical in "assessing how U.S. Black feminist thought—its core themes, epistemological significance, and connections to domestic and transnational Black feminist practice—is fundamentally embedded in a political context that has challenged its very right to exist."[11] This essay ultimately places Mary Ann Shadd Cary on the large spectrum of Black women's collectively evolving and expanding activism and thought in the long nineteenth century.

The long-held argument about the inimical relationship between Mary Ann Shadd Cary and Mary Bibb started from Bearden and Butler's *Shadd: The Life and Times of Mary Shadd Cary*, published in 1977. The book chronicles Shadd's struggle to establish her position in conflict with the Bibbs, summarizing that their feud was "long-lasting and bitter."[12] The biography in favor of Shadd depicts that, from the beginning of her hire at one of the schools under Henry Bibb's supervision of the Refugee Home Society in Windsor, she found his dishonesty and despotism to take advantage of desperate new Black settlers. Shadd's high moral standard and keen observation of his misdeeds did not keep her quiet, and his false accusation of her slander against him rather inflamed Shadd's anger to fight right back. On the same ground as Bearden and Butler, Rhodes suggests several factors that made Shadd suspect Mary Bibb's substantial role in estranging Shadd from their community operation. For example, Shadd saw that Mary Bibb designed the school system in Windsor, which did not allow her to open an integrated classroom. As many attacks publicly made by Henry Bibb came from his *Voice of the Fugitive*, Shadd also considered his wife being the real author of the damaging articles because she doubted his ability to write for newspaper publication. Rhodes calls Mary Bibb probably "the architect of the attack on Shadd, while remaining shielded by her husband's public status."[13] Shadd once did not hide her disappointment at Mary Bibb: "If Rev. H. Bibb had been trained when young he might have become a great man, but it is too late now. His lady is an incorrigible woman and rules him and all within her influence."[14] Shadd's voice here does not sound like an honest defense of Henry Bibb. Instead, her tone of resignation about the impossibility of his improvement amplifies her contempt for him. Furthermore, Shadd's frustration at Mary Bibb reveals that Shadd would have expected better from the wife, presumably because Mary, differently from Henry, could have formed a sort of sisterly alliance with Shadd in the face of sexism and corruption in their community.

The way that Henry Bibb relied on masculine authority to pillory Shadd implies a more complex aspect of the two women's relationship in the context of gender as well as race. He began to gain fame for his 1849 autobiography, *Narrative of the Life and Adventures of Henry Bibb*, which caused an immediate sensation among abolitionists and antislavery sympathizers. His harrowing experience of losing his first wife and daughter to slavery and dogged determination for freedom demonstrate how the institution of slavery emasculated him and, at the same time, how he reinstated his dignity by revising "the masculinizing imperatives of abolitionist ideology."[15] In the autobiography, Bibb also described the moment when he met his future wife, Mary E. Miles, at one antislavery anniversary meeting in New York City, in May 1847 after he had frequently heard her "very highly spoken of, for her activity and devotion to the anti-slavery cause, as well as her talents and learning[,] and benevolence in the cause of reforms, generally." After the brief courtship, he married Miles who became his "beloved wife," "bosom friend," "help-meet," and "loving companion in all the social, moral[,] and religious relations of life."[16] Nonetheless, belying his tenderness and ostensible respect for the women in the book, Bibb's unvarnished attack on Mary Ann Shadd reveals the nature of his *misogynoir*, as Shirley J. Yee observes: "Shadd's feud with Henry Bibb was also well known and illustrated the way in which gender figured heavily in the struggle for power in the Canadian black settlements."[17] Bibb's performance on "a socially acceptable style of manhood" in his effort to prove Black humanity turned out to be "patriarchal subordination" to the preexisting masculine landscape, as Hazel V. Carby argues on the concept of "race men."[18] Whereas Shadd criticized his fraudulent practice with evidence, Henry Bibb attempted to disqualify her from arguing against him because of her gender.

Henry Bibb did not naively bank on the "patriarchal retrieval" within the Black community because he was not unaware of the implications of gender and race.[19] As a matter of fact, he used both racialized and gendered performances to achieve his purposes, which Robin Winks disapprovingly calls "begging schemes."[20] He, for example, subserviently pleaded to abolitionists for their generous donations by representing formerly enslaved people as destitute and incapable of self-reliance. But he also accumulated possessions by operating the colony under his unchallenged directorship.[21] He built his patriarchal status by playing a role based on the misperception pertaining to formerly enslaved people and, at the same time, by profiting from the exploitative economy implanted in the new settlement. Therefore, Shadd's questions about Bibb's management of the settlement not only challenged his leadership but also threateneded his patriarchal status founded upon the control over the settlement. It is not coincidental that when Shadd broke female submissiveness—the quality that he had expected a Black woman to have aligned with his newly established power—Bibb asserted a "larger pattern of gendered indictment of her transgression."[22] He disproved Shadd's "credit as a lady, for there should be no insult taken where there is none intended," and discouraged young women from following the model of Shadd's leadership, saying "Girls, do you want to get married? And do you want good husbands? If so, cease to act like fools."[23] His abusive remarks on Shadd, whom he called "a designing individual whose duplicity is sufficient to prove a genealogical descent from the serpent that beguiled mother Eve, in the Garden Eden," continued until his death in 1854.[24] Furthermore, Bibb also defamed other Black male leaders with gendered terms as well, which reveals his obsession with masculinity in association with authority. When the prominent lecturer and writer Samuel Ringgold Ward accepted the editor position of Shadd's *Provincial Freeman*, Bibb ridiculed his manliness: "S. R. Ward unfortunately wandered from his orbit when he raised his voice against that [Refugee Home] Society. . . . We do not believe this fall would have happened to him however, if he had not been prevailed upon by evil counsel, spoken by a *syren* voice, like father Adam was by a similar influence when he fell."[25] Shadd's transgressive femininity, armed with her intellect and fearlessness, was intimidating to Henry Bibb, who attempted to create the new colony as a site where he could restore manhood through Black wealth and patriarchal authority.

Mary Ann Shadd apprehended Henry Bibb's domineering masculinity that ultimately weakened the Black community. In one of her letters to George Whipple, secretary of the American Missionary Association, Shadd fiercely criticized Bibb: "What a vast amount of mischief a man like *H. Bibb* can do with an organ of his own to nod, insinuate and 'fling' away the reputation of others and how much *he* has already done to persons who have had no means equally extensive to their control to counteract it is appalling."[26] She understood sexism within Black people to be no less detrimental than racism, as she recognized that her "unfortunate sex" was the basis for his attack on her.[27] One of her articles reads: "Colored men are as merciless as other [white] men, when possessed of the same amount of pride, conceit, and wickedness, and as much, if not more ignorance. They make just as bad masters as the worst of the whites, in their best moods, and infinitely worse in their worst."[28] While she did not single out Henry Bibb as one of those men,

Shadd equated their masculinity as a sign of "pride, conceit, and wickedness" or "ignorance" with racism. In her visionary effort to promote collective neighborship, she could not have failed to see the destructive force of Henry Bibb's gendered attack on her and other leaders. Here, I am careful in arguing that Shadd found the need for a sisterly bond by experiencing the masculine violence in the so-called liberatory place for Black people in Canada West, as if Black women's collective action were triggered solely by patriarchal oppression. In fact, Mary Ann Shadd was capable of defending herself from the men's assault because they could not discourage her from practicing her ideal of the Black community.[29] Shadd rather envisioned an inclusive cultural identity to "let [the] emigrants so *abolitionize* and strengthen neighboring positions as to promote the prosperity and harmony of the whole," beyond the limited boundary of Black womanhood beset by Henry Bibb's grandiose control over the new settlement.[30]

Given that Mary Bibb as an educated and independent woman had actively engaged in abolitionism and Black education before her marriage to Henry Bibb, her inaction in compliance with her husband regarding the infamous conflict with Shadd generates questions about who she really was. Indeed, Mary Bibb's position as a wife of the charismatic man complicated her leadership in the frontier town. If we conclude that Mary Bibb did not form meaningful solidarity with Shadd because of her marital obligation to her husband, we may overlook the multilayered negotiations among socio-cultural expectations that pressured Bibb rather into silence. Shadd and Bibb lived during the time of the debate on whether Black women should participate in public culture.[31] In this circumstance, Shadd would have understood that Bibb's silence on her husband hinted at more than her blind defense of him. Shadd once described Bibb as "a profane swearer and drug taking woman," which belies the latter's highly regarded reputation.[32] If her observation was true, Mary Bibb seemed to have troubles, which could not be exposed to the public eye, most likely resulting from her intimate and domestic life. In 1853 Matilda Nichols, a young Black teacher and Oberlin graduate, began her career at a school supervised by Mary Bibb in Sandwich. Then, Nichols confided to her sister that Bibb was violent and volatile to her because the former suspected the young teacher's inappropriate relationship with her husband. Nichols further witnessed that "Mrs. Bibb calls her husband a nasty infernal devil and finds fault with everything, . . . Mrs. B can be kind and has been part of the time but she is so changing."[33] Mary Bibb's cursing might be a sign of her pent-up anger and frustration, but it is also as

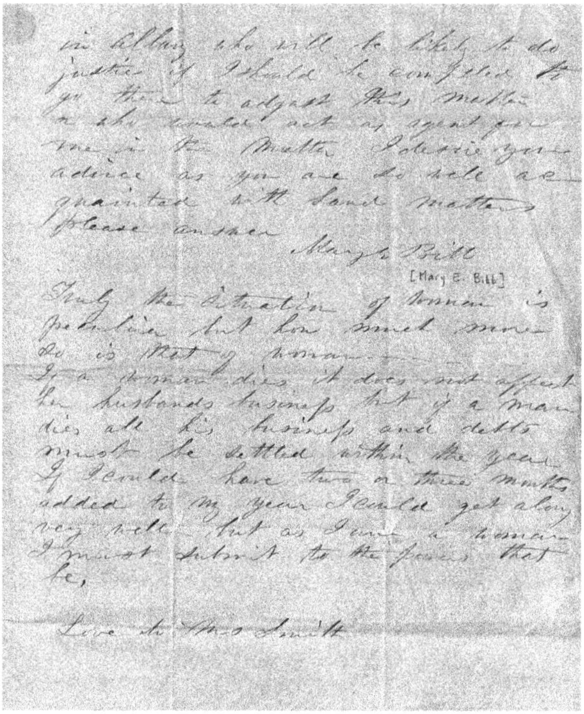

Figure 2.1. One page of Mary Bibb's letter to Gerrit Smith, July 16, 1855. Courtesy of the Gerrit Smith Papers, Special Collections Research Center, Syracuse University Libraries.

unintelligible and futile as her usual silence in the archive. Learning about Bibb's trouble, Shadd could at least suspect that Mary Bibb took drugs to control her anger and grievance, which were escalated by the unhappy domestic life with Henry Bibb. Shadd knew how the man's patriarchal desire for dominance over women could negatively affect his most intimate person, even if she did not express her sympathy for the wife.

One of the few remaining letters by Mary Bibb offers us a glimpse into her painful awareness of the sexist discrimination against women at home and in society. In 1855, about one year after her husband's death, she wrote to the famous abolitionist and philanthropist of New York Gerrit Smith to ask for his help so that she could prove her entitlement to Henry Bibb's property. According to the letter, Smith once donated a piece of land to the Bibbs, but none of the documents listed Mary as a coproprietor, most likely because her husband intentionally omitted her name, as she says, "Mr. Bibb never had his deed recorded [my name; therefore,] perhaps it would be legal for you to furnish me with a new deed in my own name." The letter does not end simply with polite closing remarks. Instead, Mary added a short passage of her lament and sorrow about being a woman:

> Truly the situation of woman is peculiar but how much more so is that of woman— – – – If a woman dies it does not affect her husbands business but if a man dies all his business and debts must be settled within the year If I could have two or three months added to my year I could get along very well but as I am a woman I must submit to the powers that be,

Love to Mrs Smith[34]

Despite Mary Bibb's fame as a skillful writer, whom Mary Ann Shadd considered an actual editor of the *Voice of the Fugitive*, this passage appears replete with stylistic errors (Figure 2.1). The multiple dashes reveal her hesitation before expressing her agony to the abolitionist and asking him to send her "love" to his wife, Ann Smith. The missing punctuations in the passage hint at Bibb's hurried writing in distress as if she burst out the thought she had suppressed for a while. Nevertheless, this letter itself also proves her independence as a capable woman. Mary Bibb persuades Gerrit Smith to support her with his legal authority, by bringing his wife as her ally in sisterly sympathy and solidarity. Mary Bibb was clearly cognizant of the necessity of women's bond for their survival in the male-dominant society. This explains that, regardless of the antagonistic relationship between Henry Bibb and Mary Ann Shadd, Mary Bibb was willing to collaborate with Shadd for a common objective such as publishing the *Afric American Repository*.

What Mary Ann Shadd and Mary Bibb actually thought about each other does not clearly appear firsthand for two reasons. First, Shadd's contemporary men downplayed her criticism of Mary Bibb, by trivializing it as mere jealousy between women, a distrust generated by same-sex competition and vanity. In her letter to Whipple, Shadd deplored the false accusation from Charles C. Foote, who operated the Refugee Home Society with the Bibbs: "Rev. C. C. Foote . . . represents me as jealous of Mrs. Bibb's superior attainments. I never wish to be as well accomplished in some things as she is."[35] Foote failed to see Shadd's higher vision for women's role in the community because of his own misogyny and ignorance of their contribution. Likewise, a powerful man's disregard for women's concerns also disrupted possible solidarity among them through constructive criticism. Second, both Marys understood that they had to regulate themselves to demonstrate their feminine quality in order that they could be treated with respect by their contemporaries. Shadd exhibited "Victorian femininity to shield her from the attacks of her enemies," even when she had to challenge Black male authority.[36] One contributor to the *Provincial Freeman* described her highly within the contemporary framework of acceptable notions of womanhood. At an antislavery meeting, he saw Shadd "nervous, hurried, and not so eloquent as Mr. [H. F.] Douglass," but her speech was "replete with original ideas and soundest logic, and unmistakably showed that she is a woman of superior intellect, of high literary cultivation, and of the most persevering energy of character," and "her manner is modest, and in strict keeping with the popular notions of the 'sphere of women'"; the article concluded that she was "truly a superior woman."[37] Mary Bibb also had to play her gender role as a social custom, by keeping her subjective voice quiet. If Bibb, "uncharacteristically" in Rhodes's term, ever presented herself in public, it was usually to defend her husband's work.[38] Mary Ann Shadd was once surprised with relief when, despite their disagreement and worsening conflict, Mary Bibb courteously introduced Samuel J. May to her classroom without any hint of her judgment against Shadd's qualification as a capable teacher.[39] Shadd and Bibb performed the gendered code for their own purpose, which caused their restraint in making their interactions public.

It is possible that Mary Ann Shadd upon her arrival at Windsor might have been hopeful that she could have collaborated with Mary Bibb because of their shared intelligence, education, and activism. Above all, they grew up in Black middle-class families in the North who had strong educational aspirations for their daughters. Shadd was born to a prominent Black family who was deeply involved in abolitionism and the Black civil rights movement. Shadd's parents ran a successful business in Delaware, but because the state made the education of Black children illegal, they moved to West Chester, Pennsylvania, to offer their children better educational and sociopolitical opportunities. Similarly, although her early life is barely known, Mary Bibb's parents, the Mileses, free Black Quakers in Rhode Island, let her be educated well. The two promising women's participation in abolitionist meetings and conventions link them more tightly. As a precocious student at a Quaker school, Shadd actively attended Black-led conventions with her father, Abraham D. Shadd, while helping self-emancipated people at her house, one of the West Chester routes for the Underground Railroad.[40] After she had attended numerous conventions and meetings by the year 1848 when Frederick Douglass asked his readers of the *North Star* about a direction for Black organizing,

Shadd at the age of twenty-five unhesitatingly asserted that "we should do more and talk less."[41] *The Black Abolitionist Papers* shows that in the 1840s, Mary Miles was a well-known intellectual and taught at several schools in urban areas where Black residents maintained vibrant communities, including Albany, Cincinnati, and Boston. She joined various antislavery meetings and conventions held in these areas. Their experiences as Black educators, activists, and convention attendees before their migration to Canada West were strikingly similar. Their contemporariness and overlapped geography lead us to assume that they would have known each other through Black news outlets and communities, if they were not directly acquainted, before Miles became Mrs. Bibb.

Mary Ann Shadd and Mary Bibb shared more commonalities than differences in their work for Canada's Black community in the 1850s. Mary Bibb and Shadd apparently had conversations about Black education, immigration, and women's work, because the Bibbs persuaded Shadd and her family to move to Canada when they met twice in 1851; first, at the North American Convention in Toronto and again, at the meeting of the citizens of Buffalo only one week after the convention. Shadd, as a secretary, transcribed the minutes in Buffalo and Henry Bibb published them on the first page of his newspaper on January 29, 1852. Their encounters both at the meetings and in print substantiate the two Marys' close acquaintance. In terms of education in Canada West, they promoted racially integrated education, in contrast to Henry Bibb's segregationist stance aligned with the Refugee Home Society as a solution for the act of 1850 that legalized barring Black children from the local common schools.[42] From the beginning of her teaching in 1851, Shadd insisted that Black children be educated with whites to become part of leadership in this chosen country. Mary Bibb, despite her supposed compliance with her husband, also occasionally ran integrated schools before and after his death. When they moved to Windsor from Sandwich in 1852, Bibb started her second school for both Black and white children, which three years later Boston abolitionist and journalist Benjamin Drew found successful: "Mrs. Mary E. Bibb, widow of the late lamented Henry Bibb, Esq., has devoted herself to teaching a private school in Windsor, and with good success. During the last spring term, she had an attendance of forty-six pupils, seven of whom were white children."[43] Mary Bibb would not have established this interracial school without friction with her husband's agenda for Black-only education.

In addition to their pursuit of integrated education, Shadd and Bibb were editors and framers of Canada's first Black newspapers despite their limited place in print because of their gender. Mary Ann Shadd as the first Black woman newspaper editor in North America has been studied well.[44] Her article "Adieu," written when she resigned from the editor position, encouraged Black women to "go to Editing," as she had "broken the Editorial ice."[45] She also utilized Black women's clubs and organizations to circulate and promote the newspaper: "Let our sisters throughout the country go to work on behalf of the defender of their rights . . . *The Provincial Freeman.*"[46] Accordingly, in 1856, the paper's editorial board, including Mary Ann Shadd Cary, held a meeting to organize a women's committee, the Provincial Union, one of whose goals was to assure "the newspaper's survival as the mouthpiece of the Black communities in Canada."[47] Although Mary Bibb in comparison to Shadd Cary has hardly been recognized as an editor, historian Afua Cooper unhesitatingly calls Bibb "Canada's first female newspaper publisher."[48] Bibb's contribution to enriching the content and broadening the scope of the *Voice of the Fugitive* is indisputable. From its beginning, the newspaper was funded through Bibb's recruitment of subscribers among her long-established acquaintances in the United States.[49] She also performed as an editor during her husband's trip for fundraising and lecturing in 1851.[50] Indeed, it is not unreasonable that C. Peter Ripley, editor of *The Black Abolitionist Papers*, believes that "the contrast between [Henry] Bibb's private correspondence and the paper's polished style suggests that his well-educated wife, Mary E. Bibb, had a good deal to do with the paper's style and content."[51] Both Shadd and Bibb often had to hide their presence behind male editors or asterisks, but they did not hide their pen to empower women as a collective force.[52]

Going further than the editorial work, they vitalized women's organizations as essential parts of Black community-building. As Peggy Bristow argues through her close examination of Black women in Canada's early settlements, these organizations were "crucial not only to the success of the family economy but also to the liberation of their people. Elevating the race from the subordinate position forced on it was a primary concern for all Black people, and so group solidarity and cooperation were constantly stressed."[53] In contrast to the prevalent belief in Shadd as a solitary protester in the Black community controlled by Henry Bibb, not only was the community itself never solely dictated by Bibb and his Refugee Home Society, but Shadd and Mary Bibb also actively participated in communal works at various women's organizations and less formal gatherings. They seemed to have meetings frequently together with other women, according to one article in the *Voice of the Fugitive* that reported on a donation party for Black churches and schools:

> There was quite a large gathering, and the ladies deserve much credit for the manner and taste in which they conducted the supper. The announcement that Miss Mary Ann Shad [sic], a lady of high literary attainments, would address the meeting on the subject of education, doubtless brought out many who otherwise would not have attended, and whom, by the by, were well paid for coming. . . . The entertainment was highly interesting, at the close of which, Mrs. M. E. Bibb proposed the formation of a Mutual Improvement Society, which was sanctioned, and to which there were 22 names attached at that time. They agreed to meet on every Thursday evening, to read, converse, or hear addresses from members of the society for intellectual improvement.[54]

Likewise, the two Marys were members of the Windsor Antislavery Society, the first abolitionist organization established in 1827 in Canada. Regardless of their apparent conflict, neither of them left the society as long as they lived in Canada. In fact, their cooperation was indispensable to introduce Black women to leadership. For example, Amelia Freeman, Oberlin graduate, came to Chatham in 1856, after Martin Delany and his wife had persuaded her to teach at a school where Shadd (Cary by then), Shadd Cary's stepdaughter Ann, and younger sister Sarah Shadd taught as well.[55] Freeman initiated a Literary Ladies Society, which emulated the Ladies Club, one organized in 1854 and presided over by Mary Bibb in Windsor. Members of these organizations met to "hear speeches and improve their minds" and were involved in various activities such as helping neighbors in need.[56] In this closely bonded community that inevitably required its members to work together, Shadd and Bibb had to put up with their animosity, if this tension continued even after Henry Bibb's death, to pursue their ideals of Black education and community-building.

In the 1850s, when she seemed to have a hard time building a supportive relationship with Mary Bibb, Mary Ann Shadd began to expand her network with other Black women leaders who demonstrated "transgressive" femininity. This indicates that Shadd indefatigably sought models for Black women's leadership and adopted their skills for her own agenda. They still lived in the time period when Black women were often ostracized from the male-dominant Black leadership, as Shadd's bitter yet victorious experience of speaking at the 1855 Colored National Convention in Philadelphia illustrates.[57] In this misogynous circumstance, instead of continuing a lonely fight with her nemeses, Mary Ann Shadd established supportive friendships among her contemporary Black women such as Sojourner Truth, Elizabeth Taylor Greenfield, and Frances Ellen Watkins Harper.[58] Just like Shadd kept her personal feelings toward Mary Bibb barely known, any evidence of her friendship with other Black women remains mostly elusive. Nonetheless, Shadd expressed her admiration for them through her private letters and editorial work for the *Provincial Freeman*, suggesting their intellectual and sisterly intimacy.

One of the most important Black women whose trajectory on Black civil rights and women's rights movements coincides with that of Mary Ann Shadd is Frances Ellen Watkins (later, Harper). Whereas Rhodes views that they did not have any notable interaction, Frances Foster Smith claims that Shadd Cary and Harper were "lifelong" friends, still collaborating in 1898.[59] How close the relationship they as friends and allies had may remain unclear. Nevertheless, they were well acquainted with each other from the 1850s to their later years. For example, when Shadd visited Philadelphia in 1853 to give a series of speeches encouraging emigration to Canada West, Watkins at the same meeting also recited two original antislavery poems.[60] Shadd did not hide her admiration for Watkins in one letter to her husband, Thomas Cary, saying that Watkins was "the greatest female speaker ever was . . . so wisdom obliges me to keep out of the way as with her prepared lectures there would just be no chance of a fabourable [sic] comparison."[61] Importantly, Shadd left a mark on her intense interest in Watkins's work, by reporting on Watkins in the *Provincial Freeman* several times. Shadd's close friend William Still sent a letter to Shadd to praise Watkins's performance as well as her writing. He asked the editor to publish her prose and poem alongside his letter in Shadd's newspaper, in order that "every unbiased and liberal-minded reader of your paper . . . feel proud of the gems of the authoress, when he shall have taken into account the fact that she is herself of the down-trodden class."[62] Accordingly, Shadd published Watkins's essay "Christianity" and poem "Died of Starvation," indicating the author's gender incontestably—"Miss Frances Ellen Watkins." By juxtaposing Still's letter with Watkins's writings, Shadd expressed her agreement with his estimation of Watkins and led her readers to recognize the promising writer and speaker. This exemplifies Shadd's subtle yet certain gesture to connect her to the Black woman peer through her editorial contribution.

This expansive vision of the Black women's network signals their radical organizing in the later nineteenth-century United States. How Shadd Cary actualized this ideal in the later years is explained well in Brandi Locke's chapter, as she notes that Shadd Cary's proto–Black feminist vision grew out of the soil that Black women had fertilized collectively from the 1830s. In a similar way to how Shadd extended her work in conjunction with Watkins, Mary Bibb actively associated herself with other Black women. Starting with the Windsor Ladies Club in 1854, she created various radical spaces for Black women. For example, Bibb occasionally ran a beauty business, even when she was busy teaching and assisting her husband's newspaper.[63] One of the remaining business directories lets us know that she operated a "fancy ladies store" in Windsor at least from 1865 to 1871.[64] Tiffany Gill points out the significance of the Black beauty industry that "since its inception has served as an incubator for black women's political activism and a platform from which to agitate for social and political change."[65] In this context, her store must have functioned as a site to politicize Black women's experience—from mundane activities like dressmaking and hairdressing to organizing a bazaar for conventions—especially when Black beauty was inconceivable in mainstream society. If Mary Ann Shadd Cary endeavored to achieve leadership for the Black community by associating herself with other women on the podium and in print, Mary Bibb kept herself involved in the Black women's network through her transgressive transitions between a printing room, classrooms, beauty salons, and her parlor. Bibb's physical spaces, in spite of the lack of documentation, still prove her solid location in Black women's organizing.

While some would perpetuate the old doubt about Shadd Cary's collaboration with other women in the 1850s Canada West because of the lack of documents to prove it, we should remember that Black women strengthened their solidarity and friendship often in non-male-centered venues. Collaborations between women were rarely documented, not only because their work was considered private and personal rather than public, as their conventional space was circumscribed within a domestic area, but also because their labor behind organizations and printed materials happened out of the public's sight intentionally and unintentionally. Not enough information about the publication of the *Afric American Repository* as a literary magazine itself is available, and the editorial collaboration of Mary Ann Shadd and Mary Bibb remains undetectable.[66] Nevertheless, we can interweave the remaining threads of Mary Bibb and Mary Ann Shadd Cary with this collective and ever-evolving net of Black women's organizing.

In 1859 Shadd Cary and Bibb became sisters to each other in one extended family circle through Mary Bibb's second marriage to Isaac Cary, who was the brother of Mary Ann Shadd Cary's late husband, Thomas, and once involved with the *Provincial Freeman*. If the two Marys' conflict was long-lasting as its bitterness remained unpatched, they were not discouraged from creating an alternative alliance with others that expanded the concept of a Black feminist coalition in practice. If their conflict somewhat faded away after Henry Bibb's masculine manipulation of them ended with his unexpected death, they demonstrated resilience to work together for a bigger purpose such as publishing a periodical, the *Afric American Repository*, to promulgate Black achievements against the white colonist agenda. In particular, living in Canada West in the 1850s, when and where new Black settlers clashed with one another over political and ideological differences in their effort to establish an ideal community, was crucial to the two women's intellectual growth as Black feminists, who emerged from the frontline adversities intersected by racism and sexism. In the end, they—interestingly, having the same name, Mary Cary—together evinced the core nature of Black feminism; that is, collectively evolving activism for human liberation.

Notes

1. The periodical would serve as a counternarrative of the *African Repository and Colonial Journal*, which the American Colonization Society issued between 1825 and 1892 to promote the migration of free Black Americans to Africa, specifically the U.S. colony of Liberia.

2. Martha S. Jones, *All Bound Up Together: The Woman Question in African American Public Culture, 1830–1900* (Chapel Hill: University of North Carolina Press, 2007), 105. Bibb attended the convention only three weeks after the death of her husband, Henry Bibb.

3. The *Voice of the Fugitive*, the first Black newspaper in Canada, was published in Windsor from 1851 to October 9, 1853.

4. Jane Rhodes, *Mary Ann Shadd Cary: The Black Press and Protest in the Nineteenth Century* (Bloomington: Indiana University Press, 1998), 53. My essay is deeply indebted to Rhodes's pioneering study of Shadd Cary.

5. W. E. B. Du Bois, *Darkwater: Voices from Within the Veil* (New York: Harcourt, Brace and Howe, 1920), 178; available at Project Gutenberg, https://www.gutenberg.org/files/15210/15210 -h/15210-h.htm#Chapter_VII.

6. Jim Bearden and Linda Jean Butler, *Shadd: The Life and Times of Mary Ann Shadd Cary* (Toronto: NC Press, 1977), 36.

7. Rhodes, *Mary Ann Shadd Cary*, xiii.

8. Elizabeth Cali, "'Why Does Not Somebody Speak Out?': Mary Ann Shadd Cary's Heteroglossic Black Protofeminist Nationalism," *Vitae Scholasticae* 32, no. 2 (2015): 36.

9. Jones, *All Bound Up Together*, 88.

10. As Afua Cooper argues, we cannot but take the dearth of evidence in itself as "a kind of evidence in the attempt to put the pieces of her life together" to picture Mary Bibb. Cooper, "The Search for Mary Bibb, Black Woman Teacher in Nineteenth-Century Canada West," *Ontario History* 83, no. 1 (1991): 39.

11. Patricia Hill Collins, *Black Feminist Thought: Knowledge, Consciousness, and the Politics of Empowerment*, 2nd ed. (New York: Routledge, 2000), 6.

12. Bearden and Butler, *Shadd*, 34.

13. Rhodes, *Mary Ann Shadd Cary*, 48.

14. Mary Ann Shadd to George Whipple, June 21, 1852, quoted in Rhodes, *Mary Ann Shadd Cary*, 48.

15. Keith Michael Green, "Am I Not a Husband and a Father? Re-membering Black Masculinity, Slave Incarceration, and Cherokee Slavery in *The Life and Adventures of Henry Bibb, an American Slave*," *MELUS* 39, no. 4 (2014): 24.

16. Henry Bibb, *Narrative of the Life and Adventures of Henry Bibb, an American Slave, Written by Himself* (New York: Published by the author, 1849), 190–91, https://docsouth.unc .edu/neh/bibb/bibb.html.

17. Shirley J. Yee, "Finding a Place: Mary Ann Shadd Cary and the Dilemmas of Black Migration to Canada, 1850–1870," *Frontiers* 18, no. 3 (1997): 4.

18. Hazel V. Carby, *Race Men* (Cambridge, MA: Harvard University Press, 1998), 33–34. Bibb's display of manhood failed to encompass the Black women subject, in apposition to that of Frederick Douglass who was keenly aware of the white patriarchy as a fundamental of slavery yet also prioritized Black manhood for Black liberation.

19. I use this term in a way that Bibb appealed to gender and familial normativity. See Grace Kyungwon Hong and Roderick A. Ferguson, introduction to *Strange Affinities: The Gender and Sexual Politics of Comparative Racialization*, ed. Hong and Ferguson (Durham, NC: Duke University Press, 2011), 8.

20. Robin Winks, *The Blacks in Canada* (New Haven, CT: Yale University Press, 1972), 207.

21. For his capitalistic vision on the Black settlement, see Roger W. Hite, "Voice of a Fugitive: Henry Bibb and Ante-Bellum Black Separatism," *Journal of Black Studies* 4, no. 3 (1974): 269–84.

22. Cali, "'Why Does Not Somebody Speak Out?,'" 35.

23. "Advice to the Girls," *Voice of the Fugitive*, May 20, 1852, quoted in Rhodes, *Mary Ann Shadd Cary*, 57.

24. *Voice of the Fugitive*, February 22, 1853, quoted in Rhodes, *Mary Ann Shadd Cary*, 73.

25. Quoted in Rhodes, *Mary Ann Shadd Cary*, 73.

26. Mary Ann Shadd to George Whipple, December 25, 1852, quoted in Bearden and Butler, *Shadd*, 77.

27. Quoted in Dorothy Sterling, ed., *We Are Your Sisters: Black Women in the Nineteenth Century* (New York: W. W. Norton, 1984), 171.

28. "A Word About, and to Emigrationists," *Provincial Freeman*, April 15, 1854, p. 2.

29. According to another leader in Canada West, Rev. Alexander McArthur, "[Miss Shadd] has been very much abused here in public meetings and through the columns of the 'Voice of the Fugitive' by the senior Editor of that paper. . . . But it is not my object to enter into a defence of Miss S.'s character and motives, she is abundantly able to defend herself from the charges which

Mr. C. C. Foote brings against her." Alexander McArthur to George Whipple, December 22, 1852, quoted in Bearden and Butler, *Shadd*, 115.

30. Mary A. Shadd, *A Plea for Emigration; or, Notes of Canada West* (Detroit: Printed by George W. Pattison, 1852), 42, https://archive.org/details/cihm_47542/page/n45/mode/2up.

31. Jones, *All Bound Up Together*, 9.

32. Mary Ann Shadd to George Whipple, June 21, 1852, quoted in Rhodes, *Mary Ann Shadd Cary*, 48.

33. Fuller to George Whipple, July 18, 1853, cites Nichols's letter to Fuller, July 15, 1853. Quoted in Bearden and Butler, *Shadd*, 122. I could not find Fuller's full name.

34. Mary Bibb to Gerrit Smith, July 16, 1855, Gerrit Smith Papers, Special Collections Research Center, Syracuse University Libraries. I thank Petrina Jackson, the former director of the Special Collections Research Center, for letting me learn about this letter.

35. Mary Ann Shadd to George Whipple, January 13, 1853, quoted in Bearden and Butler, *Shadd*, 121–22.

36. Rhodes, *Mary Ann Shadd Cary*, 22.

37. "Anti-Slavery Lectures," *Provincial Freeman*, March 29 1856, p. 2. Reference here is to H. Ford Douglas (sometimes spelled Douglass), coproprietor of the *Provincial Freeman*. He is cited as H. Ford Douglass in Demetra McBrayer's chapter in this volume.

38. On one occasion, Mary Bibb publicly defended Henry Bibb from the allegation that he operated the Refugee Home Society for his own benefit, maintaining that the allegation came from white and free Blacks who resented the fact that they were excluded from the society's distribution of land and resources. As Rhodes describes, "it was Mary Bibb who uncharacteristically moved from her husband's shadow to challenge the Shadd faction" (*Mary Ann Shadd Cary*, 63).

39. See Bearden and Butler, *Shadd*, 8; and Rhodes, *Mary Ann Shadd Cary*, 58. May, an antislavery and women's rights advocate, ran the Massachusetts State Normal School, a teacher-training institution, from which Mary Bibb graduated in 1843. May was impressed by Shadd's work, writing to Lewis Tappan, "Miss Shadd is a very capable young woman. I visited her school and inspected several exercises of several classes, all of which were well performed," quoted in Rhodes, *Mary Ann Shadd Cary*, 58–59.

40. Abraham Shadd participated in five of the first six national meetings from 1830 to 1835, and served as president of "the Third Annual Convention for the Improvement of the Free People of Colour in these United States," held in Philadelphia, 1833. Mary Shadd continued to attend conventions with her father in Canada West, such as the Great North American Anti-Slavery Convention, held in Toronto. See Rhodes, *Mary Ann Shadd Cary*, 33. As P. Gabrielle Foreman suggests, "the pantheon of Black leadership and the movement's geographic reach and generational influence beg for a consideration of not only conventions but convention culture." Foreman, "Black Organizing, Print Advocacy, and Collective Authorship," in *The Colored Conventions Movement: Black Organizing in the Nineteenth Century*, ed. P. Gabrielle Foreman, Jim Casey, and Sarah Lynn Patterson (Chapel Hill: University of North Carolina Press, 2021), 28.

41. *North Star*, March 23, 1849, p. 3. Retrieved from the Library of Congress, www.loc.gov/item/sn84026365/1849-03-23/ed-1/.

42. Afua P. Cooper, "Black Women and Work in Nineteenth-Century Canada West: Black Woman Teacher Mary Bibb," in *"We're Rooted Here and They Can't Pull Us Up": Essays in African Canadian Women's History*, coord. Peggy Bristow (Toronto: University of Toronto Press, 1994), 148. Also see Rhodes, *Mary Ann Shadd Cary*, 42.

43. Benjamin Drew, *A North-Side View of Slavery* (Boston: John P. Jewett, 1856), 321–22, https://docsouth.unc.edu/neh/drew/drew.html.

44. See Bearden and Butler, *Shadd*; Rhodes, *Mary Ann Shadd Cary*; Carol B. Conaway, "Mary Ann Shadd Cary: A Visionary of the Black Press," in *Black Women's Intellectual Traditions*, ed. Kristin Waters and Carol B. Conaway (Burlington: University of Vermont Press, 2007), 216–45; Lauren F. Klein, "Dimensions of Scale: Invisible Labor, Editorial Work, and the Future of Quantitative Literary Studies," *PMLA* 135, no. 1 (2020): 23–39; and Carla L. Peterson, *"Doers of the Word": African-American Women Speakers & Writers in the North (1830–1880)* (New Brunswick, NJ: Rutgers University Press, 1998), chap. 4 ("Colored Tourists").

45. "Adieu," *Provincial Freeman*, June 30, 1855, p. 2.

46. *Provincial Freeman*, October 6, 1855, p. 2.

47. Peggy Bristow, "'Whatever You Raise in the Ground You Can Sell It in Chatham': Black Women in Buxton and Chatham, 1850–65," in *"We're Rooted Here and They Can't Pull Us Up,"* 122.

48. Afua Cooper, "The *Voice of the Fugitive*: A Transnational Abolitionist Organ," in *A Fluid Frontier: Slavery, Resistance, and the Underground Railroad in the Detroit River Borderland*, ed. Karolyn Smardz Frost and Veta Smith Tucker (Detroit: Wayne State University Press, 2016), 143.

49. Mary Bibb to Gerrit Smith, November 8, 1850. *The Black Abolitionist Papers*, vol. 2, *Canada, 1830–1865*, ed. C. Peter Ripley (Chapel Hill: University of North Carolina Press, 1985), 108–12.

50. Cooper, "The *Voice*," 142–43.

51. Ripley, *Black Abolitionist Papers*, 2:108.

52. In "The Search," Cooper describes the difficulty in searching for Mary Bibb, whose name never appeared as a contributor to articles in the *Voice of the Fugitive*. Likewise, Jim Casey points out that searching for Mary Ann Shadd even in our digital age is challenging, as she used an asterisk to indicate her editorship. Casey argues that her asterisk as an "encoded form of editorial expression" implies "the tensions between exposure in print and self-effacement." Jim Casey, "Parsing the Special Characters of African American Print Culture: Mary Ann Shadd and the * Limits of Search," in *Against a Sharp White Background: Infrastructures of African American Print*, ed. Brigitte Fielder and Jonathan Senchyne (Madison: University of Wisconsin Press, 2019), 111.

53. Bristow, "'Whatever You Raise,'" 87.

54. "Donation Party," *Voice of the Fugitive*, November 19, 1851, p. 2.

55. Later Freeman married Shadd Cary's brother, Isaac Shadd. Bristow, "'Whatever You Raise,'" 116.

56. Bristow, "'Whatever You Raise,'" 122.

57. Her intention to deliver a speech as a delegate of Canada caused "a spirited discussion," and she was finally allowed when Frederick Douglass and other male delegates supported her. *Proceedings of the Colored National Convention, Held in Franklin Hall, Sixth Street, Below Arch, Philadelphia, October 16th, 17th and 18th, 1855*, Colored Conventions Project Digital Records, accessed August 5, 2021, https://omeka.coloredconventions.org/items/show/281.

58. Regarding Shadd's work with Truth, see Margaret Washington, "'I Am Going Straight to Canada': Women Underground Railroad Activists in the Detroit River Border Zone," in Frost and Tucker, *A Fluid Frontier*, 178; about how Greenfield and Shadd shaped each other's transnational vision, see Kristin Moriah, "'A Greater Compass of Voice': Elizabeth Taylor Greenfield and Mary Ann Shadd Cary Navigate Black Performance," *Theatre Research in Canada* 41, no. 1 (2020): 20–38.

59. See Rhodes, *Mary Ann Shadd Cary*, xvii; and Frances Smith Foster, introduction to *A Brighter Coming Day: A Frances Ellen Watkins Harper Reader*, ed. Foster (New York: Feminist Press at the City University of New York, 1990), 14.

60. It was a well-advertised affair. Robert Purvis introduced Shadd and other speakers in an article, "M.A. Shadd" in the *Pennsylvania Freeman*, Philadelphia, on May 26 and September 29, 1853.

61. Quoted in Dorothy Sterling, *We Are Your Sisters: Black Women in the Nineteenth Century* (New York: W. W. Norton, 1984), 174.

62. "W.S. Letter to the Editor," *Provincial Freeman*, September 2, 1854, p. 3.

63. Ripley, *Black Abolitionist Papers*, 2:111.

64. Cooper found Mary Bibb in the Dun and Bradstreet business directories. Cooper, "The Search," 43.

65. Tiffany M. Gill, *Beauty Shop Politics: African American Women's Activism in the Beauty Industry* (Urbana: University of Illinois Press, 2010), 1.

66. Penelope L. Bullock assumes that the *Repository* was never published. See Bullock, *The Afro-American Periodical Press, 1838–1901* (Baton Rouge: Louisiana State University Press, 1981), 66. However, the group of the nine editors and publishers organized at the second National Emigration Convention in 1856 somewhat managed to help African American writers, including James Theodore Holly, publish pamphlets. Holly's *A Vindication of the Capacity of the Negro Race* was published by the Afric-American Printing Co. in 1857 as part of the proposal for the *Afric American Repository*: "I have permitted it to be published at the request of the Afric-American Printing Company, an association for the publication, which forms a constituent part of the National Emigration Convention, over which [Rev. William C. Munroe] so ably presided, at its sessions, held in Cleveland, Ohio, in the year 1854–6." Antislavery Pamphlet Collection at the University of Massachusetts, Amherst, accessed November 25, 2022, https://credo.library.umass.edu/view/full/murb003-i162. I thank Curtis Small at the University of Delaware for introducing me to this document.

CHAPTER 3

Mary Ann Shadd Cary in Mexico

KIRSTEN LEE

In *Darkwater* (1920), W. E. B. Du Bois devotes an entire chapter to the political legacies and actions of Black women, as well as their central position in the Black community's function and flourishing. He writes in "The Damnation of Women" about the contradictory condemnations that Black women face in misogynist, patriarchal society, both inter- and intraracially. He includes a paragraph praising "Mary Shadd" alongside descriptions of Mary Still, Sojourner Truth, and Harriet Tubman. Of Shadd, Du Bois writes that "she threw herself singlehanded into the great Canadian pilgrimage when thousands of hunted black men hurried northward and crept beneath protection of the lion's paw. She became teacher, editor, and lecturer; tramping afoot through winter snows, pushing without blot or blemish through crowd and turmoil to conventions and meetings, and finally becoming recruiting agent for the United States government in gathering Negro soldiers in the West."[1] Here Du Bois offers an itinerary of Shadd's political activities throughout her migrations, giving pride of place to her part in "the great Canadian pilgrimage." Du Bois thus tracks Shadd's migrations in the Americas as phases of her political career and vice versa. He praises Shadd both for renouncing her U.S. citizenship and also for returning to the States in the face of the Civil War. But Shadd's major political positions cannot be reduced to her migratory patterns. Indeed, as this essay ventures, in her writings Shadd outlines how the geopolitical scenario of the nineteenth-century Americas requires Black peoples and their allies to prepare for expatriation acknowledging the political promise but also risks of emigration. Shadd's promotion of Canadian emigration is ultimately a hemispheric argument in service of the abolition of slavery and thus as much concerned with Central and South America as with the United States. Throughout her political career she encouraged her Black audience to be aware of the political risks of Mexico's precarious antislavery position as a territory of interest to Anglo slaveholders, while encouraging readers to be prepared to build an abolitionist Black enclave there all the same.

Some critics may note that Shadd's emigrationist platform focused on Canada as a terminus for Black out-migration in the Americas.[2] Yet in this chapter I argue that to focus only on the Canadian arm of Shadd's political awareness too closely links the settler aspirations of Shadd's platform to land ownership in North America. Looking at Mexico in Shadd's *A Plea for Emigration; or, Notes of Canada West* and in the *Provincial Freeman* shows how she argues both for and against a mass Black migration to Central America and the Caribbean, projecting "the establishment of an empire formed out of the southern United States and Mexico" either of proslavery or antislavery forces.[3] A close reading of *Plea* reveals how Shadd believed that Mexico was the wrong destination for Black out-migration, criticizing implicitly such an out-migration that was already underway, as explored by Theodore W. Cohen, Julian Lim, Christopher P. Lehman, and Cara Anne Kinnally.[4] In this reading of Shadd, I build on work by Winfried Siemerling, who explores the juxtaposition between Shadd and Martin Delany regarding the (un)suitability of Central and South America for a Black settler colony in *The Black Atlantic Reconsidered*.[5]

I argue that Shadd's confident refusal of Mexico as a Black settler colony does not refuse Central America for a mass Black out-migration but rather reacts to the ongoing pursuits of North American slaveholding interests to acquire land in Central and South America.[6] Shadd and her Black nationalist contemporaries—among them Frederick Douglass, James McCune Smith, and Martin Delany—believed that a Black antislavery politics based in North America required hemispheric strategy and migration.[7] Following Brigitte Fielder's notion of Blackness beyond the rhetoric of hypodescent, I argue that Shadd's emigrationist platform ultimately shows us "racialization is not individualistic but *spatially and temporally expansionist*," deploying migration as a means but not an end.[8] As Siemerling writes, "Shadd's call for black emigration from the United States, however, was also an explicit judgment on the United States that mapped out other Americas."[9] I propose in turning to Shadd that we find a framework beyond fugitivity and flight to think about Black freedom (of) movement in the Americas in the nineteenth century. In this chapter I imagine alongside Shadd what kinds of language can describe

Black migratory patterns in nineteenth-century Americas, of which self-emancipating peoples were a part but not the whole. I suggest that Shadd saw the expedience of a Canadian out-migration, but never saw it as the only or final destination for Black émigrés and self-emancipating enslaved peoples.

In this essay I refer to Shadd as a Black nationalist to focus on the political purposes of Shadd's multinational migration rather than on the destination. I identify Shadd in the school of what Tommie Shelby calls "pragmatic nationalism," the platform of which "inevitably draws on Western nationalist ideas . . . with a critical eye and an improvisational spirit, joined with a healthy suspicion of politicized ethno-racial identities and a steadfast commitment to justice for all."[10] Shadd was and remains an important thinker of Black nationalism, and her interest in political protest through emigration proposes a geographical register wherein Black movement and Black movements are one and the same, where we can observe a self-determined version of "the articulation of colonization with emancipation."[11] Studies of nineteenth-century Black nationalism in the Americas often frame its politics in opposition to emigrationist rhetoric, but both Black nationalist and emigrationist thought linked Black liberation to freedom of movement, migration, and property holding in their political advocacy.[12] Shadd's insistence that she and other Blacks would leave the United States of their own accord is a powerful refusal to an implicitly white nationalism in favor of colonization, but also leaves space for Black émigrés' enduring national attachment.[13] I submit that emigration and Shadd's Black nationalism are modes of apposition, in the style discussed by Fred Moten. When Moten writes, for example, that "the black radical tradition is in apposition to enlightenment," he signals a specifically Black register of improvisational deployments of freedom, or even enactments of freedom.[14] Here I read Moten somewhat literally and treat apposition as an on-the-ground choreography, as a geographic protocol, as a political cartography, and read "the performance of something like a detour" as a philological metaphor for Black liberatory practice in the nineteenth-century Americas.[15] In the case of apposition, adjacency produces not a relation between two independent elements but a relation of identification, of elaboration, of redescription. If we think of apposition as a spatial tactic at the scale of the human rather than the scale of the sentence, it makes it possible to think of migration as a relation of adjacency rather than flight alone. Shadd's emigrationist platform stands in apposition to her nationalist sensibilities rather than in opposition, in that she deploys migration as a method of multinational identification rather than separation. What makes Shadd's leaving the United States so radical is her idea not of its permanence but of its temporariness, its conditionality—leaving on her own terms, but also reserving and eventually exercising the right to return.

Shadd's *Plea* For and Against Central America

In *A Plea for Emigration; or, Notes of Canada West*, Shadd lays out her arguments in favor of a mass Black migration to a destination outside the United States. Rightly or wrongly, Shadd casts the precarity of antislavery efforts as territorial: she argues if more places were abolitionized in the Americas, antislavery efforts would be more successful. She in fact argues that though Black people in the United States have successfully rejected colonizationist schemes to deport them, they face the intractable problem that "more territory has been given up to slavery."[16] She makes clear that she sees all Black migration as a political act, enticing her kinsmen to see Canada as a proper home because its land had "the common ground on which all honest and respectable men meet . . . that of an *innate* hatred of American slavery."[17] Here Shadd imputes to Canadians a characteristic that is actually a political position, presenting antislavery sentiment as a natural resource and "common ground" of Canadian society. But as Rinaldo Walcott writes, "Blackness simultaneously unsettles Canadian-ness."[18] Enslaved Black peoples were some of the earliest residents of Canada West, and their presence has been made what Katherine McKittrick calls "erasable" over and above narratives of Canada "as a safe haven (to U.S. fugitive slaves)."[19] Throughout *Plea* Shadd relies on equivalences that establish the physical territory of Canada West, the land itself, as the basis of the political environment of antislavery. For Shadd, Canada is a good destination for Black émigrés not only for its the economic opportunities or colorblind legal protections; indeed, she works in *Plea* to derive Canadian social norms and political structure from its landscape, from the natural world itself. Shadd's envirodeterminist argument about Canadian abolition—which we might see from another angle as part of "the continual formation and reformation of race that has implications from the bodily to the national scale"—shows her belief that spatial location is also a racial technology that can be literally mobilized in pursuit of greater freedom in acts of migration.[20] Because for Shadd race is made and remade only through social contexts, as *Plea* and *Provincial Freeman* show, she contends that that migration could remake Blackness itself. When she writes to her fellow "colored people," that "the people are in a strait," Shadd establishes the notion of fording as the foundational metaphor of migration in her treatise.[21]

Shadd saw the abolitionist political scene in the United States as too quietist, as evidenced by her argument that only a Black-led mass (e)migration would be politically capable of undermining the institution of chattel slavery. In *Plea* Shadd identifies that the proslavery forces in the United States will continuously chip away at rights of free Blacks in effort to keep their kin enslaved. Shadd notes that the 1850 Fugitive Slave Law has effectively or will soon create a refugee crisis for Black peoples in the United States, regardless of their legal status. Shadd concludes that the passing of the Fugitive Law makes all Black movements subject to review and policing. "It is well known that the Fugitive Bill makes insecure every northern colored man—those free are alike at the risk of *being sent south*. Consequently many person, always free, will leave the United States and settle in Canada, and other countries, who would have remained had not that law been enacted."[22]

Shadd elaborates this point by noting that those self-emancipating enslaved peoples might find themselves overwhelmed and living destitute lives after "the accident of nominal freedom" corresponding to migration.[23] Though Shadd argues that mass exodus is imminent, she firmly rejects outmigration to Africa, saying, "neither a home in Africa, nor in the Southern States, is desireable [*sic*] under present circumstances."[24] Shadd argues that Black (e)migration is the only political tactic that would be successful as a coordinated blow to chattel slavery, and thus an act supporting the actions of abolitionists who might remain in the United States. In her "Introductory Remarks," for example, Shadd casts in the role of Scylla and Charybdis "a pro-slavery administration" and "the Colonization Society," suggesting that both phenomena are trying to dispossess and displace Black people enslaved and free.[25] Though Shadd reduces Africa to its hostile terrain, and opposes the false promise of the motherland, "teeming as she is with breath of pestilence, a burning sun, and fearful maladies," to the domesticated territories of North America, she also proposes that neither the United States nor Africa offers a suitable environment in which Black folk could prosper, unite, and organize.[26]

Indeed, Shadd talks about the advantages of the Canadian terrain in terms of its temperate zones "exempt from the steady and enfeebling warmth of *southern latitudes*."[27] Shadd emphasizes the potential moral decay of Black settlers if they move to too southern a location, which will later in *Plea* become a reluctance to encourage a migration. She further insists on the inferiority of territories farther south than Canada, suggesting that in the Great Lakes region "the people living in the States bordering, suffer more severely from the cold than Canadians."[28] Shadd's emigrationist call to action relies on establishing that the States suffer from more extreme weather than Canada West. By illustrating that Canada has fertile ground and temperate weather, Shadd shows her Black readers of all class positions that they could establish and build capital in Canada.[29] Critically, Shadd argues that theoretically all lands outside the United States hold more value for potential Black landholders because their rights as citizens would be respected, and they would be treated as free citizens, some for the first time. She does not make a distinction between the value of Mexican lands or Canadian lands for Black émigrés. In this passage Shadd begins to make her case against Mexico as a destination for Black émigrés, already fortified by her earlier case against the border states of the Great Lakes region.

> Lands out of the United States, on this continent, should have no local value, if the question of personal freedom and political rights were left out of the subject, but as they are paramount, too much may not be said on this point. I mean to be understood, that a description of lands in Mexico would probably be as desirable as lands in Canada, if the idea were simply to get lands and settle thereon; but it is important to know if by this investigation we only agitate and leave the public mind in an unsettled state, or if a permanent nationality is included in the prospect of becoming purchasers and settlers.[30]

Here Shadd makes no qualitative difference between Mexico and Canada, instead emphasizing that at the level of description both terrains would be desirable for potential Black émigrés hoping to settle there. Yet Shadd acknowledges that the best destination for a mass Black migration depends on how long migrants intend to stay in their new country. Shadd suggests, in other words, that Mexico can only seem a desirable destination in a speculative mode that leaves the "public mind in an unsettled state."

Shadd additionally insists that permanent settlement in Canada would secure a more liberated future for Black émigrés. She contends that "no equal number of colored men in the States, north or south, can produce more *free-holders*," conflating property-holding with more durable freedom for Black folks than can even be achieved en masse under American law.[31] Indeed Shadd emphasizes that "destitute" émigrés forfeit their property in the act of travel, "from having, in many instances, to leave behind them all they possessed," but Shadd only uses this to portray the state of dependence in which fugitives are kept by the constant stream of donations.[32] But Shadd also emphasizes that the colored population of the Canadas, among "those permanently settled," hold "portions of the best farming lands in the province, and own much valuable property in the several cities, etc."[33] And as further explored by scholars like Nina Reid-Maroney, Afua Cooper, and Jane Rhodes, by the mid-nineteenth century when Shadd emigrated, urban hubs like Chatham and Toronto could boast of Black communities with resources in the form of land, cultural institutions, and businesses.[34] Though many critics, among them Jane Rhodes and Christian Olbey, have pointed out the poverty and financial insecurity in which Shadd lived in Canada West, Shadd in *Plea* represents all émigrés as capable of achieving financial wealth in their new country. She stresses that there are no racial or gender limitations on who can own land or on whose landholding entitles them to voting rights.[35] Further, Shadd entices her readers to migrate based on the fact that there is "no legal discrimination whatever effecting [*sic*] colored emigrants in Canada," before later reiterating that white Americans are also moving to Canada in an effort to shape public opinion toward Black emigrants, poisoning the abolitionist culture of the Canadas.[36]

Shadd in the later parts of *Plea* finally turns to discuss in detail the position of Canada relative to other potential outposts for Black migrants. Summarizing her argument thus far in *Plea* before turning to elsewhere in the Americas and Caribbean, Shadd includes an entire section called "Recapitulation," reminding readers of the progress of her argument and drawing to something of a conclusion. "The conclusion arrived at in respect to Canada, by an impartial person, is, that *no settled country in America* offers stronger inducements to colored people. . . . The laws of the country give to them, at first, the same protections and privileges as to other persons not born subjects, and after compliance with Acts of Parliament affecting them, as taking oath, &c., they may enjoy full 'privileges of British birth in the Province.'"[37]

In her first section addressing the possibility of southward emigration, she first addresses how common "the direct advantage to the planter from such emigration" is, especially "if the emigrants consent to be mere laborers instead of owners of the soil."[38] Shadd blames this coercive labor and the resulting migratory patterns—many of which both she and her readers would have identified as the ongoing hold of chattel slavery—for the resulting racialized and class inequalities in the Caribbean, inequalities sustained by the seductive rhetorics "held out by planters to colored men."[39] Importantly, Shadd argues that the only resulting arrangement of Caribbean society will be one of inequality sustained by the plantation system.[40]

Because in *Plea* Shadd seeks strategies that will "materially elevate" her readers, she will not assent to forms of migration that continue to lock colored émigrés out of property-holding. Indeed she suggests that slaveholders have already identified their vested interests in preserving slavery in the Global South, making "large calculations of a future interest in the West Indies, Honduras, and ultimately South America."[41] Because Shadd argues that only "a system of voluntary emigration to those islands" could break up its plantocracy—and here "voluntary" signals the migration without planters' solicitation—she sees Black movements as speech acts, as always a rhetoric and an action. Neither the legacies of marronage nor the precedent set by significant insurrections like the Berbice Rebellion and Haitian Revolution seem here to shape Shadd's argument that Black American émigrés are necessary to topple West Indian plantocracies. Elsewhere in *Plea* we can see Shadd encouraging her readers to consider moving southward to shore up antislavery efforts. Shadd explains the enticements of each southern location to readers not so much in terms of the quality of land or of society, but as tactical placements in a political landscape.

> To preserve those countries [the West Indies, Honduras, and ultimately South America] from the ravages of slavery, should be motive to their settlement by colored men. Jamaica, with its fine climate and rich soil, is the key to the gulf of Mexico. It is not distant from the United States, Cuba, nor Haiti; but, as if providentially, is just so positioned that, if properly *garrisoned* by colored free men, may, under Britain, promptly and effectually check foreign interference in its own policy, and any mischievous designs now in contemplation toward Cuba and Haiti.[42]

Shadd elaborates that Black folk should move southward primarily to shore up abolitionist organizing, writing that "in view of the ultimate destiny of the southern portion of North America, it is of the first importance that colored men strengthen that and similar positions in that region."[43] Shadd's call to action to abolitionists comments on the precarity of the U.S. South as equal to that of Mexico. In fact, as will be later discussed, Shadd's editorials in *Provincial Freeman* show that after *Plea*'s publication she continued to see Mexico as a terrain of major interest for Blacks free and enslaved as well as American abolitionists concerned about Texas's de facto protections for Anglo slaveowners. Shadd sees Mexico differently than she does the West Indies, pointing out like David Walker before her that the colored population in the Caribbean far outnumbers whites, resulting in a "'balance of power'" that favors Black uprising.[44]

Shadd also discourages choosing the Global South ultimately because she doubts those nations' ability to unite, or to finalize "plans for a grant of territory from governments in that country."[45] In this Shadd differs from Martin R. Delany, who sought out Nicaragua as a potential settler site for Black American émigrés in the early 1850s, and who was further elected mayor of San Juan del Norte, Nicaragua, in 1852.[46] Shadd ends her section on geographies other than Canada by concluding that only current or former British territories could be a good home for Black American émigrés, but she briefly acknowledges that Mexico is not subject to the same faults as South America as a potential site for settlement. Shadd writes with certainty that slaveholding interests will succeed in acquiring territories in Central and South America, but she also imagines a future that points as equally to an antislavery success as to a proslavery one: "It needs no prophet to foretell the establishment of an empire formed out of the southern United States and Mexico. The settlements by colored people of those countries, with their many sympathizers, is but a preparatory step: that a step has been taken, slavery and republican rapacity will do the rest."[47]

Shadd here argues that the fastest route to a mass liberation for Black folks in the United States is ultimately expatriation. Indeed, Shadd encourages potential emigrants to confirm that, whatever their destination, their new nation has "only governments, anti-slavery in spirit and tendency."[48] She still encourages Black émigrés to choose Mexico, the West Indies, and Honduras as their destination, in preparation to thwart proslavery land interests from their new positions as Black landowners.

Shadd both discourages Black émigrés from relocating to Mexico and also conveys that emigrants to the country should form a Black separatist colony. Shadd holds Mexico apart as a special case for Black American émigrés because it borders the United States and also has a natural inclination to abolitionist sentiment. When it comes to Mexico, however, Shadd insists that the country is a false positive for a Black settler colony. She opens her section on Mexico writing that "the vicinity of Mexico to the United States, and the known hostility of Mexicans to the institution of slavery, weigh strongly with some person in favor of emigration to that country."[49] Yet she blames "the Castilians" for wanting to retain power after the revolution in Mexico and blames their hope for national autonomy for the possibility that the Mexican government would form "a coalition with American slaveholders even."[50] In Shadd's view, Mexico's strong cultural identification with Spain and the Roman Catholic Church make Mexico and other Latin American states "undesirable for colored people from the United States in the present state of things."[51] Indeed she sees Mexico as already vulnerable to being a major outpost for preserving slavery in North America. "We want a strong position. Mexico does not offer that, even though the majority are anti-slavery. The Southern United States have 'marked her for prey,' which she will be for a time; and combining with the minority, the probability is a contest for the supremacy of slavery for a long time."[52] Shadd again appeals to her readers' abolitionist leanings, appealing to them as a group self-consciously committed to seeking and protecting durable freedoms for their Black kin, pleading that "people who love liberty do not emigrate to weak governments . . . but to strong ones."[53]

Ultimately Shadd argues in *Plea* that there must be a larger abolitionist plan through which all Black peoples in the Americas understand their movements and migrations as weakening or strengthening the political project of abolition. Interestingly, she describes that master plan as one of conservation rather than acquisition. "The position of colored Americas must be a conservative one, for a time, in any foreign country (from the very nature of their relations to foreign nations), as well as for themselves in the United States; and if it were folly in them to voluntarily enter the breach between any two hostile nations until stronger in position. Their efforts to be rational should be to gain strength."[54] Shadd recommends Black Americans emigrate not as a permanent decision but as a political action, precisely because she asks them to see always their condition and the condition of Black kin in the United States as linked. Yet Shadd discourages potential Black emigrants from fully defecting from the United States or renouncing their national attachment. Shadd makes that psychic and political investment in the state of Black life in the United States an important material condition of flight and also return. In other words, as much as Shadd advocates Black mass out-migration, she also holds steady that Blacks' return to the United States should always be a tactical option, should it become necessary for the universal aim of abolition or to the immediate protection of Black property and capital, as well as the safety of Black persons. What makes Shadd's emigrationist platform radical is not its prescribed relocation or calls for permanent settlement outside the United States but its anticipation of return to the States, and return put to political use at that.

Shadd's assumption that the border between nations of North America are porous and will always be so illustrates how her emigrationist platform is built around the border space and border-crossing rather than permanent settlement; this feature of *Plea*'s geography shows that freedom of movement is the main goal for Shadd. When Shadd addresses Mexico's role in her abolitionist geography, she makes a case that Mexico may eventually be a destination for émigrés, but that it cannot house a Black settler colony in the Americas just yet. "Let Mexico, at present, take care of herself, by the efforts of her own mixed population rightly directed, and let our emigrants so *abolitionize* and strengthen neighboring positions as to promote the prosperity and harmony of the whole. This can be done without compromising away honor; in fact the sentiment 'liberty or death,' is never realized but by so proceeding as to secure the first permanently, and only courting the latter when life is no longer of utility."[55] She recommends that emigrants thus move to areas around Mexico but not Mexico so that they can strengthen efforts to resist Mexico becoming amenable to slavery, or a shelter for slaveholders and their estates. In *Plea* Shadd does not exclude Mexico as a potential settler colony, but prods her readers' to *abolitionize* regions through their migrations.

Central and South America in Shadd's *Provincial Freeman*

In *A Plea for Emigration* Shadd does indeed give a case for what the relation between North American and Central American emigration might be. Shadd's skepticism toward Mexico partially illustrates how much Shadd saw abolition as an issue of land politics, because she identified that Mexico's geopolitical vulnerability was its desire to keep territory. Part of Shadd's critique of Mexico in *A Plea* is that Mexican nationalists are so desperate to shore up their recently-acquired independent republic that they would deal with slaveholders or be vulnerable to their rhetoric. At the same time that she encourages readers to see or prepare for Canadian emigration, she also makes clear how important it is to plan to build Black settler colonies in Central America and the West Indies so that they can work to abolitionize the region.[56] What Shadd means by "abolitionize" seems first and foremost measured with reference to American antislavery efforts.

Shadd also points to other histories of dispossession that subtend Mexico's unsuitability for Black migrants, whom she casts as settler colonists. She blames Indigenous peoples for losing land to settler colonists, hinting through historical example that Black émigrés would face a similar fate if they tried to set up a settlement in Mexico before it has abolitionized neighbors. On this point, Shadd's rhetoric bears a marked resemblance to both Delany's and Douglass's on the same; in a 1849 editorial in the *North Star*, for example, Douglass asserts that "the persecuted red man of the forest, the original owner of the soil, has, step by step, retreated . . . gradually disappearing from the face of the country."[57] In a similar line of reasoning, Shadd writes in *Plea* that "the Indians have learned sense from frequent defeat, the consequence of going to war before they were prepared, and whole tribes now cultivate the arts of peace and progress. Let us learn even of savages!"[58] She portrays Native peoples as insufficiently organized against colonizers and counts those "defeats" of dispossession and displacement against Indigenous peoples.[59] Yet she warns all peoples that whatever their national affiliations, the ongoing character of primitive accumulation makes the most urgent politics hemispheric rather than local. She reminds readers in closing her section on Mexico that "the pro-slavery party of the United States is the aggressive party of the United States is the aggressive party on *this continent*. It is the serpent that aims to swallow all others."[60]

What we can see here is Shadd's bleak prognosis for continental abolition. She advises abolitionists to target the acquisition of land and creation of colonies both in North America and elsewhere, noting "they [proslavery] are strengthening themselves in the Northwest, and in the Gulf."[61] Instead she tells abolitionists to always be thinking about the hemispheric consequences and scope of their organizing; against the state-level focus, Shadd suggests a transnational coalition building to coordinate "a peaceful but decided demand for freedom to the slave from the Gulf of Mexico."[62] Critically, Shadd defines this abolitionist goal not in terms of nation, or states, but landscapes; "the slave from the Gulf of Mexico" could hail from the United States, Central America, Mexico, or the West Indies.

Shadd's arguments about Mexico find more full expression in the *Provincial Freeman*, especially since *Plea* helped Shadd eventually source funding for the latter. Shadd used her periodical platform not only to promote outmigration to her readers but to steer them toward the right destinations. In an editorial, April 15, 1854, Shadd calls on Black folk to release their impulse to "wait out their fear and despair."[63] In this editorial, "A Word About, and to

Emigrationists," Shadd invites readers to see themselves as part of "the colored British Nation" that has room for "no one color above another, but being composed of all colors."[64] To the Commonwealth she opposes the United States where "you are taxed without being represented."[65] Shadd indicates that emigrationists believe in the dignity of desire and material security and, as I would read it, built on landholding: "But we speak to you in all kindness; we wish to be where you can act like men. To talk of doing great things where you cannot get a foot hold, as anti-Emigrationists do, is questionable with us. First take a position, and then what can prevent you from accomplishing what you desire?"[66] She further posits emigrationists as empathetic and even "softened" toward their opponents in their political folly as "nominal freemen."[67] But Shadd shows the linked and also unlinked fate that Black émigrés elsewhere in North America feel with Black Americans, who not only fail to see the advantages of leaving the United States behind but also tend to frame the issues as a "national affair" rather than a North American one—a move that excludes Black Canadians who, Shadd writes, can "only hope for your 'arrival' on our shores in due time."[68] Shadd argues against emigration to Central America and South America in closing, suggesting that migrants will be forced into manual labor and won't be able to build capital:

> But you talk of emigration to Central America and other hot places. Know you not that men are there before you? Central and South America, Central Africa and Egypt, as you please, have as many great men now as they know what to do with. The black men of those countries want men to trim up their cane fields at 3s 9d at the most. . . . You can trim your own fields in Canada by paying 7s 6d an acre for the land, or another man's if you have not the energy enough to have fields of your own, at better pay than that. Now if this is not enough to induce you to come hither what will, what will?[69]

Shadd goes on to suggest that Black émigrés would suffer miserably in the heat of the African continent and their women would be afraid of the insect life of the terrains. Her editorial shows how her argument in favor of Canadian emigration always implicitly draws on her argument against Central American emigration. Indeed, she proves the Canadian case partly through the counterfactual that Central American case presents.

But as established in *Plea*, Shadd still holds out the possibility that southward mass Black migration could play a key role in abolitionizing the continent. The frequency with which the *Provincial Freeman* publishes or reprints pieces describing what borders enslaved peoples could cross and self-emancipate shows the newspaper's awareness of its multiple audiences, enslaved and free.[70] Shadd ran a reprint from the *Saturday Evening Post* in the *Provincial Freeman*, March 24, 1855, in which the author argued on the topic of Central America that Americans' voracious ongoing and coordinated land theft has damaged the United States' reputation as a leader: "Mexico, the Central American, and South American States, all looked up and revered our Government as *the great head of the American political church.*"[71] This belief in the leadership and soft power of the United States implicitly argues that the U.S. policy decisions affect the entire hemisphere. The *Provincial Freeman* in some moments praised Mexico and its policies. For example, a reprinted article from the *A.S. Standard* in the *Provincial Freeman* issue of April 25, 1857, celebrated the new constitution, which "declares that all persons born in Mexico are born free, and that slaves coming thither from other countries are free the moment their feet touch the soil, and entitled to the protection of the laws."[72] The article further claims that this element of the Mexican constitution is a personalized blow to "American Slavocracy" and especially to "slaveholders of the United States, living on the Mexican border."[73] Seeing foreign policy internal to other nations as ultimately geared toward the United States reads as American exceptionalism at first glance, but it also mirrors a strength of Shadd's ideology, because she used this interpretive tendency to signal how Black expatriation, the "longstanding porosity of the US-Canadian border for Black North Americas, particularly women," could ultimately be a political action toward domestic issues.[74]

Interestingly, in the *Provincial Freeman* Shadd focuses as much on intranational as international politics in the United States and Canada. In a summary of a letter to the *Cleveland Daily Herald* reprinted by Shadd in the *Provincial Freeman*, William Walker, a chief in the Wyandot Tribe, delivers a story revealing the links between Native sovereignty and the process of Black self-emancipatory migrations, particularly to Mexico. Walker's main complaint throughout the letter is that the courts have designated his nation's lands in Missouri a slavery territory, since "some slaves are held by the Indians by virtue of their own laws and usages," a fact that many "white people going into the territory by the authority of the government in the character of Indian agents, mechanics, licensed traders, teachers, missionaries, &c." exploit by bringing enslaved peoples with them.[75] Walker then cites a Missouri Supreme Court case where a Judge Ryland ruled in favor of the defense's claim that Indian territory was "not free soil," allowing an estate administered by Walker the ability to sue for "the value of the runaway slave" who had "managed to escape, and succeeded in reaching Mexico, and was never reclaimed."[76] Here the *Provincial Freeman* engages Indian territory and Indigenous slaveholding as a deciding factor in the balance between proslavery and antislavery actors, and related to the role of Mexico in hemispheric antislavery efforts at that.

The *Provincial Freeman* combines an awareness of the trauma and injustice of Indian Removal with an awareness that sometimes Native sovereignty directly opposes the interests of Black freedom. Walker and to a certain extent the *Provincial Freeman* hint that white slaveholders are exploiting regional legal loopholes all over North and Central America. In the face of such flagrance, Shadd argues ultimately that only Black peoples could have each other's best interests really at heart in their political actions, particularly around abolition.

Conclusion: Shadd's Movement Politics

In this chapter I have considered how Shadd's refusal of Mexico as a Black abolitionist destination dovetails with her promotion of Black emigration to Canada West. When we read these Global North and Global South spheres of Shadd's emigrationist platform together, we can see how Shadd's (trans) national political objectives ultimately prioritize a Black freedom of movement in the Americas, a freedom tied to the ability to both leave and return to any particular nation. Shadd's Canadian emigration, then, stands in apposition to her refusal of Mexico-bound Black emigration. Both gestures are part of the same political project of Black emancipation and hemispheric abolition. When Shadd writes in *Plea* of the need to "abolitionize" the Global South, she ultimately warns her readers against allowing proslavery forces based in the United States to gain territory in these known geographic targets for acquisition in Central America and the West Indies. Her major arguments in *Plea* as well as her editorial curation of the *Provincial Freeman* show how Shadd argued for and against a mass Black out-migration to the Central America, the West Indies, and Central Africa. She puts both northward and southward out-migrations to use in her arguments about Black liberation, abolition, and freedom of movement. For Shadd, abolition is movement par excellence.

Notes

1. W. E. B. Du Bois, *Darkwater: Voices from Within the Veil* (New York: Harcourt, Brack and Howe, 1920), 178.

2. Kathy L. Glass, "Bi-National Connections: Mary Ann Shadd Cary and the Afro-Canadian Community," in *Courting Communities: Black Female Nationalism and "Syncre-Nationalism" in the Nineteenth-Century North* (New York: Routledge 2006), 57–76; Jennifer Bernhardt Steadman, "Traveling Uplift: Mary Ann Shadd Cary Creates and Connects Black Communities," in *Traveling Economies: American Women's Travel Writing* (Columbus: Ohio State University Press, 2007), 85–111; Jane Rhodes, *Mary Ann Shadd Cary: The Black Press and Protest in the Nineteenth Century* (Bloomington: Indiana University Press, 1998); Jane Rhodes, "At the Boundaries of Abolitionism, Feminism, and Black Nationalism: The Activism of Mary Ann Shadd Cary," in *Women's Rights and Transatlantic Antislavery in the Era of Emancipation*, ed. Kathryn Kish Sklar (New Haven, CT.: Yale University Press, 2007), 346–64; Andrea Stone, "Ancient Ideals and the Healthy Self: Mary Ann Shadd's *Plea for Emigration* and Martin Robison Delany's *Condition, Elevation, Emigration, and Destiny*," in *Black Well-Being: Health and Selfhood in Antebellum Black Literature* (Gainesville: University Press of Florida, 2016), 51–83; Jim Casey, "Parsing the Special Characters of African American Print Culture: Mary Ann Shadd and the * Limits of Search," in *Against a Sharp White Background: Infrastructures of African American Print*, ed. Brigitte Fielder and Jonathan Senchyne (Madison: University of Wisconsin Press, 2019), 109–27; Rodger Streitmatter, "Mary Ann Shadd Cary: Advocate for Canadian Emigration," in *Raising Her Voice: African-American Women Journalists Who Changed History* (Lexington: University Press of Kentucky, 1994), 25–36; Carla L. Peterson, *"Doers of the Word": African-American Women Speakers and Writers in the North (1830–1880)* (New York: Oxford University Press, 1995); Shirley J. Yee, "Finding a Place: Mary Ann Shadd Cary and the Dilemmas of Black Migration to Canada, 1850–1870," *Frontiers* 18, no. 3 (1997): 1–16.

3. Mary Ann Shadd, *A Plea for Emigration; or, Notes of Canada West*, ed. Phanuel Antwi (Peterborough, ON: Broadview Press, 2016), 56.

4. See Theodore W. Cohen, *Finding Afro-Mexico: Race and Nation After the Revolution* (Cambridge, UK: Cambridge University Press, 2020); Julian Lim, *Porous Borders: Multiracial Migrations and the Law in the U.S.-Mexico Borderlands* (Chapel Hill: University of North Carolina Press, 2017); Christopher P. Lehman, *Slavery's Reach: Southern Slaveholders in the North Star State* (St. Paul: Minnesota Historical Society, 2019); Cara Anne Kinnally, *Forgotten Futures, Colonized Pasts: Transnational Collaboration in Nineteenth-Century Greater Mexico* (Lewisburg, PA: Bucknell University Press, 2019); Herman L. Bennett, *Colonial Blackness: A History of Afro-Mexico* (Bloomington: Indiana University Press, 2009); Elena K. Abbott, "Departure and Debate: Free Black Emigration to Canada and Mexico," in *Beacons of Liberty: International Free Soil and the Fight for Racial Justice in Antebellum America* (New York: Cambridge University Press, 2021), 77–99.

5. Winfried Siemerling, *The Black Atlantic Reconsidered: Black Canadian Writing, Cultural History, and the Presence of the Past* (Montreal: McGill-Queen's University Press, 2015), 112.

6. Marco Cabrera Geserick, *The Legacy of the Filibuster War: National Identity and Collective Memory in Central America* (Lanham, MD: Lexington Books, 2019); Rodrigo Lazo, *Writing to Cuba: Filibustering and Cuban Exiles in the United States* (Chapel Hill: University of North Carolina Press, 2005); Joaquín Bernardo Calvo, *La campaña nacional contra los filibusteros en*

1856 y 1857: Breve reseña histórica (San Jose, Costa Rica: Tip. nacional, 1909); William Walker, *The War in Nicaragua* (New York: S. H. Goetzel, 1860); Michel Gobat, *Empire by Invitation: William Walker and Manifest Destiny in Central America* (Cambridge, MA: Harvard University Press, 2018); Carmen Fallas Santana, review of *The Legacy of the Filibuster War*, by Cabrera Geserick, *Hispanic American Historical Review* 101, no. 1 (2021): 136–38; Kevin Waite, *West of Slavery: The Southern Dream of a Transcontinental Empire* (Chapel Hill: University of North Carolina Press, 2021); Matthew Karp, "The World Slaveholders Craved: Proslavery Internationalism in the 1850s," in *The World of Revolutionary American Republic: Land, Labor, and the Conflict for a Continent*, ed. Andrew Shankman (New York: Routledge, 2014), 414–32.

7. Martin Robison Delany, *The Condition, Elevation, Emigration, and Destiny of the Colored People of the United States* (Philadelphia: Published by the author, 1852); Frederick Douglass, "'What to the Slave Is the Fourth of July?': An Address Delivered in Rochester, New York, 5 July 1852," in *The Speeches of Frederick Douglass: A Critical Edition*, ed. John R. McKivigan, Julie Husband, and Heather L. Kaufman (New Haven, CT: Yale University Press, 2018), 55–92. See also Frederick Douglass, "The Present Condition and Future Prospects of the Negro People" (speech at annual meeting of the American and Foreign Anti-Slavery Society, New York City, May 11, 1853), in *Frederick Douglass: Selected Speeches and Writings*, ed. Philip S. Foner, abridged and adapted by Yuval Taylor (Chicago: Lawrence Hill Books, 1999), 250–59.

8. Brigitte Fielder, *Relative Races: Genealogies of Interracial Kinship in Nineteenth-Century America* (Durham, NC: Duke University Press, 2020), 205, my emphasis.

9. Siemerling, *The Black Atlantic Reconsidered*, 105.

10. Tommie Shelby, *We Who Are Dark: The Philosophical Foundations of Black Solidarity* (Cambridge, MA: Harvard University Press, 2009), 55.

11. David Kazanjian, *The Colonizing Trick: National Culture and Imperial Citizenship in Early America* (Minneapolis: University of Minnesota Press, 2003), 96.

12. Juliet Hooker, "'A Black Sister to Massachusetts': Latin America and the Fugitive Democratic Ethos of Frederick Douglass," *American Political Science Review* 109, no. 4 (2015): 690–702; Chris Dixon, *African America and Haiti: Emigration and Black Nationalism in the Nineteenth Century* (Westport, CT: Greenwood Press, 2000); Beverly Tomek, *Colonization and Its Discontents: Emancipation, Emigration, and Antislavery in Antebellum Pennsylvania* (New York: New York University Press, 2011); Joycelyn Moody, "'We Wish to Plead Our Own Cause': Independent Antebellum African American Literature, 1840–1865," in *The Cambridge History of African American Literature*, ed. Maryemma Graham and Jerry W. Ward, Jr. (New York: Cambridge University Press, 2011), 134–53.

13. Andy Doolen, *Fugitive Empire: Locating Early American Imperialism* (Minneapolis: University of Minnesota Press, 2005), 118.

14. Fred Moten, "Knowledge of Freedom," *CR* 4, no. 2 (2004): 269–310, quotation at 274.

15. Moten, "Knowledge of Freedom," 274.

16. Shadd, *Plea*, 62.

17. Shadd, *Plea*, 154.

18. Rinaldo Walcott, "'Who Is She and What Is She to You?': Mary Ann Shadd Cary and the (Im)possibility of Black/Canadian," *Atlantis* 24, no. 2 (2000): 137–46, quotation at 141. See also Afua Cooper, "Acts of Resistance: Black Men and Women Engage Slavery in Upper Canada, 1793–1803," *Ontario History* 99, no. 1 (2007): 5–17; Afua Cooper, *The Hanging of Angélique: The Untold Story of Canadian Slavery and the Burning of Old Montréal* (Toronto: HarperCollins,

2006); Harvey Amani Whitfield, "Black Loyalists and Black Slaves in Maritime Canada," *History Compass* 5, no. 6 (2007): 1980–97; Robyn Maynard, *Policing Black Lives: State Violence in Canada from Slavery to the Present* (Halifax, NS: Fernwood Publishing, 2017); Katherine Thorsteinson, "National Roots and Diasporic Routes: Tracing the Flying African Myth in Canada," *Diaspora: A Journal of Transnational Studies* 20, no. 3 (2011): 259–82; Robin W. Winks, *Blacks in Canada: A History* (Montreal: McGill-Queen's University Press, 1997); Sylvia Hamilton, "Naming Names, Naming Ourselves: A Survey of Early Black Women in Nova Scotia," in *"We're Rooted Here and They Can't Pull Us Up": Essays in African Women's History*, ed. Peggy Bristow (Toronto: University of Toronto Press, 1999), 13–40.

19. Katherine McKittrick, *Demonic Grounds: Black Women and the Cartographies of Struggle* (Minneapolis: University of Minnesota Press, 2006), 97.

20. Fielder, *Relative Races*, 199.

21. Shadd, *Plea*, 62.

22. Shadd, *Plea*, 41, my emphasis.

23. Shadd, *Plea*, 41.

24. Shadd, *Plea*, 19.

25. Shadd, *Plea*, 19.

26. Shadd, *Plea*, 19.

27. Shadd, *Plea*, 21, my emphasis.

28. Shadd, *Plea*, 22.

29. Shadd, *Plea*, 26–27.

30. Shadd, *Plea*, 24–25.

31. Shadd, *Plea*, 48.

32. Shadd, *Plea*, 49.

33. Shadd, *Plea*, 48.

34. Nina Reid-Maroney, "Possibilities for African Canadian Intellectual History: The Case of 19th-Century Upper Canada/Canada West," *History Compass* 15, no. 12 (2017); Jane Rhodes, "The Contestation over National Identity: Nineteenth-Century Black Americans in Canada," *Canadian Review of American Studies* 30, no. 2 (2000): 175–86; Boulou Ebanda de B'béri, Nina Reid-Maroney, and Handel Kashope Wright, eds., *The Promised Land: History and Historiography of the Black Experience in Chatham-Kent's Settlements and Beyond* (Toronto: University of Toronto Press, 2018); Barrington Walker, "'Set Apart for the Children of Colored Taxpayers of the Entire Town': Race, Schools, and Citizenship in Nineteenth-Century Chatham, Ontario," in *Who Pays for Canada? Taxes and Fairness*, ed. E. A. Heaman and David Tough (Montreal: McGill-Queen's University Press, 2020), 113–28; Heike Paul, "Out of Chatham: Abolitionism on the Canadian Frontier," *Atlantic Studies* 8, no. 2 (2011): 165–88.

35. Shadd, *Plea*, 44–46.

36. Shadd, *Plea*, 43, 52.

37. Shadd, *Plea*, 54, original emphasis.

38. Shadd, *Plea*, 54.

39. Shadd, *Plea*, 54.

40. Katherine McKittrick, "Plantation Futures," *Small Axe* 17, no. 3 (2013): 1–15; Sylvia Wynter, "Novel and History, Plot and Plantation," *Savacou* 5 (1971): 95–102.

41. Shadd, *Plea*, 55.

42. Shadd, *Plea*, 55, original emphasis.

43. Shadd, *Plea*, 55.

44. Shadd, *Plea*, 56.

45. Shadd, *Plea*, 57.

46. Hooker 692–95. Jake Mattox, "The Mayor of San Juan del Norte?: Nicaragua, Martin Delany, and the 'Cotton' Americans," *American Literature* 81, no. 3 (2009): 527–54.

47. Shadd, *Plea*, 56.

48. Shadd, *Plea*, 56.

49. Shadd, *Plea*, 58.

50. Shadd, *Plea*, 58.

51. Shadd, *Plea*, 59.

52. Shadd, *Plea*, 59.

53. Shadd, *Plea*, 59.

54. Shadd, *Plea*, 59.

55. Shadd, *Plea*, 60.

56. Shadd, *Plea*, 60.

57. Frederick Douglass, "The Destiny of Colored Americans," *North Star*, November 16, 1849, in Foner, *Frederick Douglass*, 148–49. See also Martin R. Delany, *Blake; or, The Huts of America: A Corrected Edition*, ed. Jerome McGann (Cambridge, MA: Harvard University Press, 2017); Douglass, "Present Condition."

58. Shadd, *Plea*, 60.

59. See María Josefina Saldaña-Portillo, *Indian Given: Racial Geographies Across Mexico and the United States* (Durham, NC: Duke University Press, 2016); Mark Rifkin, *Settler Common Sense: Queerness and Everyday Colonialism in the American Renaissance* (Minneapolis: University of Minnesota Press, 2014); Audra Simpson, *Mohawk Interruptus: Political Life Across the Borders of Settler States* (Durham, NC: Duke University Press, 2014).

60. Shadd, *Plea*, 60, my emphasis.

61. Shadd, *Plea*, 62.

62. Shadd, *Plea*, 62.

63. Mary Ann Shadd Cary, "A Word About, and to Emigrationists," *Provincial Freeman*, April 15, 1854.

64. Shadd Cary, "A Word."

65. Shadd Cary, "A Word."

66. Shadd Cary, "A Word."

67. Shadd Cary, "A Word."

68. Shadd Cary, "A Word."

69. Shadd Cary, "A Word."

70. For more on overlaid Black reading publics, see Elizabeth McHenry, *Forgotten Readers: Recovering the Lost History of African-American Literary Societies* (Durham, NC: Duke University Press, 2002); Robyn Maynard, "Reading Black Resistance Through Afrofuturism: Notes on Post-Apocalyptic Blackness and Black Rebel Cyborgs in Canada," *Topia* 39 (2018): 29–47; Kinohi Nishikawa, *Street Players: Black Pulp Fiction and the Making of a Literary Underground* (Chicago: University of Chicago Press, 2018).

71. "Central America," *Provincial Freeman*, March 24, 1885, my emphasis.

72. "Freedom in Mexico," *Provincial Freeman*, April 25, 1857.

73. "Freedom in Mexico."

74. Kristin Moriah, "'A Greater Compass of Voice': Elizabeth Taylor Greenfield and Mary Ann Shadd Cary Navigate Black Performance," *Theatre Research in Canada* 41, no. 1 (2020): 20–38, quotation at 22. See also Judith Madera, *Black Atlas: Geography and Flow in Nineteenth-Century African American Literature* (Durham, NC: Duke University Press, 2015).

75. "Slavery Existing in Nebraska—A Letter from William Walker," *Provincial Freeman*, May 20, 1854.

76. "Slavery Existing in Nebraska."

CHAPTER 4

Mary Ann Shadd Cary's Black Soil Ecology

EUNICE TOH

In the summer of 2020, Black farmers in Detroit rejoiced when the GoFundMe campaign they organized to raise money for African American land access reached its goal in just twenty minutes.[1] Described by the campaign creators as "a matter of equity," the fund was a crucial starting point for tackling the deep-seated disparity of land acquisition among Black and white farmers.[2] While urban farmers are predominantly African American and Latino/a, research has shown an uneven distribution in farming land, which is mostly white owned. In the face of this structural disparity, however, Black farmers are ceaselessly striving to fulfill urban farming's civic purpose, with neighborhoods working together to advocate for communal agricultural projects. Such efforts are a continuation of a Black ecological tradition that centers community, practices of care, and a mutual respect for the earth.

Following the troubling set of issues that the contemporary urban farming movement raises, this essay considers the racial politics of U.S. agriculture in relation to Black emigration in the nineteenth century. I do so by turning to a discreet text—Mary Ann Shadd Cary's *A Plea for Emigration; or, Notes of Canada West, in Its Moral, Social, and Political Aspect* (1852)—that takes up these ecological themes in its promotion of Black emigration from the United States to Canada.[3] In her widely disseminated pamphlet, Shadd Cary positions Canada (over South America, West Africa, and the Caribbean) as a space of possibility for Black settlement in the mid-nineteenth century. While one might expect this pamphlet to focus on the moral, social, and political conditions of the region (as its subtitle suggests), Shadd Cary begins instead with extensive information on the quality of the region's climate and soil. These sections have been interpreted by critics as a laying out of indisputable facts before getting into the more contentious conditions of Canadian life.[4] This essay, however, argues for the material and symbolic possibilities of Shadd Cary's ecological meditations. Her habitual articulation of Canadian soil quality and climate health suggests an affinity with the land that is pragmatic while also signaling a form of Black belonging.

Such a reading of *A Plea* engages with questions of emigration, extraction, and agriculture that have been a concerted point of inquiry for fields focusing on Black ecologies and Black diasporas.[5] When situating these fields within current conversations of the Anthropocene, Black scholars have argued against the physical environment's neutrality, raising questions about the embedded racialization of Black bodies among material deposits and reserves.[6] While this conflation of Black life and mineralogy demands greater interrogation, there is also a need to address their incommensurability so as to resist reinscribing this violence onto Blackness and the earth. In the face of this aporia, scholars have instead questioned how Black bodies negotiate the ecological and environmental ruptures of the world in ways that engender and expand forms of Black belonging. Sonya Posmentier's *Cultivation and Catastrophe* (2017), for instance, situates Black modernists and their ecological writings as markers of "diasporic differences" (84). Meanwhile, in his essay "In Bondage When Cold Was King: The Frigid Terrain of Slavery in Antebellum Maryland" (2017), Tony Perry focuses on how enslaved men and women utilized cold weather to subvert slaveholder authority. Crucially, he notes, that while weather was something the enslaved deployed, it remained a force "impossible to harness" (32). Posmentier's and Perry's works demonstrate the fruitfulness of centering environmental phenomena in the historiography of American slavery and colonialism.[7] Thus, in considering *A Plea*'s depictions of soil's centrality to Black emigration, this essay extends the above critical insights to questions of citizenship in nineteenth-century studies, raising possibilities for different configurations of national and Black belonging.

As this essay will show, *A Plea*'s double relationship to "soil" and "land" offers a layered look at the independent and interdependent nature of Black ecology. In identifying Shadd Cary's imagination of a "soil ecology," I mean to suggest how it paradoxically creates a potentially liberatory space through the fraught context of land ownership and settlement.[8] While the terms "land" and "soil" are often used interchangeably in nineteenth-century rhetoric, "land," in this chapter, functions as storied ground—that which is a physical referent of a nation. In contrast, "soil"—a thin covering over land encompassing organic materials, minerals, air, and water—represents contingency and collaboration. Notwithstanding the provisional definitions of "land" and "soil" in this essay, "soil" can be viewed as a deeply compromised term given its historical usage and deployment. "Free soil" in the nineteenth century, for instance, began as a slogan for "land reform" before becoming shorthand for Jacksonian antislavery (Earle 13). However, "soil" as a term remains compelling insofar as its dynamic and potential nature signals both a space of sustenance for Black emigrant communities and a form of belonging that reconfigures notions of nationhood.

Moreover, this essay's use of "soil," as opposed to "land" or "territory," allows us to think outside of the settler colonial paradigm that has dominated discourses around Indigenous land rights. Insofar as *A Plea*'s call for Black U.S. fugitives to build new livelihoods in Canada West (now known as Ontario), such emigration can arguably be viewed as complicity in settler colonialism. After all, Kent County, where Shadd Cary was based, was an administrative district set up in the mid-1840s. This district was settled on the traditional land of the Odawa, Potawatomi, and Ojibwa, following the McKee Purchase Treaty of 1790.[9] However, the vocabulary of "settler" is fraught when applying it to Black emigrants. Here, I follow Tiya Miles who eloquently states, "Yes, they settled on Native lands appropriated by a colonial state . . . we should also note, in our expositions, that they did so in a state of near-permanent exile that always shaped their relationship to settler colonial social and political structures" (425). Thus, in focusing on "soil" over "land" in this essay, I hope to build on Miles's exhortation for new vocabularies that will nuance these important discourses around settler colonialism, particularly as they involve Black emigrants.

In the sections that follow, this chapter takes us through the material and metaphoric resonances of "fertile soil," as depicted in Shadd Cary's *A Plea* and her larger body of work.[10] Given the importance of her writings in nineteenth-century Black emigration politics, I read her work alongside that of interlocuters Frederick Douglass and Martin Delany, tracking the language of soil across her Colored Convention speeches and editorials in the *Provincial Freeman*. The first section attends to the relationship between soil and independence, arguing that Shadd Cary's ethos of self-reliance allows for extralegal forms of economic and civic citizenship. The next section goes on to explore how "soil" operates in tandem with "blood," another metaphor often used as a stand-in for a larger body (politic). Unlike Delany, whose principles of emigration reflected Black nationalist ideals, Shadd Cary's heralding of Canada reconfigured essentialist notions of what constitute a Black diaspora. At the same time, her espousal of Canada, troublingly, depended on a logic of settlerism while failing to acknowledge the British province's colonial dimensions. Despite being a text that remains dependent on residual notions of gender and settler colonial politics, the contradictory politics of Shadd Cary's soil aesthetics in *A Plea* highlights the urgency of examining the confluences between imperialism, nationalism, and self-subsistence. While Shadd Cary's vision of Black belonging is intertwined with the imperial impulses of the British Empire, the cultural and material resonances of soil in her writings showcase the potential for a Black soil ecology to undermine the colonial logics from which *A Plea* emerges, thereby revealing possible directions for negotiating the tensions inherent in Black ecologies, citizenry, and nationhood.

On Free Soil

> Ecology: the branch of biology that deals with the
> relations of organisms to one another and to their physical
> surroundings; the political movement that seeks to protect
> the environment, especially from pollution.
>
> —Christina Sharpe, *In the Wake:*
> *On Blackness and Being* (2016)

While ecology has mostly been focused on natural phenomena, Christina Sharpe introduces another dimension to (Black) ecology, that of politics. As noted earlier, multiple scholars have disarticulated *A Plea*'s political arguments from its descriptions of Canadian climate and soil. However, as Sharpe eloquently shows, these elements cannot be so easily disentangled. If one of the main factors driving African American emigration was equal rights, then soil played a central role in allowing for this independent personhood. In this section, I contemplate the relationship between soil and autonomy as they emerge in *A Plea*. In so doing, I build on the work of Black studies scholar Salamishah Tillet, whose paradigm of a "democratic aesthetic" looks to African American heritage tourism as an alternative site of democratic discourse (16). As Tillet writes in *Sites of Slavery* (2012), the extralegal markers of citizenship entail the "economic (the right to earn) and the civic (the right to recognition)" (6). I extend Tillet's insights to Shadd Cary's soil ecology, reckoning with the concept of citizenship in light of Black emigration. To demonstrate the intertwining of soil, economic independence, and national belonging, Shadd Cary's representation of the landscape, I maintain, allows her to enact an understated evaluation of a nation's "character."

What do Shadd Cary's intimations of soil in *A Plea* offer? Or more precisely, what does it mean to hone in on the relationship between soil and Black belonging, to speak of soil as a marker of citizenship and nationhood? In one of *A Plea's* opening sections, Shadd Cary proclaims, "So far as colored people are interested in the subject of emigration to any country, their welfare, in a pecuniary view, is promoted by attention to the quality of soil" (49). Though she speaks of the availability of land in countries such as Mexico, she insists that the prospect of becoming "purchasers and settlers" needs to be thought alongside "permanent nationality" (50).[11] This assertion, then, is where the quality of soil becomes crucial. As T. Sowell in *Migrations and Culture: A World View* (1996) argues, "Soil has profound effects on the kinds of agriculture that is [sic] possible and therefore the kinds of societies that are possible" (qtd. in Calloway-Thomas 247). In Shadd Cary's eyes, "soil" supersedes "land" when thinking about the potentialities for settling in a new nation. To index the multiple possibilities that Canadian soil can engender, Shadd Cary elucidates that the varieties of soil are a "black loam, sandy loam, clay, and sand" (*A Plea*, 51). In presenting these various categories, Shadd Cary demonstrates the fertile nature of Canada's landscape for agricultural growth.[12]

A Plea's insistence on soil is propelled by the economic independence it would grant Black emigrants. Shadd Cary declares, "There are, and must be for a time, few experimental and scientific farmers, as it [farming] is more as a means of present subsistence than to test the capacity of different soils" (52–53).[13] While the advancement of science is undoubtedly an important endeavor, Shadd Cary categorizes "intelligence" and "wealth" as lower priorities for the time being, asserting that the soil should be reserved for the farmer laboring to "procure a crop" (53). In looking out for the welfare of Black fugitives, Shadd Cary argues for soil's centrality to a life of self-subsistence. Such an ethos of self-reliance was in line with her disdainful stance toward charity. Near the end of the section "Churches and Schools," Shadd Cary disparages the "benevolent act[s]" of U.S. charitable organizations, questioning: "What good purpose was accomplished, or even what sort of vanity was gratified, by emptying the useless contents of old libraries on destitute fugitives?" (67). In refuting support from such entities, her tirade not only exposes the self-serving nature of charity but also advocates for the self-sufficiency of Black fugitives. To drive the message home, *A Plea* includes testimonials from several emigrants who were "supporting themselves by their own industry" (84).[14]

Further, Shadd Cary's investment in the "character" of Canadian soil and its churches, schools, and other institutions demonstrates the intertwining of soil with the social, moral, and political conditions of the nation-state. The word "character" also denotes mental and moral qualities, thereby making it a quizzical term to describe the nonhuman nature of soil. However, in describing the character of Canadian soil as "rich, dark . . . heavy" with "depth," Shadd Cary subtly plants that word in readers' minds as she sets up her later argument for civic recognition in Canada (*A Plea* 50).[15] Declaring that the nation's "political character" leaves no room for chattel slavery and prejudice of color, the word "character" thus ties the economic desirability of Canada with the affective potential of permanent national belonging (60). Highlighting Shadd Cary's articulations of soil thereby reifies the importance of a country's climate—symbolically and materially—in one's decision to emigrate.

The political grounding of Shadd Cary's soil ecology extends beyond *A Plea*, playing a notable role in her introduction at the National Convention of Colored People in 1855. In her first appearance as a delegate of any such Black conventions, Shadd Cary uses the platform to amplify the importance of agriculture for Black independence. Following what scholars like Brandi Locke have spoken about the gender politics of reports and responses to Shadd Cary's participation, it is interesting to note how her speech at this 1855 convention was framed.[16] As not all newspapers thought it important to mention this point when covering her participation, I focus on an article from Savannah, Georgia's *Daily Morning News*, which offers a couple of sentences on Shadd Cary's agricultural sensibilities. "The Black Convention" article reports that Shadd Cary was "anxious" for Black people to "turn their attention to farming" and that there was no group better off than those who had "settled in Canada on farms" (*Daily Morning News*, October 23, 1855). Despite the inclusion of this message, the crux of it is lost in the layout of this subsection (at the end of the report) and its heading ("A Woman on the Floor"). Between the misogynistic undertones of this title and the lack of coverage on Shadd Cary's soil aesthetics lies a reminder that ecology often gets subsumed in the focus on social or political "character." But perhaps we can also imagine the "floor" that Shadd Cary is standing on, as per the newspaper heading, as its own plot of soil laying the groundwork for new forms of political discourse. In carving out a space in this male-dominated arena, Shadd Cary's advocation of Black Canadian independence is exemplary of what a "soil ecology" can yield.[17] Her speech, in this sense, offers as much about the independent nature of soil, as it does for soil's potential for greater civic engagement within the convention movement. This relationship between soil and the body politic is something I explore further in the next section.

Soil, Water, and Blood

> Having watered your soil with our tears, enriched it with
> our blood, performed its roughest labor in time of peace,
> defended it against enemies in time of war . . . we deem it
> no arrogance or presumption to manifest now a common
> concern with you for its welfare, prosperity, honor, and glory.
> —Frederick Douglass, oration delivered before
> the National Convention of Colored Men,
> Louisville, Kentucky, September 24, 1883

What kind of difference might a focus on soil offer to our understanding of Black diaspora and the politics of emigration? Frederick Douglass's deployment of the rhetoric of soil in a speech delivered in Louisville, Kentucky, at the National Convention of Colored Men provides a possible answer to this question. In emphasizing the difference between "your" and "our" in reference to the fertility and protection of American soil, Douglass amplifies the metaphoric significance of soil as a stand-in for the nation's body politic. The speech relies on this metaphor as a means of contesting the nation's indifference to African Americans' labor and care for the soil, hence insisting on a shared stake for its "welfare, prosperity, honor, and glory." However, the cultural force that marks Douglass's speech—its insistence on soil as enriched by *blood*—offers yet another metaphoric turn in his oration. As the adage "Blood is thicker than water" goes, the metaphor of blood as lineage thus affords soil's association with not only a nation-state but a Black nationalist politic as well. By using the word "nationalism" in an ideological sense, I follow Jane Rhodes's definition of the word's rootedness "in a people's ties to a geographical region which they feel entitled to possess" (87). Thus, Douglass's invocation of soil and blood, as I will show in this section, corresponds with the cultural work put forth by Shadd Cary to link material soil with the larger Black diasporic body (politic).[18]

This section interrogates the interdependent nature of soil by considering its articulations of Black belonging in Shadd Cary's *Provincial Freeman* editorials alongside the work of fellow author and activist Martin Delany. In assessing Shadd Cary's and Delany's articulations of soil in relation to one another, I mean to think through the possibilities and limitations of soil as a metaphor for Black diasporic belonging and community.[19] While Delany and Shadd Cary were arguably the most fervent spokespersons of Black emigration in the nineteenth century, their choices and rationales for destinations diverged greatly. In his pamphlet *The Condition, Elevation, Emigration, and Destiny of the Colored People of the United States* (1852), Delany championed a Pan-African consciousness by espousing Liberia and Central and South America. Meanwhile Shadd Cary cultivated a different sense of Black belonging, one that was less committed to a romanticized Africology. As Rhodes notes, Shadd Cary "refused to adhere to notions of black superiority or nobility" and thus preferred an integrationist approach grounded in agriculture (86). Such an integrationist approach, however, meant that Shadd Cary's idealization of Canada relied on an embrace of British colonial structures and a failure to condemn the province's imperial practices of resource extraction. Thus, in focusing on both the progressive and less progressive aspects of Shadd Cary's ecological aesthetics, this section demonstrates the emergent possibilities of her Black soil ecology to envision alternative forms of Black diasporic belonging, even if such formulations were not actualized in her own time.

First, Delany's instrumentalization of soil for essentialist purposes demonstrates the attendant pitfalls of soil's symbolism. By including the word "destiny" in the title of his emigrationist text (published a few months before *A Plea*), Delany offers a view of Black ecology that heralds an ethos of predestination. Critics such as Grant Shreve have noted the theological dimensions of Delany's argument, such as his proclamation that South and Central America were the "providentially selected homes" for Black peoples in America (Shreve 471). Indeed, *The Condition* empathetically concludes, "What part of mankind is the 'denizen of every soil, and the lord of terrestrial creation,' if it be not the black race? . . . The land is ours—there it lies with inexhaustible resources; let us go and possess it" (appendix). This language (the use of the term "land" rather than "soil"), coupled with the logic of racial essentialism, allowed Delany to construct a nationalist consciousness purporting Black peoples as the lords of "terrestrial creation."[20] Further, this line of reasoning precipitated a straightforward dismissal of emigration to Canada, for, as Delany asserts, "the Canadians are descended from the same common parentage as the Americans on this side of the Lakes—and there is a manifest tendency on the part of the Canadians generally, to Americanism" (chap. 19). Ironically, however, Delany's utilitarian view of land as "inexhaustible" and ripe for possession reveals an ethos of domination not unlike the "manifest tendency" of white settler imperialists.

With this example in mind, I turn to Shadd Cary's writings in the *Provincial Freeman* for an alternative reading of the resonance of soil. Shadd Cary's and Delany's differing emigrationist views were palpable in her early editorials, including an especially contentious piece published on April 15, 1854, titled, "A Word About, and to Emigrationists." Writing in anticipation of the National Emigration Convention to be held later that year in August, Shadd Cary offered her rationale for emigration to Canada over other countries. Grounding her argument in pragmatic factors, such as the opportunity to "have fields of [one's] own" in Canada, she ends the editorial with reasons against Central America and "other hot places." She justifies her preference by alluding to the harsh and inhospitable landscape of these regions, questioning, "What will your women say ... when surrounded by big spiders, lizards, snakes, centipedes, scorpions and all manner of creeping and biting things?" This pointed question speaks to both the progressive and conservative dimensions of Shadd Cary's emigrationist ideology. On one hand, she is relying on stereotypical gender dispositions and assumptions about tropical climates. Yet, her invocation of "What will your women say" suggests an ignorance on the part of Black male emigrationists who might be speaking on behalf of their larger families and communities and who have failed to consult them on this decision.[21] By emphasizing the importance of physical environment and opportunity for economic independence, Shadd Cary's envisioning of diasporic soil is both pragmatic and more representative of the heterogeneous Black nation. The ecological logics that produce Shadd Cary's "pragmatism" also provide the context in which Shadd Cary responds, "You *cannot* be a whole African Nation here brethren, but you can be *part* of the Colored British nation." In her invocation of Canadian emigration, Shadd Cary is aware of the limits that come with being part of a nation. Yet, she highlights the opportunity of being integrated into a Black diasporic community within the territorial borders of this nation-state. Such a mindset might be utopic, but it also reveals her naïveté (or willful ignorance) of the colonial workings in the rest of the British province. While her advocation of self-reliance through agriculture appears to be part of a progressive Black soil ecology, it is also reliant on a global produce system facilitated by imperial trade.

Indeed, the interplay between the global and domestic aspects of Shadd Cary's soil ecology is best seen in her work as the editor of the *Provincial Freeman*, the first North American newspaper edited by a Black woman. Despite the paper's editorials' using of collective language to downplay Shadd Cary's role, her influence and control remained visible in the writing. In one of the *Provincial Freeman*'s first few editorials ("Number Two," March 25, 1854), she declares: "WHY ESTABLISH THIS PAPER? . . . We answer, Because the interests of the large and growing colored population of Canada demand such an organ, for several reasons. . . . Such need intelligent information of our climate, soil, productions, institutions, customs, laws, progress, &c., &c." In this piece, she writes that one of the core reasons for establishing the *Provincial Freeman* was to provide information on climate and soil. Fascinatingly, she states these reasons before the seemingly more important factors such as "laws" and "progress." With its "Agricultural" section as a staple, the paper provided its readers resources for essential quotidian practices like soil management. A February 1855 edition, for instance, included an article titled "Facts About Guano," which offered tips on how this specific manure could be used. The "factual" nature of the article, however, belies the violent origins that allowed for the product's export to North America. As Tao Leigh Goffe posits in her essay "'Guano in Their Destiny': Race, Geology, and a Philosophy of Indenture," "Flowing through the world in what was a multi-million-dollar industry, guano was a global commodity in the mid-nineteenth century extracted by estimates of 100,000 Chinese indentured contract laborers shipped to Peru" (28). Reckoning with the extractive practices that undergird agricultural products like guano thus demonstrates the contradictory politics of Shadd Cary's Black soil ecology. Her prioritizing of agricultural items is evidence of how material ecology was deeply intertwined with the "progress" of the Black body politic in Canada, even as it was set against a troubling—even if unsurprising—imperial backdrop.

Having analyzed the editorial apparatus of Shadd Cary's soil ecology, we can view Shadd Cary's choice of Canada as foregrounding what Rinaldo Walcott calls a "queer black diaspora." "Black diaspora queers," he notes in "Outside in Black Studies" (2005), "live in a borderless, large world of shared

identifications and imagined historical relations" (92). Shadd Cary, he artic-
ulates in a separate article ("'Who Is She and What Is She to You?'" 2000),
sits "between Canada and the USA ... between Canadian Studies and Black
Studies" (139). In so doing, her politics "complicates the category of citizen"
("'Who Is She'" 143). Kirsten Lee, in her contribution to this volume, likewise
echoes the radical potential in Shadd Cary's emigration sensibilities: "What
makes Shadd's leaving the United States so radical is her idea not of its permanence but of its temporariness, its conditionality—leaving on her own
terms, but also reserving and eventually exercising the right to return." Yet
this visionary imagination of Shadd Cary's politics is not without acknowledgment of its limits. Citing her critique and rejection of Haiti as a possible
destination, Walcott rightly highlights the imperialist dimensions of Shadd
Cary's diasporic thinking ("'Who Is She'" 145). A look at the Black ecological themes of Shadd Cary's work, however, offers a possibility for ways to
think beyond the limits of the nation. In her reformulation of Black sociali-
ties with the land, Shadd Cary demonstrates the potentialities of diasporic
soil that exist outside of national jurisdictions. With the Fugitive Slave Law of
1850 pushing African Americans farther north, Shadd Cary's advocation of
Canada demonstrates how material soil emphasizes the fictive nature of legal
borders.[22] A focus on material soil allows for a thinking beyond the X/Y axis
of territorial land and instead highlights the three-dimensionality of soil that
its topography necessitates. In so doing, she disrupts conventional notions of
cultural nationalism, thereby showcasing that the locales of the Black diaspora are limitless.

Conclusion: Soil as Skin or Kin

Earlier in this essay, I opened the question of how Black belonging relates
to land ownership through the mutual aid initiative of urban Black Detroit
farmers. I began with this contemporary example to show how the current
landscape of Black ecology in North America continues to revolve around
questions of independence, recognition, and, of course, racial (in)justice.
And yet, the communal tactics that Black farmers employ in the fight for land
ownership suggest the continuous potentiality of diasporic soil for the sus-
tainment of Black belonging. For this reason, I close this essay by reflecting
on an unlikely link between contemporary Black urban farmers and Shadd
Cary's A Plea: the space (or soil) of Detroit.

Despite its subject matter and Shadd Cary's situatedness in West Canada, *A Plea for Emigration* was published "across the river" in Detroit (Almonte 18). Likewise, notwithstanding Shadd Cary's fervent emigrationist activism, she ultimately returned to the United States in the years following the Civil War, with her first relocation being the city of Detroit.[23] In the two years she lived there with her family, Shadd Cary taught in the public school and was involved in local politics, including the Black labor movements in Detroit. How might this contextual knowledge situate our ultimate understanding of her soil ecology? Why (e)migrate in the first place? How much was "soil" a factor in her movement? Instead of viewing her mobility through the carto-graphic lens of moving from nation to nation, what if we view Shadd Cary's travel through the lens of soil? While the land might be storied and static, American soil had been watered (by tears) and enriched (by blood); it was not a returning or a restoring, but a *recovering* of land that persists with the Black urban farmers of Detroit. When viewed this way, soil is also skin (or kin), a covering of the larger body (politic).

Soil as skin recalls Frantz Fanon's meditation on epidermic schemata as prompted by a white young child's hailing, "Look, a black man!" This encounter on the street leads Fanon in "The Fact of Blackness" to ponder the relationship between the social and the biological as theorized through layers of the skin. He remarks, "Below the corporeal scheme I had sketched a historico-racial schema" (258). The relationship between one's skin color and the psychological, dehumanizing realities of racialization demands a reconsideration of the taxonomies that have structured inter- and intraracial relationships.[24] Might ecology be the ground (or soil) that cultivates interra-cial solidarity? Giving the waning of the emigration and resettlement move-ments in the ensuing Civil War, it is hard to tell how Shadd Cary and her contemporaries might have addressed these issues or expanded their views to engage more capacious forms of democracy. Perhaps, however, the current urban farming movement, and its national initiatives—not just in Detroit but in California and New York, among others—demonstrate how activists are working to promote "land and food sovereignty" among Black, Indigenous, and people of color farmers (McCauley). Thus, while Shadd Cary's formula-tion of a Black soil ecology in *A Plea* remained dependent on the dominant gender, racial, and national ideas of her time, how we might embrace the emergent ideals grounding her aesthetics is something that warrants further attention as we as scholars continue to meditate on the intertwining of race and ecology. By focusing on that which is both rooted and porous, Shadd

Cary's Black soil ecology allows for an understanding of Black belonging that ties dynamism with diaspora, and Black being with the earth.

Notes

1. Rhonda J. Smith, "It Took a Group of Black Farmers to Start Fixing Land Ownership Problems in Detroit," *Civil Eats*, November 6, 2020, https://civileats.com/2020/11/06/it-took-a -group-of-black-farmers-to-start-fixing-land-ownership-problems-in-detroit/.

2. The urban farming movement, as it has been known in the last decade, is a form of agriculture that celebrates income-generating food production. Melissa N. Poulsen's article "Cultivating Citizenship, Equity, and Social Inclusion? Putting Civic Agriculture into Practice Through Urban Farming," *Agriculture and Human Values* 34, no. 1 (2017): 135–48, offers an incisive look at how urban farming leads to greater civic engagement.

3. This essay joins the work of R. J. Boutelle and Marlas Yvonne Whitley in this collection on Shadd Cary's emigrationist ecologies. In situating Shadd Cary as a "theorist of Black community-building at the intersection of Black nationalism and Black feminism," they look at the role that horticulture and family farms played in nineteenth-century emigration to Canada West.

4. In his introduction to *A Plea for Emigration*, Richard Almonte suggests that Shadd Cary begins with the factual, such as farms, weather, and saw mills, before engaging more debatable topics (schools, religion, segregation) (35). Similarly, Nele Sawallisch posits that the pamphlet's opening with Canadian climate "rejects an imaginary geography" of a cold and inhospitable land propagated by enslavers to prevent Black fugitives from moving north ("North American Counterterritoriality," 234).

5. Christina Sharpe's *In the Wake* interrogates the "moral debt" of slavery's afterlives and the continual practices of rendering Black people as "objects of transaction" (60). Meanwhile, Kathryn Yusoff has argued for geology's perpetuating role in the ongoing "instrumentalization of dominant colonial narratives" in this system (*Billion Black Anthropocenes*, 2).

6. See Tao Leigh Goffe's recent piece on the "ecology of Black extraction" as it relates to citational practices and Black thinkers (https://doi.org/10.17658/issn.2058-5462/issue-18/conversation/008).

7. Recent trends in Black studies scholarship have interrogated the relationship between Blackness and Indigeneity and their seemingly perpetual antagonism. See Tiffany Lethabo King, Frank Wilderson, and Jared Sexton. While this essay is responsive to the ontological claims posited by these theorists, my focus is on Shadd Cary's soil ecologies (even as they sit uneasily against the backdrop of settler colonial and imperial logics). I expand on this in later sections.

8. Shadd Cary's attention to soil was contemporaneous with two other key movements in the mid-nineteenth-century. Free soil as an ideology, a movement, and later, a political party emerged from the radical land reform movement in the 1830s to convey both "agrarian (free farms) and antislavery (free of slavery) meanings" (Earle 14). The Free Soil Party, however, was less concerned with advocating for equal rights for Black peoples as its focus was on free labor programs that benefited white farmers. Another movement worth noting is the free-produce movement, a form of consumer activism that boycotted slave labor goods. The movement, which had its origins in seventeenth-century Quaker movements, was in decline by the late nineteenth century (Holcomb 3).

9. For more on Kent County's history, see the district's Traditional Territory Acknowledgment, https://www.chatham-kent.ca/livingck/communities/landacknowledgment/Pages/default.aspx.

10. Criticism on Mary Ann Shadd Cary and her work largely focuses on her emigrationist ideologies and the gender and racial politics that undergird this activism. One such foundational text is Shirley Yee's "Gender Ideology and Black Women as Community-Builders in Ontario, 1850–70" (1994), which identifies Shadd Cary as part of a collective of Black women who facilitated the foundation of Black Canadian life in the mid-nineteenth century. More recently, Calloway-Thomas, Stone, and Fraser and Griffin have explored *A Plea*'s integrationist and emigrationist ideals in relation to themes of respectability politics, rhetoric, and Black health.

11. On the point of Mexico, see Kirsten Lee's essay in this collection for more on Shadd Cary's ambivalence toward Mexico, which includes her sentiments on Mexico's desirability as a destination for Black emigrants.

12. In attending to Shadd Cary's soil ecology, Calloway-Thomas highlights the empirical value of the descriptions of Canadian soil. Such descriptions, argues Calloway-Thomas, are representative of Shadd Cary's "quantitative approach" in promoting Canada West's viability (241). While Calloway-Thomas reads Shadd Cary's soil ecology with a focus on how its factual nature affords the pamphlet credibility, this essay is more interested in the metaphorical possibilities of Black belonging that soil indexes.

13. Beyond pragmatic factors, Shadd Cary's anxieties about experimentation could be related to antebellum racial science, which often pathologized racial groups. This is not to say that Black scientific knowledge was sidelined in the nineteenth century, in contrast, as Britt Rusert outlines, there were oppositional, practical, and speculative forms of fugitive science. See Rusert's *Fugitive Science* for more.

14. An investment in such self-sufficiency is further seen in Shadd Cary's work with Toronto's Provincial Union, founded in 1854. As Jennifer Harris details in her article on Black Canadian literary culture, "Notably, when Mary Ann Shadd drafted the constitution of the Provincial Union, she explicitly accounted for Black Canadians interested and actively engaged in literary production" (7).

15. By characterizing Canadian soil as "rich and dark," Shadd Cary is also, troublingly, relying on racial connotations in her bid to persuade Black emigrants.

16. For more on the gendered nature of Shadd Cary's legacy, see Brandi Locke's work in this collection, as well as the Colored Conventions digital exhibit she curated: "Mary Ann Shadd Cary's Herstory in the Colored Conventions," https://coloredconventions.org/mary-ann-shadd-cary/.

17. At times, Shadd Cary herself was guilty of reinforcing gender stereotypes. The next section explores this in greater detail.

18. The language of soil was fairly common in nineteenth-century emigration discourse. While the Kentucky speech is one of his more well-known instances, Douglass's deployment of soil can also be seen in his earlier speeches in the 1850s.

19. For a different focus on Shadd Cary's and Delany's emigration politics, see Andrea Stone's *Black Well-Being* (2016), which looks at the authors' "valorization of health . . . through a reworking of classical ideals" so as to promote Black emigration (57).

20. Despite his nationalist views here, critics have pointed out that Delany's 1850s essentialism needs to be thought alongside his later views in life, which become more integrationist.

See Tunde Adeleke's biography *Without Regard to Race: The Other Martin Robison Delany* (2004) for more on Delany's political thinking.

21. While Shadd Cary's conservative gender ideology has crucially received much critical attention, my focus here is on Shadd Cary's comments on acclimation and agriculture. For more on the gendered politics of this editorial and on her gender politics, see Rhodes; also Locke's essay in this volume.

22. Crucially, emigration debates heightened following the Fugitive Slave Law of 1850, which threatened the livelihood of free African Americans in the North. The law essentially meant that no Black person could feel safe in the United States.

23. For more information on Shadd Cary's two years in Detroit, see Rhodes's biography.

24. Such thinking has been prompted by Sylvia Wynter's work on reenchanting humanism and decolonial *scientia* (see interview with David Scott).

Works Cited

Adeleke, Tunde. *Without Regard to Race: The Other Martin Robison Delany.* Jackson: University Press of Mississippi, 2004.

Almonte, Richard. Introduction to *A Plea for Emigration*, by Mary A. Shadd, ed. Almonte, 9–41. Toronto: Mercury Press, 1998.

"The Black Convention." *Daily Morning News* [Savannah, GA], October 23, 1855.

Calloway-Thomas, Carolyn. "Mary Ann Shadd Cary: Crafting Black Culture Through Empirical and Moral Arguments." *Howard Journal of Communications* 24, no. 3 (2013): 239–56.

Delany, Martin R. *The Condition, Elevation, Emigration, and Destiny of the Colored People of the United States.* 1852. Project Gutenberg.

Douglass, Frederick. "Address of Hon. Fred. Douglass, delivered before the National Convention of Colored Men, at Louisville, Ky., September 24, 1883." Colored Conventions Project Digital Records, accessed December 12, 2020, https://omeka.coloredconventions.org/items/show/554.

Earle, Jonathan H. *Jacksonian Antislavery and the Politics of Free Soil, 1824–1854.* Chapel Hill: University of North Carolina Press, 2004.

Fanon, Frantz. "The Fact of Blackness." In *Theories of Race and Racism: A Reader*, ed. Les Back and John Solomos, 257–66. New York: Routledge, 2000.

Fraser, Rebecca J., and Martyn Griffin, M. "'Why Sit Ye Here and Die?': Counterhegemonic Histories of the Black Female Intellectual in Nineteenth-Century America." *Journal of American Studies* 54, no. 5 (2020): 1005–31.

Goffe, Tao Leigh. "'Guano in Their Destiny': Race, Geology, and a Philosophy of Indenture." *Amerasia Journal*, vol. 45, no. 1 (2019): 27–49.

———. "Human Resources: Art's History and the Ecology of Black Extraction." In "The Arts, Environmental Justice, and the Ecological Crisis," *British Art Studies* 18 (2020), https://doi.org/10.17658/issn.2058-5462/issue-18/conversation.

Harris, Jennifer. "Peter Susand, Lost Texts, and Black Canadian Literary Culture of the 1850s." *Canadian Literature* 236 (Spring 2018): 15–32.

Holcomb, Julie. *Moral Commerce: Quakers and the Transatlantic Boycott of the Slave Labor Economy.* Ithaca, NY: Cornell University Press, 2016.

King, Tiffany Lethabo. *The Black Shoals: Offshore Formations of Black and Native Studies.* Durham, NC: Duke University Press, 2019.

McCauley, DJ. "In California, Michigan, and New York, How Urban Agriculture Combats Food Security." *GreenBiz*, March 4, 2021, https://www.greenbiz.com/article/california-michigan -and-new-york-how-urban-agriculture-combats-food-insecurity.

Miles, Tiya. "Beyond a Boundary: Black Lives and the Settler-Native Divide." *William and Mary Quarterly* 76, no. 3 (2019): 417–26. muse.jhu.edu/article/730604.

Perry, Tony. "In Bondage When Cold Was King: The Frigid Terrain of Slavery in Antebellum Maryland." *Slavery & Abolition* 38, no. 1 (2017): 23–36.

Posmentier, Sonya. *Cultivation and Catastrophe: The Lyric Ecology of Modern Black Literature.* Baltimore: Johns Hopkins University Press, 2017.

Poulsen, Melissa N. "Cultivating Citizenship, Equity, and Social Inclusion? Putting Civic Agriculture into Practice Through Urban Farming." *Agriculture and Human Values* 34, no. 1 (2017): 135–48.

Rhodes, Jane. *Mary Ann Shadd Cary: The Black Press and Protest in the Nineteenth Century.* Bloomington: Indiana University Press, 1998.

Rusert, Britt. *Fugitive Science: Empiricism and Freedom in Early African American Culture.* New York: NYU Press, 2017.

Sawallisch, Nele. "North American Counterterritoriality: Nineteenth-Century Black Activism and Alternative Legal Spatiality." *Journal of Transnational American Studies* 11, no. 1 (2020): 231–52.

Scott, David. "The Re-Enchantment of Humanism: An Interview with Sylvia Wynter." *Small Axe* 8 (September 2000): 119–207.

Sexton, Jared. "The Vel of Slavery: Tracking the Figure of the Unsovereign." *Critical Sociology* 42, no. 4–5 (2016): 583–97.

Shadd [Cary], Mary Ann. "Number Two." *Provincial Freeman*, March 25, 1854.

———. *A Plea for Emigration.* Edited by Richard Almonte. Toronto: Mercury Press, 1998.

———. "A Word About, and to Emigrationists." *Provincial Freeman*, April 15, 1854.

Sharpe, Christina Elizabeth. *In the Wake: On Blackness and Being.* Durham, NC: Duke University Press, 2016.

Shreve, Grant. "The Exodus of Martin Delany." *American Literary History* 29, no. 3 (2017): 449–73.

Smith, Rhonda J. "It Took a Group of Black Farmers to Start Fixing Land Ownership Problems in Detroit." *Civil Eats*, November 6, 2020. https://civileats.com/2020/11/06/it-took-a-group -of-black-farmers-to-start-fixing-land-ownership-problems-in-detroit/.

Stone, Andrea. *Black Well-Being: Health and Selfhood in Antebellum Black Literature.* Gainesville: University Press of Florida, 2016.

Tillet, Salamishah. *Sites of Slavery: Citizenship and Racial Democracy in the Post-Civil Rights Imagination.* Durham, NC: Duke University Press, 2012.

Walcott, Rinaldo. "Outside in Black Studies: Reading from a Queer Place in the Diaspora." In *Black Queer Studies: A Critical Anthology*, ed. E. Patrick Johnson and Mae G. Henderson, 90–105. Durham, NC: Duke University Press, 2005.

———. "'Who Is She and What Is She to You?': Mary Ann Shadd Cary and the (Im)possibility of Black/Canadian Studies." *Atlantic: Critical Studies in Gender, Culture and Social Justice* 24, no. 2 (2000): 137–46.

Wilderson, Frank B. *Red, White & Black: Cinema and the Structure of U.S. Antagonisms.* Durham, NC: Duke University Press, 2010.

Yee, Shirley. "Gender Ideology and Black Women as Community-Builders in Ontario, 1850–70." *Canadian Historical Review* 75, no. 1 (1994): 53–73.

Yusoff, Kathryn. *A Billion Black Anthropocenes or None.* Minneapolis: University of Minnesota Press, 2018.

PART II

"To Display Her Powers"

Black Theater, Sound, and Performance

CHAPTER 5

Mary Ann Shadd Cary, Her Life and Legacy

A Production

LYNNETTE YOUNG OVERBY, DIANNA RUBERTO,
A. T. MOFFETT, AND ROSALYN GREEN

I pass the torch
and let it spread. Let it leap to the masses
because education—reading and staying informed
Is walking toward freedom. See the light.
Once you are warmed by it
You will never go cold again.
You will know your worth.

—Glenis Redmond

Creating and performing a production based on the life and times of Mary Ann Shadd Cary required time, creativity, and collaboration. Research exploration meetings began in spring 2019. The project continued with a first performance in August 2019 and evolved in 2021 with performances, oral history research, and educational extensions. A multidisciplinary array of researchers, composers, poets, choreographers, educators, and performers collaborated to create this work. The production was inspired by the research of MacArthur Fellow Gabrielle Foreman, who set the historical context of the production. The production and the educational and research extensions were coordinated by artistic director Lynnette Young Overby. Other team members included choreographers Teresa Emmons, Desiree Cocroft,

Rachel DeLauder, Amber Rance, Ikira Peace, Lynnette Young Overby, Kimberly Schroeder, and Marion Hamermesh. Composers included Ralph Russell, Christian Wills, and Jordan Lloyd. The poets included Glenis Redmond, Bebe Coker, and Rachel DeLauder, and the research team included Rosalyn Green, A. T. Moffett, and Dianna Ruberto. The performers, who brought the story to life on stage, included Amber Rance, April Singleton, Ikira Peace, Chelsey Gbemudu, Marlene Jones Boddy, Marion Hamermesh, Gabrielle Shubert, Omi Davis, Ralph Russell, and Christian Wills. The narrator for the production was Michelle Peebles. The production was captured by photographer Sierra Watkins.

This chapter will tell the story of the immersive journey from the initial inspirations to the continuing extensions that emerged from creating a Mary Ann Shadd Cary (MASC) production.

Who Was Mary Ann Shadd Cary?

It was essential for us to tell a truthful story of Shadd Cary by reviewing the literature, accessing archival materials, and viewing videos. Our research focused on specific aspects of her life, beginning with her birth in Wilmington, Delaware, to her education in Pennsylvania, the move to Canada where she was editor of the *Provincial Freeman*, to her continued legacy of inspiration for today's women of color.

We read books about Shadd Cary's life and times, viewed videos about her life, listened to lectures by literary scholar P. Gabrielle Foreman and librarian Carol Rudisell, and participated in embodied research.[1] During the embodied research sessions, artistic director Overby facilitated a process that allowed the performers to review a specific aspect of Shadd Cary's life, then imagine a specific scenario, where the performers could envision the scene. Following this imaginary journey, the performers focused on content and emotions as they embodied the scene. For example, the performers read about and discussed the circumstances leading to her immigration to Canada. They then discussed the feelings that occurred during the move, the conflicts that arose, and finally the overcoming of conflicts to become a successful editor of the *Provincial Freeman*. This embodied process allowed the dancers to fully engage in the historical data and express their understanding through movement. This process utilized arts-based research strategies.[2] All collaborators focused on creating an arts-based work that illuminated the struggles and achievements experienced by Shadd Cary as an African American educator, journalist, orator, suffragist, and pioneering African American female newspaper publisher and editor.[3] Shadd Cary used her skills as an orator and journalist to express her views on issues impacting the lives of African Americans in the United States and Canada, agitate for the civil rights of African Americans and women, and persuade others to join the cause. She used her skills as an educator and attorney to directly impact the lives of individuals by giving them the tools they needed to improve their own lives. She was a trailblazer for women of color, who understood the power of the written and spoken word to move public opinion. The methods that she used and the degree of success that she achieved made it possible for others, particularly African American women, to continue the struggle and benefit from the gains that she made.

Arts-Based Research as a Critical Race Methodology

As the artistic collaborators continued creating the production, the research team, affiliated with the production, Rosalyn Green, A. T. Moffett, and Dianna Ruberto, selected an arts-based research (ABR) and critical race methodology (CRM) that led to a post-performance survey for audiences to complete.

CRM provided an overarching perspective for the assessment of the outcomes of this project. Through counterstorytelling, scholars tell the stories of people whose experiences are not often told or centered in history. With this methodology, scholars can recognize and give voice to silenced Black women. The artistic method of collaborative choreography presents a novel approach to creating counterstories that reflect the story of Shadd Cary as a historical figure with contemporary resonance.

Critical race theory (CRT) is a theoretical lens that illuminates and examines systems of racial oppression in society and the impact these systems have on victims of racism to incite transformational change.[4] While there are several widely accepted principles of CRT, this project focused on the tenet of voice or counternarrative.[5]

Counternarrative refers to the practice of telling the stories of racially oppressed groups through their voice to counteract the erasure of their perspectives in white hegemonic storytelling.[6] The act of counterstorytelling derives from the assumption that stories reflect a point of view and illuminate what the teller, audience, society, and/or those in power believe to be important and often valorizes Eurocentric perspectives.[7] Without counter-storytelling, the stories and experiences of Black women, like that of Shadd Cary, are subject to being oversimplified, misrepresented, or erased.

While CRT is a well-developed theoretical framework, CRM is a developing area of scholarship.[8] Critical race scholars are exploring new avenues for integrating CRT in their methodological practices. Counterstorytelling has emerged as an invaluable strategy for merging CRT and methods.[9] By using creative strategies to tell the stories of racially oppressed people, many scholars are using counternarratives to explore the complex dimensions of racialized oppression as it manifests in the real-life experiences of Black individuals and reveals how these individuals make sense of their oppression.[10]

ABR is a viable strategy for counterstorytelling through the lens of CRT as a critical race methodology. ABR is "the systematic use of the artistic process, the actual making of artistic expressions . . . as a primary way of understanding and examining experience by both researchers and the people involved in their studies."[11] ABR acknowledges the synergy of artistic creation and academic scholarship in that they are both centered on critical and creative inquiry. It is a research paradigm that has grown from the desire of researchers to elicit and share understandings that are not fully accessed through more traditional scholarly approaches. ABR utilizes the arts in one or more stages of the research design.[12] Artistic methods are used alongside complementary, qualitative methods to study a social, educational, or artistic phenomenon.

ABR aligns with CRT in terms of its potential to engage aesthetics, form and technique, and real-world social content.[13] More specifically, a critical-theoretic approach to ABR engages the arts as a means for critical reflection around invisible assumptions, values, and norms to critique and change systems of oppression.[14] When ABR is used to study and understand racialized ideologies, it can be a tool for furthering CRT research agendas that aim to address the pervasiveness of racism in society.

Modern dancers have a documented history of actively engaging with their time's social and political climate in the dance field. There are choreographic works in this genre that range from social commentary to outright embodied social activism to advocate for social changes such as better working conditions and addressing racial inequality.[15] The work of African American modern dance scholars Pearl Primus and Katherine Dunham combined aesthetic forms of dance, dialogue, social content, embodied research, and pedagogy to create dances that challenged the social injustices of racial segregation on Black lives in America during the 1940s. Dunham's research on performance methodology brought scholarship to the concert stage as she performed her anthropological fieldwork findings and used the body's language to educate audiences on Black cultural heritages and experiences.[16]

The Production

The previous sections of this chapter have provided a brief introduction to the embodied explorations, the historical background, and the theoretical perspectives that grounded the production. In this section, artistic director Lynnette Young Overby shares her process of creating and assessing the entire collaborative production.

As artistic director of the MASC production, my goal was to tell the story of Shadd Cary's life through artistic expression. In addition to telling her story, I wanted to allow audiences to empathize with the circumstances of her life and be inspired by her journey.

I first became aware of Shadd Cary through research and conversations about the Colored Convention Movement. Colored Conventions took place in several locations in the United States prior to the establishment of the NAACP. The Colored Conventions provided African Americans a venue to discuss political and social issues that impacted their community. Gabrielle Foreman, founding director of the Colored Conventions Project, introduced me to Shadd Cary as a participant in the Colored Conventions.

The process of transforming the written historical literature into an artistic production took several steps, including (1) inviting potential choreographers, poets, composers, dancers, educators, and researchers to become part of a community of learners who would ultimately contribute to the creation, performance, and assessment of the final production; (2) outlining potential themes to be presented in the production; (3) allowing the artists to select a specific focus for their work; (4) developing research questions and strategies; (5) creating, rehearsing, and finalizing the production; (6) sharing the production; (7) collecting, analyzing, and reporting on audience and artists perceptions.

Composer Ralph Russell collaborated closely with the choreographers in the process of creating the production. Describing his work, he said, "My compositions were structured to capture different aspects of [Shadd] Cary's life. They reflect her dedication to providing quality education to African American children and securing human rights to African Americans."[17]

A Community of Learners

We began to have weekly meetings in the spring of 2019. During the meetings, we learned about and discussed Shadd Cary from readings, research presentations, and videos. After the discussions, we moved into smaller groups of composers, researchers, dancers, poets, and choreographers, to discuss specific contributions of each group. During meetings, we shared excerpts of music, poetry, and movement ideas and received feedback from all participants.

Composer Ralph Russell reflected on the process of gaining knowledge about Shadd Cary in the following statement:

> Before I began composing pieces for the production, I read several chapters from *Mary Ann Shadd Cary: The Black Press and Protest in the Nineteenth Century* by Jane Rhodes and watched a short video of her life to understand her role and importance in American history. I found chapters such as "The Making of an Activist," "Emigration Furor and *Notes of Canada West*," and "Reconstructing a Life—Reconstructing a People" helpful in composing pieces that portrayed her passion and dedication to equal rights. The compositions were in simple ABA or AB forms and unified with recurring melodies and countermelodies. Moreover, the pieces were both interwoven in particular scenes to accentuate the stories and functioned as backdrops to create atmosphere for the dances.[18]

Outlining the Production

After meeting for several weeks, an outline of potential aspects of Shadd Cary's life emerged. They included (1) her life as a child in Wilmington; (2) being educated in Pennsylvania; (3) the impact of the fugitive slave act on her family; (4) her experiences in Canada—becoming an editor; and (5) her experiences as a suffragette.

The next section of this chapter will include narration from the production, descriptions of the original works, and the artists' reflections.

Narration Scene 1: "This is for Mary"

Mary, born free, did not have to endure slavery, however, she fought for the rights of enslaved and disenfranchised African Americans. We will now look at a reflection of Mary Ann Shadd Cary's legacy throughout her lifetime. This is for Mary.

This piece, choreographed and performed by Rachel DeLauder, provided an introduction to Mary's life through poetry and choreography (figure 5.1). As DeLauder explained, "'This is for Mary' was a choreographic reflection as a 'call for action,' where I begin to embody Shadd, the activist. I used three metaphors for the choreographic motif, 'rebel,' 'strength,' and 'visionary.' Finally, the piece shifts to the voice of Shadd stepping into her role as an activist, educator, and emigrationist, journalist, and lawyer, as she continues to shed light on her journey and legacy. Shadd brings together the new legacy, Shadd's daughter, and the next generation of women to continue pushing the needle and social policies forward for social change."[19]

Figure 5.1. Mary Ann Shadd Cary is expressing her strength and independence with her arms rounded and outstretched in high relief facing upstage. Photography by Sierra Watkins. Choreographer and Dancer Rachel DeLauder.

Figure 5.2. At the end of the dance "Games," members of Mary Ann Shadd Cary's childhood community are reaching toward the center person who is tapping a stick in defiance of a law that indicates that girls cannot be educated in Delaware. Photograph by Sierra Watkins. Choreography: Lynnette Young Overby. Dancers: Ikira Peace, April Singleton, Amber Rance, Gabrielle Shubert, Omi Ames Davis, Chelsea Gbemudu, Marion Hamermesh, and Marlene Jones Boddy.

Narration Scene 2: "Games"

In the 1800s Wilmington, where Mary Ann grew up, playing fun games was an important part of childhood. However, it was also a time when educational opportunities were denied to African American girls.

"Games," choreographed by Lynnette Young Overby, included children's games played in the streets during the 1800s (figure 5.2). The playful attitude turns serious as an individual with a sign stating "No Schools for Colored Girls" passes through their play area. The dance ends with a strong verbal statement of "We will get an education. . . . Yes!"

Narration Scene 3: "Becoming"

Mary Ann and her family then moved to Pennsylvania, where she was educated. Her Papa was a leader in the Colored Conventions movement

Figure 5.3. Mary Ann Shadd Cary, dressed in red, is holding a book used for teaching a child. They are both joyful and enthusiastic about learning and teaching. Photograph by Sierra Watkins. "Becoming" Choreography: Teresa Emmons and Lynnette Young Overby. Dancers: April Singleton and Gabrielle Shubert.

and her family provided a stop on the underground railroad—Her father inspired her.

In this work, choreographed by Teresa Emmons, with vocals by Ralph Russell, we see Mary as an educator, teaching a younger sibling (figure 5.3). The piece concludes with Mary dancing with her father, who escorts her off stage while singing "Deep River."

Teresa Emmons reflected on her choreographic process: "This was the hardest part . . . deciding what is the best way to get this message across . . . this is where using a prop, the 'black book' became a focal point. As in the use of any prop, its purpose needed to be clear, and movements expressing this needed to be carefully selected and shaped. I selected the dancers (April [Singleton] and Gabby [Shubert]) to represent a teacher and student relationship. What would trigger a child to want to learn? Curiosity? Encouragement? Raising the bar? Will it be a simple task? A struggle? How will it be resolved?"[20]

Figure 5.4. As a response to the Fugitive Slave Law, the dancers are embodying African rhythms and movements as they hear dogs barking in the background. Photograph by Sierra Watkins. "The Fugitive Slave Act" Choreography: Desiree Cocroft. Dancers: Ikira Peace, April Singleton, Omi Ames Davis, and Chelsea Gbemudu.

Narration Scene 4: "The Fugitive Slave Law"

This law made it a challenge for free and enslaved African Americans to feel safe. It was passed by the United States Congress on September 18, 1850, as part of the Compromise of 1850 between southern slaveholding interests and northern Free-Soilers. Abolitionists nicknamed it the "Bloodhound Law," for the dogs that were used to track down runaway slaves.

Desiree Cocroft describes her choreographic process: "I did a lot of improvisation with dancers as I was highly interested in seeing the dancers take on feelings and emotions of what Mary and other Blacks felt during that time. I wanted their bodies to tell a story that truly embodied those experiences. I wanted this dance to encompass the beauty and power of African roots as well as transformation of how we bring a new form of dance expression to forms similar to ballet and modern. Similar to the work that Katherine Dunham brought to modern dance in America" (figure 5.4).[21]

Narration Scene 5: "Oh Canada"

After the Fugitive Slave Law was established, Canada became a refuge for many African Americans—challenges existed there as well as in the United States. However, Mary Ann overcame the challenges to become

Figure 5.5. This photo represents a triumph for Mary Ann Shadd Cary—she holds a copy of the *Provincial Freeman*, while her supporters form a tableau of support. One dancer in the photo represents Mrs. Bibbs with arms crossed, who made life challenging for Mary Ann Shadd Cary. Photograph by Sierra Watkins. "Oh Canada" Choreography: Lynnette Young Overby. Dancers: Ikira Peace, April Singleton, Amber Rance, Gabrielle Shubert, Omi Ames Davis, Chelsea Gbemudu, Marion Hamermesh, and Marlene Jones Boddy.

the first African American woman to serve as editor of a major newspaper—the Provincial Freeman, *June 30, 1855. The paper ceased publication in 1857.*

"Oh Canada," choreographed by Lynnette Overby, was initially explored in the studio with ideas of fear resulting from passage of the Fugitive Slave Law of 1850, to confrontation with Mr. and Mrs. Bibb, to a sense of accomplishment as Mary establishes her school and becomes editor of the *Provincial Freeman* (figure 5.5).

Narration Scene 6: "Women of the 1800s"

At the 1855 Colored Convention, Mary Ann demonstrated her formidable oratory skills. In this scene, Mary speaks at the 1855 Colored Convention while audience members react in call and response to her powerful words (figure 5.6).

Figure 5.6. Mary Ann Shadd Cary is reciting her 1858 speech "Break Every Yoke and Let the Oppressed Go Free". The dancers on stools represent the audience embodying a response to her powerful words. Photograph by Sierra Watkins. "The Colored Convention Speech" Speaker: Rachel Delauder. Dancers: Ikira Peace, April Singleton, Amber Rance, and Chelsea Gbemudu.

Narration Scene 7: "We as Women"

As a supporter of women's right to vote, Mary Ann Shadd Cary spoke on behalf of all women—even when African American women were left behind. In 1871, Mary Ann Shadd Cary, with several other women, attempted, unsuccessfully, to register to vote in Washington, D.C.

"We as Women" was choreographed by Kimberly Schroeder and demonstrated through movement the collaborative strength of women to make change by working to ensure their right to vote (figure 5.7).

Scene 8. "Legacy"

We concluded the first half of the program with the African American national anthem and poetic description of Shadd Cary's legacy by poet Bebe Coker (figure 5.8). In describing her motivation to create her poem "Legacy" Coker stated: "I would say that my writings fit within the life of Mary Shadd

Figure 5.7. The women in this photo have fists raised high and banners with the words "Vote for women." The dancers are demonstrating the support Mary Ann Shadd Cary provided to the suffragette movement. Photograph by Sierra Watkins. "We As Women," Choreographer: Kimberly Schroeder. Dancers: Ikira Peace, April Singleton, Amber Rance, Gabrielle Shubert, Omi Ames Davis, Chelsea Gbemudu, and Marion Hamermesh.

Cary's . . . because I make efforts to write out of a sense of expression that can be easily understood; and/or as sharing thoughts others might want to express and are either hesitant to do so or not aware of just how to say what they are thinking. I write because like Shadd Cary I am free to do so and have an obligation to share "truths."[22] The second half of this production moved us into modern times with artistic interpretations of Shadd Cary's life and legacy.

Narration Scene 9: "Breaking Boundaries"

Mary Ann Shadd Cary was a woman of many talents and passions. Many times she had to move or push against barriers to live out her plans for herself and her people.

Figure 5.8. The performers are reciting the poem "Legacy" by Bebe Coker, then singing the African American national anthem. Photograph by Sierra Watkins. Performers: Ralph Russell and Rachel DeLauder.

Marion Hamermesh choreographed this piece as an abstract depiction of Shadd Cary's boundary-breaking accomplishments (figure 5.9). The poetry of Christian Wills and music by Ralph Russell combined to engage the dancers and audiences. The dance concluded with performers making a bridge out of benches, chairs, and boxes, then slowly, one at a time walking across the bridge, with help from their friends.

Hamermesh indicated her creative process in the following statement:

I began with my vision of running back and forth across the space, parallel to the proscenium, to represent crossing lines. I invited 4 of the women to create short movement phrases about different aspects of MASC's life—being a student, an editor, a suffragette, and keeping away from those who would catch and enslave her. They used as source material other dances in the show which characterized these moments. I created a plan for when these would interrupt the running. I used the other dancers as a sort of chorus. The ending came

Figure 5.9. The dancers represent society forming walls that block access by African Americans to the ballot box. Photograph by Sierra Watkins. "Crossing Lines/Breaking Barriers, Composer and Spoken Word Artist: Christian Wills. Choreographer: Marion Hamermesh. Dancers: Amber Rance, Gabrielle Shubert, Omi Ames Davis, and Marlene Jones Boddy.

to me when I heard jazz musician Kendrick Scott Oracle say, about a piece he wrote, that sometimes . . . "A Wall Becomes a Bridge."[23]

Scene 10: "Super Woman"

This dance provides a contemporary look at the strength of women today, with music by artist Alicia Keys (figure 5.10).

Amber Rance and Ikira Peace created this contemporary piece as an inspiration to women of today. The lyrics of the song, combined with the dynamic movements of the dancers, gave a clear message of empowerment.

Narration Scene 11: "Three Etudes to Freedom"
We may go the way our blood beats, have different forms of resistance, and disagree on strategies and approaches to obtain freedom; however,

Figure 5.10. The dancers, costumed in contemporary attire, dancing to music by contemporary artist Alicia Keys, and with bodies and arms and eyes moving upward, demonstrating a unison movement of empowerment of women. Photograph by Sierra Watkins. "Super Woman" Choreographers: Ikira Peace and Amber Rance. Dancers: Ikira Peace, April Singleton, Amber Rance, Omi Ames Davis, and Chelsea Gbemudu.

freedom cannot be obtained without unity and without our resilient community for tangible social change.

"Three Etudes to Freedom" was choreographed by Rachel DeLauder (figure 5.11). In response to a question about her choreographic process, DeLauder responded as follows:

The "Three Etudes to Freedom" was my original choreography in the dance genres of Guinea, West African dance forms, and modern dance. The choreographic staging pattern started with the soloist who represents the social activist for Human Rights. The cast emerges on stage with "Hello" and "Wait" to show the disparity of being told to wait for justice, receive services and rights, while the rest of the cast who expressed "Hello" were to receive second-class treatment from

Figure 5.11. Two groups of dancers show a disparity between those who are being told to "wait" and those who can move forward. Photograph by Sierra Watkins. "Three Etudes to Freedom," Choreographer: Rachel DeLauder. Dancers: Ikira Peace, April Singleton, Amber Rance, Omi Ames Davis, Chelsea Gbemudu, Marion Hamermesh, and Marlene Jones Boddy.

a capitalist society. The cast represents political identities such as assimilationist, nationalist, emigrationist, activist, feminist, and separatist. . . . As the piece concludes, the bodies transform into a flocking improvisation and join as a united front for freedom.[24]

Scene 12: "Torch Bearer"

This poem was written by Glenis Redmond. In the poem, Redmond traces Shadd Cary's life with a focus on the contributions she was able to make against all odds.

Responding to the question of how she created the poem, Redmond revealed the following: "I researched Mary Ann Shadd Cary. Brainstormed about history. I tried to put myself in her place and tried to write from that perspective. I came up with the imagery of fire, a light leading us through darkness. Her life was the momentum that pushed my poem into existence. There need to be more poems and art forms celebrating Mary Ann Shadd Cary."[25]

Narration Scene 13: "Finale"

We have taken the journey with Mary Ann Shadd Cary from 1800s Delaware, through Canada, and then back to the United States. We have illuminated some of the essential characteristics of Mary Ann's life through dance, music, and poetry.

The finale, choreographed by Lynnette Overby with contributions from the dancers, was a final ode to women from the past and present (figure 5.12). The dancers, dressed in costumes from all previous dances, moved across the stage with photos of accomplished Black women.

Christian Wills, who composed and performed the music, said this about his process:

Figure 5.12. The dancer in red portrays Mary Ann Shadd Cary reaching high, while the other dancers are connecting to her and to each other. Photograph by Sierra Watkins. "Finale," Choreographer: Lynnette Young Overby, with contributions from the dancers. Dancers: Ikira Peace, April Singleton, Amber Rance, Gabrielle Shubert, Omi Ames Davis, Chelsea Gbemudu, Marion Hamermesh, Rachel DeLauder, and Marlene Jones Boddy.

From the beginning, I knew I wanted the song to be focused on ending Mary Ann's story as a legacy and having that legacy be the starting point for others to follow in her footsteps. Working with Jordan [Lloyd], the singer and vocalist on the project, we came together to compose the song with piano and drum elements. We infused lighter moments for the chorus and her vocals; highlighting Mary Ann's life as a legacy. The added percussion for the rapping portion of the song contained verses celebrating black women who made enormous changes through time. Overall, each line of poetry and verse throughout the song was carefully constructed to send a specific message to the audience and pull the show together through the use of spoken word.[26]

Wills performed a rap to music and lyrics by Jordan Lloyd that conclude with these words: "This is our legacy."

Impacts of the Production

The research group led by Dianna Ruberto, with contributions from A. T. Moffett, Rachel DeLauder, and Rosalyn Green, created surveys to assess the knowledge gained by audience members after observing the production. The research team designed the survey instrument to collect quantitative and qualitative data about what the audience gained or learned from watching the MASC production. The researchers used the survey responses to address the following research questions:

1. What knowledge did the audience members gain about Shadd Cary's life?
2. What knowledge did the audience members gain about the ability of the arts to inform and provoke critical discourse about African American history?

The surveys included eight Likert scale questions and four open-ended questions about the production. The Likert scale questions asked respondents to choose a number from 1 to 5 to best represent how strongly they agreed or disagreed with a given statement. Selecting 1 meant that they strongly disagreed and choosing 5 meant they strongly agreed with the given statement.

Audience members, including 110 high school students (ages fourteen to nineteen) and 112 adults (ages twenty to seventy-four), completed the surveys immediately following each performance in Delaware, Texas, and Belize.

When asked how much they knew about Shadd Cary before watching the production, a vast majority of respondents reported little to no knowledge about her as a historical figure. On a scale of 1 to 5, the average response to the statement "I knew about Mary Ann Shadd Cary before attending the production" was a 1.6, and the most frequent response was 1 (71% of respondents). The average respondent strongly disagreed with that statement.

After watching the production, almost all respondents who claimed to know little to nothing about her reported that the MASC production helped them learn more about her life. On a scale of 1 to 5, the average response to the statement "I learned a great deal about Mary Ann Shadd Cary from the production" was a 4.02, and the most frequent response was 5 (46.8% of respondents). This data demonstrates that the average respondent agreed with that statement.

In the open-ended responses, the respondents listed things they learned about Mary Ann Shadd Cary, including her work as a founder of a school for Black girls, editor of the *Provincial Freeman*, and suffragette. Additionally, they were able to speak to her attributes, including her resilience and tenacity. Some of the adult respondents commented on what they had learned from the production, including this from Respondent A: "I didn't know anything, sadly, about this great Black woman but I learned: she was from Delaware, she did learn to read and became and highly educated, her family was by the 'Evils' law (Fugitive Slave Act) of 1850, she moved to Canada and became an editor."

Additionally, the student respondents were able to recall specific aspects of Shadd Cary's life after watching the production: Respondent D commented, "I learned that she had to travel places because she couldn't fulfill her dreams where she lived due to racism." Respondent E said, "I learned that she was the first Black woman publisher."

Several adult audience respondents (19.4%) claimed to have known about Shadd Cary's story before they watched production. Those who knew about Shadd Cary responded that the production helped them learn more about her life and contributions. Respondent F commented, "I learned about MASC via genealogy research (on Geni.com), but wasn't aware of her gender fight."

A vast majority of survey respondents reported that they believed the arts to be a powerful tool for bringing history to life. On a scale of 1 to 5, the average response to the statement "I believe the arts are a useful tool in bringing history to life" was 4.52, and the most frequent response was 5 (71.6% of respondents). This data means that the average respondent strongly agreed with that statement. In their open-ended answers, both adult and student respondents shared how the multiple artistic mediums in the production, including dance, music, poetry, and the narration, inspired or moved them. Respondent H, one of the adult respondents, had the following to say about the use of arts in storytelling: "Using dance to express powerful themes in the time of slavery and oppression and suffrage issues is an ineffable form of art. Dance expresses art that words cannot express by embodying the personal and social challenges she faces." Student respondents also shared what they gained from the arts being used to tell Shadd Cary's story, including this from Respondent J: "I found it most powerful when the man started singing. I believe that singing brings a different experience and I found myself listening to the message more openly."

The audience members' survey responses answered both research questions 1 and 2 affirmatively. Both adult and student audience members learned about Shadd Cary's life and appreciated the role of the arts in telling her story. These results demonstrate the potential impact of using ABR as a critical race methodology to educate public audiences about Black history.

Extensions of the Production

EDUCATIONAL MATERIALS

Collaborators taught arts-integrated, standards-based lessons focused on the MASC production's themes in Delaware, Alabama, Texas, and Belize. Each location was unique with audience members and students from elementary school age to senior adults. However, the response was always positive with individuals able to relate to the lesson topics presented in the production and become inspired by Mary Ann Shadd Cary's story of triumph over racist and oppressive conditions. The lesson topics included an overview of the Colored Conventions, the importance of education in the Colored Conventions Movement, and Black women activists during the Colored Conventions and today. Educational materials also included video excerpts from the production and creative alternatives for summative assessment, which will be piloted in an eleventh-grade history class in Delaware.

PRESERVATION

The Delaware Historical Society, the University of Delaware Library, and the Colored Conventions Project will preserve the production videos, educational materials, and oral histories to contribute to future scholarship and artistic inquiry on her life and legacy.

PUBLICATION PRESENTATIONS

Collaborators presented the MASC production and "Shadd's Daughters" oral history project outcomes at a virtual Colored Conventions Project symposium, the Engaged Scholarship Consortium Conference, and the Delaware Afro-American Historical and Genealogical Society Conference.

Conclusion

Critical race theory provided an umbrella for the creation of this multidisciplinary arts-based research project by incorporating a critical race methodology. CRM in the form of counterstorytelling told the story of Mary Ann Shadd Cary through the arts of choreography, theater, poetry, and music. Evaluation of the impact on audiences' knowledge of Mary Ann Shadd Cary's life as portrayed in this production was assessed by using artist interviews and audience surveys.

The arts were used to explore, share, and critically engage with the lived experience of Shadd Cary through counterstorytelling. This artistic work illuminated an important historical figure who is not widely known due to interlocking systems of racism and sexism that suppressed knowledge of her contributions to social justice movements in the late 1800s. Since her story was originally recorded and archived through a white patriarchal hegemonic lens many vital aspects of her life and personhood were overlooked and forgotten. The process of exploring and telling her story through ABR created an informed imagining of her life for which the public record did not account.[27] Scholar artists imagined Shadd Cary's personality, motivations, mannerisms, emotions, and relationships with others in unprecedented ways and did so in a way that reached both public and academic audiences. By using the arts as a CRM for Counter Storytelling to tell Shadd Cary's story, artists contributed and exchanged knowledge about the critical role she played in furthering racial justice movements for Black diasporic communities in the U.S. and Canada. In addition, through public performance, artists contemporized history to foster more rich connections between Shadd Cary's life and the audience's personal experiences.

Our journey to illuminate the life and times of Shadd Cary has continued evolving in exciting ways. The contributions of researchers, composers, choreographers, poets, and performers brought her story to life in ways that would not have been possible through one approach or one disciplinary perspective. We created a multidisciplinary production, shared it with audiences of many ages, and developed additional components for educational purposes. As we continue to expand on various ways to inform and inspire our audiences, we will remember to walk in Shadd Cary's footsteps and help others gain knowledge and appreciation of her challenging yet successful contributions.

Notes

Note to epigraph: Glenis Redmond, "Torch Bearer" (unpublished poem, July 30, 2021).

1. Jane Rhodes, *Mary Ann Shadd Cary: The Black Press and Protest in the Nineteenth Century* (Bloomington: Indiana University Press, 1998); Jeri Chase Ferris, *Demanding Justice: A Story of Mary Ann Shadd Cary* (Minneapolis: Lerner Publishing Group, 2003); "Mary Ann Shadd Cary," January 29, 2015, Colgate University Academic Video, video, 8:33, https://www.youtube.com/watch?v=Zc-QvADH5qI; Allison Margot Smith, "Mary Ann Shadd Revisited: Echoes from an Old House," March 1, 2016, ActiveHistory.ca, video, 27:21, https://www.youtube.com/watch?v=uGH0m3NChM0.

2. Carl Bagley and Mary Beth Cancienne, "Educational Research and Intertextual Forms of (Re)presentation," in *Dancing the Data*, ed. Carl Bagley and Mary Beth Cancienne (New York: Peter Lang, 2002), 3–19; Celeste Snowber, "Living, Moving, and Dancing," in *Handbook of Arts-Based Research*, ed. Patricia Leavy (New York: Guilford, 2018), 247–66; Celeste Snowber, "The Zen of Laundry," November 11, 2010, video, 4:41, https://www.youtube.com/watch?v=j7kz8yyzrCM; Dwight Rogers, Paul Frellick, and Leslie Babinski, "Staging a Study: Performing the Personal and Professional Struggles of Beginning Teachers," in Bagley and Cancienne, *Dancing the Data*, 53–69.

3. Rhodes, *Mary Ann Shadd Cary*, xi–xv.

4. Richard Delgado and Jean Stefancic, introduction to *Critical Race Theory: An Introduction*, 3rd ed. (New York: New York, University Press, 2017), 1–15; Gloria Ladson-Billings, "Critical Race Theory—What It Is Not!," in *Handbook of Critical Race Theory in Education*, ed. Marvin Lynn and Adrienne Dixson (New York: Routledge, 2013), 34–47.

5. Richard Delgado and Jean Stefancic, "Legal Storytelling and Narrative Analysis," in *Critical Race Theory*, 43–53; Ladson-Billings, "Critical Race Theory," 34–47.

6. Delgado and Stefancic, "Legal Storytelling and Narrative Analysis," 43–53.

7. Ladson-Billings, "Critical Race Theory," 34–47.

8. Daniella Ann Cook, "Blurring the Boundaries: The Mechanics of Creating Composite Characters," in Lynn and Dixson, *Handbook of Critical Race Theory in Education*, 181–94; Daniel G. Solórzano and Tara J. Yosso, "Critical Race Methodology: Counter-Storytelling as an Analytical Framework for Education Research," *Qualitative Inquiry* 8, no. 1 (February 2002): 23–44, doi:10.1177/107780040200800103.

9. Cook, "Blurring the Boundaries," 181–94; Solórzano and Yosso, "Critical Race Methodology," 23–44.

10. Cook, "Blurring the Boundaries," 181–94; Daniella Ann Cook and Adrienne D. Dixson, "Writing Critical Race Theory and Method: A Composite Counterstory on the Experiences of Black Teachers in New Orleans Post-Katrina," *International Journal of Qualitative Studies in Education* 26, no. 10 (November 2012): 1238–58, https://doi.org/10.1080/09518398.2012.731531; Solórzano and Yosso, "Critical Race Methodology," 23–44; Dawn N. Hicks Tafari, "Whose World Is This? A Composite Counterstory of Black Male Elementary School Teachers as Hip Hop Otherfathers," *Urban Review* 50, no. 1 (December 2018): 795–817, https://doi.10.1007/s11256-018-0471-z.

11. Shaun McNiff, "Art-Based Research," in *Handbook of the Arts in Qualitative Research: Perspectives, Methodologies, Examples, and Issues*, ed. J. Gary Knowles and Ardra L. Cole (Thousand Oaks, CA: Sage, 2008), 29–40, quotation at 29.

12. Patricia Leavy, "Social Research and the Creative Arts: An Introduction." in *Method Meets Arts: Arts-Based Research Practice*, 2nd ed. (New York: Guilford Press, 2015), 1–38.

13. Joe Norris, "Towards the Use of the 'Great Wheel' as a Model in Determining the Quality and Merit of Arts-Based Projects (Research and Instruction)," *International Journal of Education & the Arts* 12, no. 1.7 (June 2011): 1–24, http://www.ijea.org/v12si1/; Tom Barone and Elliot W. Eisner, "Why Do Arts Based Research?," in *Arts Based Research* (Thousand Oaks, CA: Sage., 2012), 13–44.

14. James Haywood Rolling, Jr., "A Paradigm Analysis of Arts-Based Research," in *Arts-Based Research* (New York: Peter Lang, 2013), 1–38.

15. Lisa Wilson and A. T. Moffett, "Building Bridges for Dance Through Arts-Based Research," *Research in Dance Education* 18, no. 2 (October 2017): 135–49, https://doi.org/10.1080/14647893.2017.1330328.

16. Rosemarie Roberts, "Research-to-Performance Methodology: Embodying Knowledge and Power from the Field to the Concert Stage," in *Katherine Dunham: Recovering an Anthropological Legacy, Choreographing Ethnographic Futures*, ed. Elizabeth Chin (Santa Fe, NM: School for Advanced Research Press, 2014), 17–30.

17. Ralph Russell, email message to author, August 1, 2021.

18. Russell, email message, August 1, 2021.

19. Rachel DeLauder, email message to author, August 7, 2021.

20. Teresa Emmons, email message to author, August 1, 2021.

21. Desire Cocroft, email message to author, August 2, 2021.

22. Bebe Coker, email message to author, July 20, 2021.

23. Marion Hamermesh, email message to author, July 19, 2021.

24. DeLauder, email message, August 7, 2021.

25. Glenis Redmond, email message to author, July 30, 2021.

26. Christian Wills, email message to author, August 17, 2021.

27. Emilie-Andree Jabouin, Charles E. Smith, Lynnette Young Overby, Ralph Russell, April Singleton, and Kristin Moriah, "Mary Ann Shadd Cary and the Power of Black Art" (virtual symposium, Mary Ann Shadd Cary Event Series, October 9, 2020), https://www.youtube.com /watch?v=pcjuoKTP7mI.

CHAPTER 6

"A Greater Compass of Voice"

Elizabeth Taylor Greenfield and Mary Ann Shadd Cary Navigate Black Performance

KRISTIN MORIAH

First, there is the fact of the ambrotype,[1] not just the form of early photography itself, but the fact of the object's existence. The delicate portrait, probably taken between 1854 and 1865,[2] represented the female subject's singularity and was meant to be treasured. Technically, perhaps poetically, it is a pane glass negative whose image is only fully visible when put into relief against a dark background, like the reverse of a Glenn Ligon stencil.[3] Enclosed in a small black wooden case lined with flocked red velvet, the ambrotype fits in the palm of one's hand. The interior edges of the case are gilded and the image itself is nestled in a gold mat. The subject's left arm rests crooked upon a table covered with delicate pink-tinged lace. Even more delicate lace extends from the sleeves of her dress and stark white lace is gathered around the fashionable but not too revealing neckline of her gown. Her hair is neatly braided and tastefully adorned with black ribbon.[4] An ornately carved dark wooden chair peeks out from behind her. The gold brooch at the subject's neckline, her gold bracelet, gold pocket watch, and the attached gold chain were all painstakingly hand painted on the surface of the glass negative at an additional cost. This is a portrait that speaks to the subject's upward and outward mobility, a remarkable feat of self-fashioning[5] for a formerly enslaved Black woman who was a celebrity and a very real object of curiosity before the Civil War.[6]

The ambrotype is the only extant photograph of antebellum African American concert singer Elizabeth Taylor Greenfield (Figure 6.1). It is just

Figure 6.1. Photographic portrait of concert singer Elizabeth T. Greenfield, *The Black Swan*, portrait of concert singer Elizabeth T. Greenfield circa 1850s. Courtesy of Library and Archives Canada.

one of a number of material clues that demonstrate the importance of Black feminist performance along the U.S.-Canadian border, testifying to the unexpected and unhailed presence of Black diasporic performance in Canada. Today, the ambrotype is part of the Frederick H. J. Lambart fonds at Library and Archives Canada (LAC) in Ottawa, Ontario. It is one of the oldest photographs of a Black woman there. Lambart is an unlikely collector of this material. A white settler born in Ottawa in 1880, Lambart was a surveyor for the Canadian government who was noted for his "extensive experience of the Northern wilderness" and his love of photography (Scott 99). His daughter Evelyn Lambart was the first woman to work as an animator for the National Film Board of Canada. Mary Margaret Johnston Miller, art archivist at LAC, believes the ambrotype likely came into Lambart's possession through the family's connection to Hiram Edward Howard, a wealthy Buffalo banker, president of the Buffalo Music Association, and an early Elizabeth Taylor Greenfield supporter. Taylor Greenfield provided childcare for Hiram E. Howard's family when she lived in Buffalo in the early 1850s (Chybowski, "Becoming" 141) and maintained close connections with them until at least the late 1860s ("Amusements"). The Howards were related to and intermarried with Canadian families, including the Lambarts. The crisscrossing of these family ties and objects reveals both the ephemerality of the

U.S.-Canadian border and the ubiquity of Black popular culture in the antebellum period. Thus, the Elizabeth Taylor Greenfield ambrotype is a launching point for my investigation into the forms of Black feminist performance
that accrued along the Canadian border in the nineteenth century.

Rarely, if ever, recognized as such, Elizabeth Taylor Greenfield was almost
certainly the first Black woman to sing art music professionally on stage in
Canada. Born into slavery in Natchez, Mississippi, around 1819, Elizabeth
Taylor's family was once owned by Elizabeth Halliday Greenfield, a white
Philadelphian with Welsh roots who had married into the plantocracy. Shortly
after she was born, Elizabeth Taylor was legally emancipated and emigrated
to Philadelphia with her mistress, who joined the Friends' Society. Some
of the Black laborers formerly enslaved by Elizabeth Halliday Greenfield
migrated to Liberia, including Elizabeth Taylor's parents.[7] Encouraged by
Mrs. Elizabeth Halliday Greenfield, young Elizabeth Taylor began to develop
her musical talent. She also adopted her mistress's last name. Eventually, by
means of her own proficiency, the aid of white benefactors and promoters,
and the support of the Black community in the North, Elizabeth Taylor
Greenfield became a professional concert singer hailed as the "Black Swan."
Her 1853 tour of England propelled her to international fame and continues
to be the focus of much study.[8] But England was not her first international
sojourn. Her work frequently brought her to U.S.-Canadian border cities and
into Canada; she concertized in Toronto, Ontario, and towns near Black settlements like Chatham, Ontario.

Nina Sun Eidsheim insists that along with later Black concert singer
Sissieretta Jones, Elizabeth Taylor Greenfield's "performance practices and
reception by audiences—where listeners based their opinions on related artists' work and on the work of white artists in blackface— . . . influenced the
later reception of African American classical singers" (70). Her work follows
Eric Lott's assertion that Elizabeth Taylor Greenfield provided the inspiration
for the stock minstrel character Lucy Neal (235). However, like Julia Chybowski, whose detailed research sheds much needed light on the granular
details of Elizabeth Taylor Greenfield's education and early life, Eidsheim's
main concern is not the distinction between the singer's impact in Canadian or American contexts. This is not always the rule; Jennifer Lynn Stoever
examines Mary Ann Shadd Cary's interest in Elizabeth Taylor Greenfield and
"how free black people in the North constructed and understood listening as
a political and potentially self-defining act" (124). Extending the work of Eidsheim, Chybowski, and Stoever, I maintain that Elizabeth Taylor Greenfield's

Figure 6.2. Mary Ann Shadd Cary, circa 1855–60. Courtesy of Library and Archives Canada.

early performances in Canada West testify to the long-standing porosity of the U.S.-Canadian border for Black North Americans, particularly women.

What follows is a case study in the way Black feminist performance in Canada relied on the crossing of national boundaries. Black North American women in the 1850s seized on performance as a site of shared concern, and early Black performance in Canada owed much to the crossing of national boundaries. Mary Ann Shadd Cary (Figure 6.2) wrote about Elizabeth Taylor Greenfield's offers to perform in Europe in the very first issue of the *Provincial Freeman*, immediately before a longer item about Black thespian Ira Aldridge who was traveling abroad ("Miscellany"). These news items highlight the social and political importance of travel and mobility for Black North Americans. Greenfield's performances in Canada West, or what is now Southern Ontario, and her coverage in the *Provincial Freeman* demonstrate how solidarity between Black North American women was sustained through performance and surpassed national boundaries. Furthermore, Elizabeth Taylor Greenfield's connection to Mary Ann Shadd Cary reveals the centrality of

Black performance, and Black feminism, to the formation of Black Canada's burgeoning community. These women were acutely sensitive to the radical potential embedded in Black feminist performance along the border between Canada West and the United States. They pushed racial, gender, and national boundaries together. In fact, a consideration of Black women's transnational performances can effectively change our understanding of borders.

"A Place Where Things Can Both Come Together and Break Apart"

The U.S.-Canadian border is a 5,525-mile-long figurative line that has meant very real freedom for some; for the fugitives who fled slavery before the Civil War and the refugees seeking asylum there today. Theorizing the U.S.-Mexico border, Gloria Anzaldúa writes that "borders are set up to define the places that are safe and unsafe, to distinguish *us* from *them*" (3). But the U.S.-Canadian border often fails at that task. The dominant white cultures represented on either side of the dividing line are like fraternal twins. They are Western nations founded on settler colonialism and white supremacy, built by exploited labor, and they share similar languages and customs. Inhabitants of these borderlands often have a pragmatic approach to citizenship and nationhood. In cities like Detroit and Windsor, it is not uncommon for citizens of one nation to commute daily across the border for work and to have family on either side of the dividing line.[9] Until 2019,[10] border cities like Buffalo and Niagara Falls held an annual Friendship Festival celebrating the positive relations between Canada and the United States after the War of 1812. While Canada continuously struggles to establish its autonomy and moral distance from its powerful neighbor, at the border there is an overwhelming acknowledgment of similarity and shared interests between relatively homogeneous groups of North Americans. The cultural work of the U.S.-Canadian border is often more about affirming a Eurocentric *us* than defining a *them*.

At the same time, Katherine McKittrick has shown that for Black Canadians, such "nation-borders are called into question because they do not sufficiently speak to the ways in which Black geographies in Canada are made and upheld" (103). During the nineteenth century, Black North Americans were mobile in the face of openly hostile nation-states and frequently traversed the U.S.-Canadian border. Early Black communities on the border occupied a precarious place on the edges of citizenship and nationhood. Black radical abolitionist and journalist Martin R. Delany was wary of the dangers inherent in the British territory's proximity to America.[11] Rinaldo Walcott has argued that the peripatetic movements of nineteenth- and twentieth-century African Americans and Black Canadians "demonstrate that for Black North Americans, the border between Canada and the United States was permeable" (144). Some of the first African Americans who crossed the border to the British colony of Canada came as a result of the American Revolutionary War, either as the chattel of white American Loyalists or as soldiers who were granted freedom by the British. The War of 1812 and the Underground Railroad also resulted in the cross-border migration of Blacks who had been enslaved in America. The Fugitive Slave Act of 1850 resulted in a significant increase in the number of refugees from U.S. slavery entering Canada West. Black migration moved both ways. Winfried Siemerling reminds us that beginning in the eighteenth century, and before slavery had been abolished there, enslaved people from Upper Canada fled to Vermont, New York, Ohio, and other free territories (68). During the Civil War hundreds of Black Canadians from Canada West crossed the U.S.-Canadian border to fight for the Union Army (Prince 12). After the Civil War, many Black Americans who had settled along the U.S.-Canadian border returned to America to be reunited with their kin. Clearly for Black North Americans in the United States and Canada, nationhood and belonging remained fraught throughout the century, and the U.S.-Canadian border often represented a site of recognition and coalescence rather than separation.

In the midst of this back-and-forth, while provinces like Quebec and Nova Scotia became vital hubs of Black life, Ontario and its border cities emerged as prime locations for Black North Americans who chose to live in Canada. The places in Canada West where Elizabeth Taylor Greenfield performed in the 1850s and 1860s were part of British colonial territory in a state of violent erasure and becoming. Like their American counterparts, early Black communities in this region saw performance as political. Theater historian Robin Breon has identified the 1840s as a pivotal moment in theatrical engagement for Black Torontonians, who recognized the danger of racist entertainment imported from America and the importance of representation on the popular stage. From 1840 to 1843, "members of the Black community petitioned the mayor's office to restrict the presentation of traveling minstrel shows which came up from the U.S. and toured widely in Canada" (Breon). Breon also notes that in 1849 the Toronto Coloured Young Men's Amateur Theatrical Society advertised in the *Toronto-Mirror* for a three-night engagement in which they presented *Venice Preserved* by Thomas Otway and selected scenes from Shakespeare (Breon). These performances seem calculated to counteract the racist tropes of blackface minstrelsy. In the next decade, Elizabeth Taylor Greenfield would sing art music in cities like Toronto, Hamilton, and Chatham, a further cross-border rejoinder to such racist depictions.

Boundary-defying notions of race, space, and place characterized descriptions of Elizabeth Taylor Greenfield's voice during the height of her career. *A Brief Memoir of the "Black Swan"* (1853) opens with the assertion that "genius belongs especially to no country, nation, race, or colour. The gift of Providence—it is scattered over the world" (2), connecting genius to diaspora. Both *A Brief Memoir* and *The Black Swan at Home and Abroad* (1855), biographical sketches available for purchase at her concerts, contain numerous reviews using the technical term "compass" to describe the singer's extraordinary vocal range, the latter explaining that "her compass of voice is probably greater than that of Parodi, Catherine Hayes, or Jenny Lind" (20), a line frequently repeated.[12] One of her first Black feminist biographers, Pauline Hopkins, tells us that "her voice was of immense compass. She struck every note in a clear and well-defined manner, and reached the highest capacity of the human voice with great ease" (47). In a practical sense, the term "compass of voice" refers to the wide range of musical notes available to a singer. Elizabeth Taylor Greenfield performed in traditionally masculine and feminine registers as both a soprano and a tenor, ranging from an upper extension to E6 down to a G2 in the bass clef (Eidsheim 73). The term "compass" was often used as a point of comparison between Greenfield and a set of white European vocalists with whom Greenfield was frequently classed. Daphne Brooks explains that the singer "both entered into the realm of classical singing uninvited as an African American woman and bastardized the sphere by vocally traveling outside the boundaries of vocal categories" (312). As Jennifer Lynn Stoever notes, Elizabeth Taylor Greenfield's unusual voice was "a threat to the sonic color line" (111). But this geographic terminology also hints at the way Greenfield's cultural reach exceeded that of white artists. To the shock and horror of some, her vocal compass allowed her to navigate and breech both Black and white cultural spaces. It guided her toward figurative and physical borders.

Black geographies were then, as now, manifest across a wide range of cultural sites. Judith Madera has demonstrated the importance of navigation as a recurring motif in African American literature during this period, claiming that "nineteenth-century African American literature is starkly geographic" (8). I contend that this stark geography extends to antebellum Black performance, too. The descriptor "compass of voice" was applied to Elizabeth Taylor Greenfield's voice shortly after the passing of the Fugitive Slave Act, when Black refugees from the United States were fleeing north in higher numbers. "Compass" was a multivalent term in the nineteenth century. But compasses were invaluable tools for these refugees, and in the antebellum era the recurring motif of the compass, alongside that of an abolitionist figure like Greenfield, could have potentially conjured discourses of freedom.

With this geographic imperative in mind, the U.S.-Canadian borderlands are a prime location to theorize Black feminist performance. Farah Jasmine Griffin has shown that representations of African American women's voices are "like a hinge, a place where things can both come together and break apart" and that "the black woman's voice can be called upon to heal a crisis in national unity as well as provoke one" (104). Griffin's work suggests that as a medium, Black women's vocals can encapsulate the border's potentiality. In this framework, Black women's vocality offers an important way to transcend geographic boundaries. Griffin also reminds us that "voices create an aural space where listeners can momentarily experience themselves as outside of themselves, as 'home' or as 'free.' This space can be simultaneously political, spiritual, and sensual" (110–11). In nineteenth-century North America, Black women's hinge-like voices could both delineate and destabilize national boundaries. Analysis of coverage in one of the first Black Canadian newspapers, the *Provincial Freeman*, and other abolitionist newspapers reveals the significance of Elizabeth Taylor Greenfield's and Mary Ann Shadd Cary's vocals within the Black diaspora and their contributions to dialogues about Black (trans)national identity in Canada and the United States, particularly among Black women.

The Voices of Feminists, Fugitives, and Free(wo)men

Elizabeth Taylor Greenfield spent her early career working in U.S.-Canadian border cities with abolitionist leanings like Buffalo and Rochester. The singer was raised and educated in Philadelphia, but after her wealthy benefactor died she was shut out of a generous inheritance. Greenfield "found herself compelled to look about for some addition to her diminished means. Having some relatives and friends in the city of Buffalo[13] . . . she resolved to visit them, and at the same time to seek her fortune in some other way" (*Brief Memoir* 6). In Buffalo she gained the attention of local elites and was invited to give a series of (segregated) public concerts at venues including the Buffalo Musical Association starting in early 1852. Following those performances, Greenfield traveled up and down the East Coast, from "Canada and most of the New England States," to the slave state of Maryland (*Brief Memoir* 8). The extreme danger of such travels for Black performers is readily apparent to readers of narratives like Solomon Northrup's *Twelve Years a Slave* (1853). But her early biographers are strangely silent about those perils. They were similarly unconcerned with the boundary represented by the U.S.-Canadian border. Instead, they focused on Elizabeth Taylor Greenfield's trip to England when considering the international extent of her cultural reach. In both James Monroe Trotter's (1878) and Monroe A. Major's (1893) influential biographies, Greenfield's Canadian appearances are treated with little fanfare or distinction. Both sources follow a similar format and a review of her 1852 Toronto performance from the Toronto *Globe* is sandwiched between reviews from Rochester, New York, and Brattleboro, Vermont. Occurring only a few months after her Buffalo debut, the Toronto performance was technically her first international appearance. But Canada may have been too culturally similar (read: conversant in anti-Black practices) for some critics, as per Martin R. Delany. In fact, Trotter's work shows that some Canadian theaters at the time were just as racially segregated as American theaters.[14]

For some critics, in the early phases of her career Elizabeth Taylor Greenfield did not so much trespass or cross racial boundaries as she was co-opted or consumed. Her triumphant early concerts were followed by a controversial 1853 New York City debut. Black patrons were barred from Metropolitan Hall and there were rumors that the New York concert would be subject to white supremacist riots. Frederick Douglass's newspaper published a stinging rebuke of white audience members whose racial prejudices remained unchallenged, nay, were even bolstered by Greenfield's performances ("Conduct"). Martin R. Delany, who had previously exposed the racist practices of her manager J. H. Wood, fueled further criticism of Greenfield in *Frederick Douglass' Paper*. Delany's 1853 exposé of the singer's living conditions was fiery. Criticizing her white American manager, Delany reported that Greenfield was "the merest creature of a slave, in the hands of this fellow Wood, and his associates, and does not know what she is getting for her services; as she does not handle her own money, but the person whom Wood appointed, one of his own troup [*sic*], being her treasurer, and holding, as they pretend, the money for her!" ("Letter"). Delany also claimed that Wood censored Greenfield's correspondence and barred her from receiving Black visitors. The alleged state of near slavery and isolation in which Greenfield was kept, or even worse, perhaps consented to, was clearly at odds with the radical political work the Black community sought, and needed, from her concerts. The use of the Black female voice in public lay at the core of much of the anger expressed by Delany, Douglass, and others. To them, Elizabeth Taylor Greenfield lacked awareness of the social importance of her newfound role. Southern newspapers had long seized on Greenfield as an object of ridicule. Taken together, depictions that appear in a broad spectrum of media foreclose readings of the radical nature of Greenfield's work and her ability to navigate the public sphere and interracial spaces.

And yet, Juanita Karpf avers that "when Elizabeth Taylor Greenfield crossed race and gender divides in the 1850s by pursuing a career in the white male world of concert performance, music in the cultivated tradition—whether composed, performed, taught, or written about—became activist and feminist discourse" (625). The significance of this boundary-defying work was not lost on all her contemporaries. Jennifer Lynn Stoever asserts that "only the *Provincial Freeman* reported consistently on [Elizabeth Taylor Greenfield's] career" (125). Here, we might take "consistently" to mean "positively." Through her editorial choices, Mary Ann Shadd Cary would steadfastly attempt to resuscitate Greenfield's reputation in the pages of the *Provincial Freeman*, reaffirming the singer's exceptional role in nineteenth-century African American culture and the importance of Black feminist performance to Black diasporic communities across both sides of the U.S.-Canadian border.

Frequently commented upon in Elizabeth Taylor Greenfield historiography and scholarship, the Metropolitan Hall controversy also resulted in one of the earliest discussions of Black feminist performance in Canadian print. In an 1854 editorial ("The Black Swan"), Shadd Cary addressed the brouhaha and dismissed the complaints against Greenfield. Noting that Greenfield had been charged in the *Providence Daily Journal* with "being direlect [*sic*] to her duty, and the cause of humanity, by not singing substantial songs, such as would interest the masses" and "not associating with colored people," Shadd Cary parsed the artist's choices and affirmed her artistic freedom: "About what Miss Greenfield does, or what she does not, we know but little; neither do we know whether she professes to be a reformer or not; nor are we going to presume that she does, merely because she has a black skin and may have been a slave." Shadd Cary challenged the racial reductivism that defined the singer's career and demanded that Greenfield be afforded the same wide berth as white artists, writing, "The majority of popular singers the world over . . . are not often noted as champions of human rights." This comment can be read as a backhanded compliment, given the great personal sacrifices Shadd Cary made as a lifelong activist, and a reminder that her contemporary Jenny Lind was, in fact, known for her philanthropy. But it is clear that Shadd Cary's focus on Elizabeth Taylor Greenfield in the *Provincial Freeman* was more nuanced, if not altogether forgiving, than coverage found in outlets like *Frederick Douglass' Paper*. In her editorial Shadd Cary framed Black performance as a means of reconsidering the limits of Black identity and collective responsibility. Her pragmatism is especially striking given her own notoriety and the importance of Black performance[15] to the abolitionist movement.

Mary Ann Shadd Cary was born free into a free Black family in Wilmington, Delaware, in 1823. The Shadds were well-known abolitionists and active conductors on the Underground Railroad, even while living in the slave state of Delaware. Shadd Cary attended the first North American Convention of Colored Freemen held in Toronto, at St. Lawrence Hall in 1851. Soon after, she published *A Plea for Emigration* (1852). Mary Ann Shadd Cary and her brother eventually immigrated to Windsor, Ontario. As a journalist and political activist, Shadd Cary wrote enthusiastically about the benefits of migration for African Americans. She founded the *Provincial Freeman* in 1853, becoming the first Black woman publisher in North America. She then migrated back to the United States, eventually becoming one of the only Black women from Canada to recruit Union soldiers during the Civil War. After the Civil War, she went on to become one of the first Black women in the United States to earn a law degree, after graduating from Howard University. Since 1994, she has been officially recognized as a person of historical significance in Canada and continues to represent the both the Black diaspora and displacement in Canada's cityscapes. In Chatham, Ontario, a commemorative bust of Shadd Cary (Figure 6.3) stands only a few blocks away from the site of her former home and one of the offices of the *Provincial Freeman*, both of which have been torn down (Smith). In Malvern, Scarborough, a working-class neighborhood of Toronto composed predominately of Caribbean and South Asian immigrants, an elementary school has been named for her. In 2021 a mural-sized portrait of Shadd Cary created by Black Canadian artist Yung Yemi was installed on the side of Mackenzie House, a historic building in downtown Toronto that was once home to the city's first mayor, William Lyon Mackenzie (see Figure 1.1). In 2022, a statue of Mary Ann Shadd Cary created by sculptor Donna Jean Mayne was installed on the downtown campus of the University of Windsor. These gestures are

Figure 6.3. Bust of Mary Ann Shadd Cary by Artis Lane, Chatham, Ontario. Photograph by Kristin Moriah.

significant, but as Rinaldo Walcott notes in his contribution to this volume, despite her increasing public recognition, "the radical project of liberation for Black people that Shadd Cary concerned herself with is often stalled by EDI measures" (see chapter 1).

In terms of scholarship, Shadd Cary's intellectual investment in Black performance and the power of the Black voice remains critically neglected. As one of the few Black feminist speakers in antebellum Black political life, Shadd Cary was in all practical senses a skilled performer. She frequently crossed the U.S.-Canadian border to give lectures. Colored Convention attendee and AME bishop Daniel Payne describes hearing Mary Ann Shadd Cary lecture on Blacks in Canada as a "pleasure" due to "her familiarity with facts, her knowledge of men, and her fine power of discrimination" (127). Her listeners were not equally pleased. Carla Peterson notes that "Shadd Cary's speeches were . . . often perceived not only as pertinent but as impertinent"

(102) and her "'unfeminine' speaking style led even those who appreciated the substance of her lectures to admit her lack of eloquence, to label her delivery as 'nervous, hurried'" (103). Her insistence on the right to be heard in public courted controversy. Jane Rhodes explains that while "black Americans seemed to encourage—and even require—women's participation in the public sphere as necessary for racial progress" during the antebellum period, "black women were expected to adhere to the cult of domesticity" (53). Speaking out on stage and in the pages of her newspaper, Shadd Cary was no angel of the house.[16] She consistently ran afoul of gendered expectations that insisted upon Black women's silence, subservience, and respectability.[17] Shadd Cary was certainly not the only nineteenth-century Black thinker to consider the intertwined revolutionary power of the voice and stage in this way. In fact, Frederick Douglass argued for Shadd Cary's right to address the 1855 Colored Convention in Philadelphia as a male delegate would, stating: "It is too late in the day to make opposition to a woman because of her sex. As to the impossibility of a woman's taking part in public meetings, our citizens have decided that long ago. They have decided that by going to hear Miss [Elizabeth Taylor] Greenfield sing, by having ladies in church choirs, singing; aye, AND singing much louder than Miss Shadd promised to speak" ("Young Africa in Convention").

Shadd Cary's foray into the world of publishing was as iconoclastic and controversial as Elizabeth Taylor Greenfield's operatic performance. I consider the *Provincial Freeman* to be an extension of Mary Ann Shadd Cary's voice and its pages a space of Black vocal experimentation. As Alex Black claims, "When we read an abolitionist text we perceive a material process in which sound is realized as an image that has the force of a statement" (619). This was no less true of Black Canadian print culture. For her readers, the vocal qualities of Mary Ann Shadd Cary's literary activism solicited response. She challenged the circumscribed limits of antebellum gender norms linked to sound and speech through her editorial choices. In contrast to the rampant sexism of North American public discourse, "the early issues of the *Freeman* established the paper as a forum for Shadd's growing interest in women's rights, especially within the context of anti-slavery and other reform movements" (Rhodes 91). In the *Provincial Freeman*, Shadd Cary frequently reprinted material by feminist abolitionists, including a speech by Harriet Beecher Stowe, "An Appeal to the Women of the Free States of America on the Present Crisis of Our Country" (Rhodes 91). Unlike her *Plea for Immigration*, Shadd Cary's newspaper contained an early assemblage of Black feminist discourse that was intersectional and drew few cultural distinctions between Canada and the United States. Like Elizabeth Taylor Greenfield, vocal performance was a key element of her feminist practice.

"Desiring to Do Her Full Share"

The most relevant example of how boundary-defying vocal performance united the careers of these two women is an 1855 Philadelphia benefit held for Shadd Cary. Shadd Cary made several public appearances in Philadelphia while attending the city's mid-October Colored National Convention that year. Traveling from Ontario, she challenged gender conventions and successfully lobbied to be recognized as the delegate from Canada. The convention minutes note that the question of whether she should be admitted to the floor resulted in "spirited discussion" (*Proceedings*). The *National Anti-Slavery Standard* reported that her suit was aided by Frederick Douglass, who "exposed, in a masterly manner, the fallacy of the objections to Miss Shadd's admission" ("Our Philadelphia Correspondence"). Shadd Cary reportedly gave "one of the best speeches" about emigration at the convention despite strong resistance against admitting female speakers to the floor (Peterson 100). Still, criticism dogged her. Writing about the convention, a reporter for the *British Banner* claimed that "had 'Miss Shadd' not had in her bosom more the male than that of the female heart, she would have felt ashamed of her position, and hastened to hide herself amid the soft obscurities of her own sex" (qtd. in Peterson 100).

Recognizing that the young activist typically engaged in activist work for free and needed financial support for her travel, women from Philadelphia's Shiloh Baptist Church "voted to organize a fund-raising gala 'in view of her faithful services in the cause of Reform'" ("Correspondence"). The event was held at Sansom Street Hall on Saturday, November 9, 1855. The Philadelphia venue, which served as a public bathhouse, lyceum, and event hall in the 1850s, had also housed the 1854 National Women's Rights Convention. The "brilliant affair" was initially advertised as an "Anti-Slavery meeting" featuring the speeches of abolitionist Passmore Williamson. Instead, attendees were treated to a surprise performance by Elizabeth Taylor Greenfield and speeches by J. M. McKim and Mary Ann Shadd Cary. The *National Anti-Slavery Standard* reported that "the room was packed as full as it could hold: aisles, platform, every place was filled" ("Anti-Slavery Meeting"). Elizabeth

Taylor Greenfield had previously sung at a fundraising benefit for Shiloh Baptist Church in 1853 (Chybowski, "Becoming" 141), raising the possibility that she had ties to the congregation. McKim "spoke to the character and labours of Miss Mary Ann Shadd among the fugitive slaves in Canada, and strongly recommended her to the good will of the audience" ("Anti-Slavery Meeting"). For her part, Shadd Cary gave a speech in which she extolled the virtues of Canada and "complimented" Elizabeth Taylor Greenfield as the "Jenny Lind of America'" ("Correspondence"). Shadd Cary's play on Green-field's traditional moniker, the "Black Jenny Lind," emphasized the unifying power of Greenfield's incredible voice. In Shadd Cary's formulation, Eliza-beth Taylor Greenfield embodied the operatic talent of a nation.

The *Freeman* report depicts Greenfield as a genteel hostess and philan-thropist deeply engaged in the world of Philadelphia's Black middle class. The presence of refreshments like ice-cream and refined entertainment trans-formed the public concert hall into an intimate domestic parlor-like space. Arthur LaBrew explains that vocal and instrumental music was practiced almost universally among Black Philadelphians and was frequently per-formed for friends and guests at home (17). Sarah Lampert suggests that the singer "surely maintained ties with members of Philadelphia's large black middle class whom she met through her schooling" (82), and thus would have been keenly aware of the role music played in their domestic lives. The impact of Greenfield's social world and Black musicians on her musical prac-tice was often overlooked by nineteenth-century journalists and biographers who conceived of the singer as a product of racial exceptionalism. But in this instance, we can see Greenfield signifying on tropes of Black respectabil-ity, domesticity, and femininity in order to intervene in the public sphere in socially acceptable ways. Music, particularly "the singing of songs" (Peter-son 101), was one of the only acceptable forms of women's participation at antebellum Colored Conventions. Singing at the Shiloh Baptist Church ladies benefit afforded Elizabeth Taylor Greenfield a nonconfrontational means of participation in discourses around Black immigration and Black feminist political participation.

Provincial Freeman readers also learned that "the Sansom Street Hall was literally packed to overflowing, with a mixed audience of white and colored, all waiting impatiently for the exercises to commence ("Correspondence"). Mention of the interracial composition of the audience was undoubt-edly directed toward Greenfield's and Shadd Cary's critics. For Greenfield, the event symbolized a break with her controversial past and affirmed her commitment to racial progress. This opportunity to hear "Miss Greenfield's liberality and charming melodies" in person was unusual for Black North Americans who were not part of the singer's inner circle, and, incidentally, for white Northerners who had not flocked to, or could not afford admission to, Greenfield's earlier U.S. concerts. In her work as a schoolteacher in Windsor and her *Plea for Emigration* (1852), Shadd Cary had demonstrated an abiding, if controversial, interest in the integration of public spaces like schools and churches. Attendees at the Sansom Street Hall benefit heard Greenfield's voice in a space comparatively free from racial and class boundaries, experiencing that voice as constitutive free space in the way that Farah Jasmine Griffin has confirmed and that mirrored the Canada West Shadd Cary imagined and promoted. That interracialism captured the essence of much of the singer's and the journalist's work.

The *Freeman's* anonymous "Philadelphia correspondent," who may well have been Shadd Cary,[18] noted that "too much praise cannot be expressed" for Elizabeth Taylor Greenfield's performance of antislavery songs and, "to her credit be it said, instead of singing only 'too [sic] ballads,' for which a handsome sum was offered, when first invited, she very magnanimously sung more than she is accustomed to do at her ordinary Concerts, evidently desiring to do her full share, not only in making the occasion interesting, but likewise, in making it as beneficial to Miss S. as possible, refusing to receive anything for her services." The antislavery songs Greenfield sang for the Shadd Cary benefit concert would have been disappointing to her first public audiences, who were often attracted to her because of the promise of racial spectacle.[19] But the antislavery songs she sang revealed Greenfield's politicization. It would not be the first or the last such revelation. Neither the *Provincial Freeman* nor the *Anti-Slavery Standard*, two contemporary sources that reported the concert, lists the songs that Greenfield performed at the benefit. However, *The Black Swan at Home and Abroad* (1855) includes a list of songs from the concert she gave at the Queen's Concert Rooms in England in 1853 under the patronage of Harriet Beecher Stowe and the famed British abolitionist the Duchess of Sutherland. That program includes a song entitled "The Vision of the Negro Slave," which is strikingly similar to the scene of Tom's death in *Uncle Tom's Cabin*. In 1859, the Anti-Slavery Society would report that Greenfield "sung, with thrilling effect, the song 'Pity the Slave'" at the Pennsylvania Anti-Slavery Society's annual meeting ("Twenty-Third Annual Meeting"). The absence of qualitative descriptions of Elizabeth Taylor Greenfield's voice at the Sansom Hall concert can perhaps be attributed to the rhetorical power of the abolitionist sentiment of her performance and the ability of her apparent politicization to eclipse other considerations, and complaints, within the Black community.

The Shiloh Baptist Church women who organized the activities of the 1855 Philadelphia Colored Convention used the concert hall and Black feminist performance as a site of resistance and critique. Their organizing efforts provide an alternative way of understanding how Black women used speech and voice to intervene in Black political discourse around immigration and border crossing at a time when openly doing so resulted in censure. Unlike at the 1855 Philadelphia Colored Convention, at the Sansom Street Hall concert the voices of Elizabeth Taylor Greenfield and Mary Ann Shadd provided the main attraction and were well received. Instead of being marginalized for their work, their boundary-defying talents provided an opportunity to reframe public opinion about Black women's public activism and emigration. The nameless women who organized the Sansom Street Hall concert worked to affirm the relevance of Black women's voices in the public sphere and demonstrated a deep interest in questions around Black migration to Canada.

Conclusion

The Sansom Street Hall benefit was a pivotal event, but it would not be a singular one. Elizabeth Taylor Greenfield would go on to accompany Black political figures like Frederick Douglass and Frances Ellen Watkins Harper at their speaking events, too.[20] Through her work as an orator, activist, and editor, Mary Ann Shadd Cary paved the way for those moments and played a central role in Elizabeth Taylor Greenfield's rehabilitation in the Black press. Shadd Cary did this work onsite in the United States and in the pages of her newspaper where the work of the two women was aligned, by both Shadd Cary herself and others. For some, the two would continue to be associated with one another long after the Shiloh Baptist Church Women's event at Sansom Street Hall event. Writing to the *Provincial Freeman* from Philadelphia in 1856, John A. Spraig remarked that "in pro-slavery Pennsylvania . . . I take pleasure in alluding to Miss Elizabeth T. Greenfield, the 'Black Swan,' Miss M. A. Shadd, and other young ladies, whose genius and talent entitle them to praise and respect. The admiration and honor which has been so largely awarded to the 'Black Swan,' both in this country and Great Britain, by the highest classes in society, settles this fact. That humble, poor, proscribed and black, and the colored man or women may be, with such commendable zeal and resolution as is here evinced, all obstacles may be triumphantly overcome." The women struck a powerful chord with their listeners and readers who approved of their transnationalism and recognized their abilities to overcome racial boundaries. Following the Shadd Cary benefit, Elizabeth Taylor Greenfield continued to concertize in Canada and centers of Black life like Toronto and Chatham, Ontario. Those performances were reviewed positively in the *Provincial Freeman* and Toronto's *Globe*. From 1855 to the 1860s, after her return from England, performances in Toronto, Hamilton, Chatham, London, and Windsor were still enthusiastically received. In 1855 the *Globe*, like others before, remarked upon Greenfield's "wonderful compass of voice" and insisted that "her extraordinary natural powers, and their cultivation, give her a permanent power of gratifying the public" ("Miss Greenfield's Concerts"). In 1857, the *Globe* pronounced Elizabeth Taylor Greenfield "a singer of high order" ("The Ship"). Even further afield, that year, the *Montreal Pilot* reported that "she was frequently *encored*, and as the assemblage broke, every face seemed to beam with satisfaction and delight, as if its owner would say, 'I feel it was worth while [*sic*] coming here'" ("Miss Greenfield's Second Concert"). Here, the reviewer might have been obliquely commenting on the supposed contentment of Greenfield's Black audience members and their satisfaction with the concert and their decision to emigrate.

The 1850 Fugitive Slave Act prompted a series of events that drew the women into the public sphere and into conversation with one another. Elizabeth Taylor Greenfield's performances became common currency for Black communities north and south of the U.S. border. They also contributed a context in which performance was imbued with increasing social and political importance for Black communities. Mary Ann Shadd Cary demonstrated canniness about the power of gender, race, and performance in her coverage of Elizabeth Taylor Greenfield. Shadd Cary's engagement with Greenfield's work reveals the power of representation for Black communities in Canada West and for Black women in the mid-nineteenth century. Their work created sites at which Black identity could coalesce and where legacies of U.S. racialization could begin to be dismantled. Their work predicts the way that border crossing remains an important part of Black feminist methodology and translates to the present. Black diaspora remains predicated upon a shared set of identities and concerns that conflict with national borders. In point of fact, research for this essay was completed on both sides of the U.S.-Canadian border. As a Black feminist scholar in the present, cross-border movements are still, for me, a performative act. When I cross over into the United States, I make simultaneous promises to go away and to come back. I promise not to get too comfortable. I promise that I am who I say I am. These gestures suggest acquiescence and deference to power. But borders are actually a site of Black feminist (re)invention. I am always changing. Always at home. Always clinging to something beyond the horizon. Always hoping to be heard.

Notes

I owe many thanks to those who read early drafts of this work and provided feedback and encouragement, including Colleen Kim Daniher, Katherine Zien, Katherine McKittrick, Kate Broad, and Jesse Schwartz.

1. Ambrotypes were an early form of photography invented by Frederick Scott Archer and patented by James Ambrose Cutting in 1854. Ambrotypes are essentially glass negatives that rely on dark backing to make the image appear positive; "in terms of image, what appeared on the glass-negative was a thin light brown-yellow transparent coating of collodion carrying the image" (Frizot 95). Ambrotypes, or collodion positives as they were known in Great Britain, "were made in the same size as daguerreotypes and were similarly treated—hand-colored, framed behind glass, and housed in a slim case" (Rosenblum 59). Because ambrotypes were less expensive to create than daguerreotypes, great numbers of people could afford to have their photograph taken for the first time in North American history.

2. Ambrotypes reached the height of their popularity in the mid-1850s but had begun to fall out favor by the 1860s. They remained popular until the end of the American Civil War, when they were overtaken by more advanced photographic processes (Maurice 50).

3. One notable print in African American artist Glenn Ligon's famed *Untitled: Four Etchings* (1992) contains the repeated phrase "I feel most colored when I am thrown against a sharp white background." The line is taken from "How It Feels to Be Colored Me," an essay by African American writer Zora Neale Hurston.

4. Greenfield's sartorial choices received intense scrutiny and the singer was subject to detailed, if condescending, fashion advice from her supporters, including feminist reformer Elizabeth Smith Miller, daughter of abolitionist Gerrit Smith (LaBrew 38).

5. Jasmine Nichole Cobb explains that "every aspect of the self demanded perfect execution for picture taking in the mid-nineteenth century" (1). Cobb also argues that "Black women activists were intensely aware of public perceptions of their femininity, especially since early abolitionism depended on Black women's credibility to advance the antislavery movement" (70) and that "Black women cultivated new ways of seeing themselves and seeing free Black womanhood against the backdrop of slavery's visual culture" (70). Within this context, Greenfield's photographic self-presentation can be read as a strategic deployment of what Cobb has termed the "optics of respectability," an early practice of Black feminist spectatorship that allowed Black women to subvert dominant modes of seeing and being seen within visual culture.

6. The portrait subtly invites yet another comparison between its sitter and Jenny Lind, whose 1854 visit to J. P. Ball's studio made American headlines thanks to a syndicated column from *Gleason's Pictorial*, which was even reprinted in *Frederick Douglass' Paper*. For performers

like Jenny Lind and Elizabeth Taylor Greenfield, images mattered. Art historian Naomi Rosenblum has suggested that "the moderately gifted Lind" owed much of her tremendous popularity in the United States to her "promotion through *carte [de visite]* portraits" (63).

7. See LaBrew 9; *Brief Memoir* 4; and *Black Swan at Home and Abroad* 3.

8. Notable scholarship about Elizabeth Taylor Greenfield includes Stoever's *Sonic Color Line*; Chybowski's "Blackface Minstrelsy"; Lampert's "Black Swan/White Raven"; and Eidsheim's *Race of Sound*.

9. See "Windsor/Detroit Friendship Festival," USC Digital Folklore Archives, May 17, 2022, https://folklore.usc.edu/windsor-detroit-friendship-festival/.

10. James Culic, "Farewell to the Friendship Festival in Fort Erie," *NiagaraThisWeek.com*, 23 January 2020. Accessed 21 February 2024.

11. In *The Condition, Elevation, Emigration, and Destiny of the Colored People of the United States*, Delany writes: "The Canadians are descended from the same common parentage as the Americans on this side of the Lakes—determined to, and will have the Canadas, to a close observer, there is not a shadow of doubt; and our brethren should know this in time" (174).

12. Italian opera singer Teresa Parodi (1827–78); Irish opera singer Catherine Hayes, known as the "Swan of Erin," or "Irish Swan" (1818–61); and Swedish opera singer Jenny Lind, known as the "Swedish Nightingale" (1820–87). Arthur R. LaBrew explains that "the names of birds" were "the mode of distinguishing one singer for another" during that era (24). Throughout her career reviewers drew racialized comparisons between Elizabeth Taylor Greenfield and Jenny Lind; Greenfield was sometimes referred to as the "Black Jenny Lind." In this moniker, we see race supplanting nation at the same time bird monikers were used to compare her to other white singers. Similar forms of racialized description were used for Black singers throughout the nineteenth century.

13. Lillian Serece Williams notes that Buffalo was an important center of commerce and industry in upstate New York in the nineteenth century (9) and while the African American population remained comparatively small, "Blacks were attracted to Buffalo because of its proximity to Canada and the freedom from slavery that it promised and because Buffalo offered plenty of job opportunities. Buffalo was also a site on the Underground Railroad. Despite its attractions, on the eve of the Civil War, the Black populace numbered only about 500, many of whom were fugitive slaves or their descendants" (11).

14. Trotter's work reveals that when "Dr. Brown," a Black doctor, purchased several seats for himself and his friends to see Black pianist Thomas J. Bowers perform in Hamilton, Ontario, Bowers was informed that "colored people were not admitted to first-class seats in Canada" (Trotter 135). Bowers protested and this noble stand against discrimination resulted in granting to Dr. Brown the seats he had purchased; after this time, no attempt was made to exclude colored persons from the troupe's concerts (Trotter 135). This is an example of how discriminatory seating practices usually ascribed to the United States were also present in Canada.

15. Here, I am particularly attuned to the recent scholarship that examines the impact of performance and music on Frederick Douglass's abolitionism, most notably David Blight's biography *Frederick Douglass* (2018).

16. Shadd Cary's feud with Henry Bibb "over philosophical differences over what was the best direction for building and sustaining Canada's black communities" (Rhodes 53) spilled onto the pages of his Ontario newspaper *Voice of the Fugitive* (1851–53), where Shadd Cary "was made to embody the most despised characteristics of Victorian womanhood: the temptress, the contaminator, the evil yet shrewd manipulator who could not be trusted" (Rhodes 72).

17. See Black 621–22; and Glass 67.

18. Jim Casey situates the editor within a broader schema of pseudonymous Black editorship within the nineteenth century (115). Jane Rhodes (in her chapter "We Have 'Broken the Editorial Ice,'" in *Mary Ann Shadd Cary*) and Casey conclude that Shadd Cary often used asterisks to both indicate and shield her authorship.

19. Daphne Brooks explains that the artist typically "negotiated a mixed repertoire of classical standards by Handel and Bellini with the minstrel folk songs of Stephen Foster and weathered an elixir of gushing praise of her 'genuine art' with the race-based aspersions of critics who dismissed her act as burnt-cork aberration and 'untaught' 'imitation'" (312).

20. Evidence to this effect is contained in the Leon Gardiner Collection's American Negro Historical Society papers at the Pennsylvania Historical Society.

Works Cited

"Ambrotype." The Historic New Orleans Collection, www.hnoc.org/virtual/daguerreotype-digital/ambrotype. Accessed 21 February 2024.

"Amusements." *Buffalo Morning Express and Illustrated Buffalo Express*, May 28, 1867.

"Anti-Slavery Meeting in Philadelphia—Speech of J. M. McKim." *National Anti-Slavery Standard*, November 17, 1855.

Anzaldúa, Gloria. *Borderlands/La Frontera: The New Mestiza*. 2nd ed. San Francisco: Aunt Lute Books, 1999.

"Biography/ Administrative History." Frederick H. J. Lambart fonds [textual record, graphic material, moving images, sound recording]. Library and Archives Canada. https://central.bac-lac.gc.ca/.redirect?app=fonandcol&id=102422&lang=eng.

Black, Alex W. "Abolitionism's Resonant Bodies: The Realization of African American Performance." *American Quarterly* 63, no. 3 (September 2011): 619–39.

"The Black Swan." *Provincial Freeman*, November 18, 1854.

The Black Swan at Home and Abroad; or, A Biographical Sketch of Miss Elizabeth Taylor Greenfield, the American Vocalist. Philadelphia: Wm. S. Young, Printer, 1855.

Blight, David W. *Frederick Douglass: Prophet of Freedom*. New York: Simon & Schuster, 2018.

Breon, Robin. "The Growth and Development of Black Theatre in Canada: A Starting Point." *Theatre Research in Canada/ Recherches théatrales au Canada* 9, no. 2 (1988). https://journals.lib.unb.ca/index.php/TRIC/article/view/7342. Accessed February 21, 2024.

A Brief Memoir of the "Black Swan," Miss E. T. Greenfield, the American Vocalist. London, 1853.

Brooks, Daphne A. *Bodies in Dissent: Spectacular Performances of Race and Freedom, 1850–1910*. Durham, NC: Duke University Press, 2006.

Casey, Jim. "Parsing the Special Characters of African American Print Culture: Mary Ann Shadd and the * Limits of Search." In *Against a Sharp White Background: Infrastructures of African American Print*, ed. Brigitte Fielder and Jonathan Senchyne, 109–27. Madison: University of Wisconsin Press, 2019.

Chybowski, Julia J. "Becoming the 'Black Swan' in Mid-Nineteenth-Century America: Elizabeth Taylor Greenfield's Early Life and Debut Concert Tour." *Journal of the American Musicological Society* 67, no. 1 (Spring 2014): 125–65.

———. "Blackface Minstrelsy and the Reception of Elizabeth Taylor Greenfield." *Journal of the Society for American Music* 15, no. 3 (2021): 305–20.

———. "Elizabeth Taylor Greenfield's Mid-to-Late Career, Philanthropy, and Activism in Nineteenth-Century America." *American Music* 40, no. 2 (2022): 211–44.

Cobb, Jasmine Nichole. *Picture Freedom: Remaking Black Visuality in the Early Nineteenth Century.* New York: New York University Press, 2015.

"Correspondence: From Our Philadelphia Correspondent, No. XII." *Provincial Freeman*, December 1, 1855.

Delany, Martin R. *The Condition, Elevation, Emigration, and Destiny of the Colored People of the United States.* Philadelphia: Published by the author, 1852.

———. "Letter from M. R. Delany." *Frederick Douglass' Paper*, April 22, 1853.

Douglass, Frederick. "The Conduct of the Black Swan." *Frederick Douglass' Paper*, February 26, 1852.

Eidsheim, Nina Sun. *The Race of Sound: Listening, Timbre, and Vocality in African American Music.* Durham, NC: Duke University Press, 2019.

Frizot, Michel. *A New History of Photography.* Cologne: Könemann, 1998.

Glass, Kathy L. Courting Communities : Black Female Nationalism and "Syncre-Nationalism" in the Nineteenth-Century North. New York: Routledge, 2006.

Griffin, Farah Jasmine. "When Malindy Sings: A Meditation on Black Women's Vocality." In *Uptown Conversation: The New Jazz Studies*, ed. Robert G. O'Meally, Brent Hayes Edwards, and Farah Jasmine Griffin, 102–25. New York: Columbia University Press, 2004.

Hopkins, Pauline E. "Famous Women of the Negro Race: I. Phenomenal Vocalists." *Colored American Magazine*, November 1901, 45–53.

Karpf, Juanita. "'As with Words of Fire': Art Music and Nineteenth-Century African-American Feminist Discourse." *Signs* 24, no. 3 (1999): 603–32.

LaBrew, Arthur R. *The Black Swan: Elizabeth T. Greenfield, Songstress.* Detroit: LaBrew, 1969.

Lampert, Sarah. "Black Swan/White Raven: The Racial Politics of Elizabeth Greenfield's American Concert Career, 1851–1855." *American Nineteenth Century History* 17, no. 1 (2016): 75–102.

Lott, Eric. *Love and Theft : Blackface Minstrelsy and the American Working Class.* New York: Oxford University Press, 1993.

Madera, Judith. *Black Atlas: Geography and Flow in Nineteenth-Century African American Literature.* Durham, NC: Duke University Press, 2015.

Majors, Monroe A. *Noted Negro Women: Their Triumphs and Activities.* Chicago: Donohue & Henneberry, 1893.

Maurice, Phillipe. 1993. "Ambrotypes: Positively Capturing the Past". *Material Culture Review* 38 (1).

McKittrick, Katherine. *Demonic Grounds: Black Women and the Cartographies of Struggle.* Minneapolis: University of Minnesota Press, 2006.

Miller, Mary Margaret Johnston. "Library and Archives Canada/Query 96374." Email interview received by Kristin Moriah, August 1, 2019.

"Miscellany: Mrs. Stowe and the People of Color—The Wesleyan." *Provincial Freeman*, March 24, 1853.

"Miss Greenfield's Concerts." *Globe* (Toronto), May 26, 1855.

"Miss Greenfield's Second Concert at the Mechanics' Hall." *Provincial Freeman*, April 11, 1857.

"Our Philadelphia Correspondence." *National Anti-Slavery Standard*, October 27, 1855.

Payne, Daniel Alexander. *Recollections of Seventy Years*. Nashville: A. M. E. Sunday School Union, 1888.

Peterson, Carla L. *"Doers of the Word": African-American Women Speakers and Writers in the North (1830–1880)*. New York: Oxford University Press, 1995.

Prince, Bryan. *My Brother's Keeper: African Canadians and the American Civil War*. Toronto: Dundurn, 2015.

Proceedings of the Colored National Convention, Held in Franklin Hall, Sixth Street, Below Arch, Philadelphia, October 16th, 17th and 18th, 1855. Colored Conventions Project Digital Records. Accessed January 2, 2024. https://omeka.coloredconventions.org/items/show/281.

Rhodes, Jane. *Mary Ann Shadd Cary: The Black Press and Protest in the Nineteenth Century*. Bloomington: Indiana University Press, 1998.

Rosenblum, Naomi. *A World History of Photography*. New York: Abbeville Press, 2007.

Scott, Chic. *Pushing the Limits: The Story of Canadian Mountaineering*. Calgary, AB: Rocky Mountain Books, 2000; 2002.

Shadd, Mary Ann. *A Plea for Emigration; or, Notes of Canada West*. Edited by Phanuel Antwi. Peterborough, ON: Broadview Press, 2016.

Siemerling, Winfried. *The Black Atlantic Reconsidered: Black Canadian Writing, Cultural History, and the Presence of the Past*. Montreal: McGill-Queen's University Press, 2015.

Smith, Allison. "Reflections on 'Mary Ann Shadd Cary Revisited.'" *ActiveHistory*. http://activehistory.ca/papers/reflections-on-mary-ann-shadd-revisited/. Accessed February 24, 2024.

Spraig, John. "Letter to the Publisher of the Provincial Freeman." *Provincial Freeman*. February 23, 1856.

Stoever, Jennifer Lynn. *The Sonic Color Line: Race and the Cultural Politics of Listening*. New York: New York University Press, 2016.

Stowe, Harriet Beecher. *Sunny Memories of Foreign Lands*. London: Dodo Press, 2006.

"The Ship 'City of Toronto.'" *Globe* (Toronto). September 4, 1857.

Trotter, James Monroe. *Music and Some Highly Musical People*. 1878. Reprint, New York: Johnson Reprint, 1968.

"Twenty-Third Annual Meeting of the Pennsylvania Anti-Slavery Society." *National Anti-Slavery Standard*, October 15, 1859.

Walcott, Rinaldo. "'Who Is She and What Is She to You?': Mary Ann Shadd Cary and the (Im)possibility of Black/Canadian Studies." *Atlantis* 24, no. 2 (2000): 137–46.

Williams, Lillian Serece. *Strangers in the Land of Paradise: Creation of an African American Community in Buffalo, New York, 1900–1940*. Bloomington: Indiana University Press, 2000.

"Young Africa in Convention." *New York Herald*, October 21, 1855.

PART III

"Led as by Inspiration"

Black Feminist Activism

CHAPTER 7

Plotting New Gardens

The Black Feminist Roots of Community-Building in *A Plea for Emigration*

R. J. BOUTELLE AND MARLAS YVONNE WHITLEY

> In Canada we find the vegetation of as rank growth as
> in the middle and northern United States. In order to
> promote a luxuriance in the products of a country equally
> with another, the conditions necessary to that end must be
> equal,—if by reference to facts, an approach to similarity
> can be made, that part of the subject will be settled for the
> present.
>
> —Mary Ann Shadd, *A Plea for Emigration* (1852)

As our epigraph from Mary Ann Shadd's *A Plea for Emigration; or, Notes of Canada West* (1852) illustrates, the pamphlet is an unusual document, sliding smoothly between factual, empirical descriptions of Canada West as a prospective site for Black emigration and rhetorical, even metaphorical language (growth, equality, settled) whose double meanings convey nuanced arguments about the pragmatic and moral aspects of emigrationism. On the one hand, as both Richard Almonte and Phanuel Antwi note in their respective critical editions of this work, it exemplifies the settler guide genre. Related to travel writing, settler guides offered detailed descriptions of agriculture, climate, demographics, labor, wages, and culture; but unlike travel writing, these texts—usually short pamphlets printed and circulated inexpensively—were governed by an eminently practical purpose: they were "designed to inform prospective immigrants of conditions in one part or another of North America."[1] Shadd's *Plea* spoke directly to African Americans in the United States who considered fleeing to Canada after the passage of the 1850 Fugitive Slave Law rendered Black lives and livelihoods in the U.S. American North intensely precarious. On the other hand, *Plea* acts as what Nassisse Solomon calls a "treatise"—an early articulation of Shadd's developing arguments and beliefs regarding Black emigrationism, Black womanhood, and the kinds of community-building that would best serve Black settler colonists in Canada West.[2] In contending that Shadd's "transnational politics" and critiques of Black women's subjection to "Victorian ideals of womanhood" were mutually informative, Solomon leads us to the central question that this essay examines: How did Shadd's experiences as a Black woman contributing to the overwhelmingly masculinist discourse of Black nationalism and Black emigrationism shape her ideological vision of community-building in Canada? And to what extent is that vision distinctive from her interlocutors?

In delimiting the scope of our analysis to *A Plea for Emigration*, we take seriously the pamphlet form as a snapshot of her vision for Black life in Canada West shortly after her arrival and as an interlocutor with similar pamphlets issued in the debates over Black emigrationism that were unfolding in the mid-nineteenth century. This comparative analysis enables our discussion of the subtle ways that Shadd argues for the centrality of Black women to the practical project of community-building that emigrationism often overlooked. That is, while her contemporaries authored manifestos that theorized Black nationalism and prospectuses for emigration that weighed their geopolitical implications, Shadd's pamphlet grappled with the material conditions and social dynamics of relocation. Because her emigrationist vision was developed concomitantly with the practical matter of settling Canada West, we argue that *A Plea for Emigration* should be read as part of the intellectual tradition of Black feminism—theories fundamentally grounded in intersectional critiques of socioeconomic inequalities, coalitional approaches to activism, and specific "context[s] of Black community development efforts and other Black nationalist-inspired projects."[3] Shadd's attention to the cultivation of land in arguing for the usefulness of horticulture further establishes *Plea* as unique among the genre as it proposes a clear alternative to the capitalist enterprises of cash-crop agriculture that was popularly promoted within her contemporaries' guides.

Moreover, we locate *Plea* in an intellectual genealogy of Black feminist theory regarding gardening and land use. Alice Walker's famous essay "In Search of Our Mothers' Gardens," for example, portrays her mother's garden as a locus to illustrate Black women's intellectual and creative prowess and serves as a site to understand meaning-making under systems of anti-Black and patriarchal oppression. Although Shadd deigns to circumvent explicit discussions of gender politics in *Plea*, we argue that her attention to the land centers Black women's contributions to community-building and aligns *Plea* with Black feminism's toil toward a more equitable and sustainable society— even as the liberatory Black feminist geography in *Plea* is nevertheless fraught by its complicity in settler-colonialist methods of community development, cultivating land stolen from the Algonquin, Mississauga, Ojibwa, Cree, Odawa, Potawatomi, Delaware, and the Haudenosaunee. Spotlighting this tension allows us to read *Plea* for its Black feminist theorizations of equity, women's empowerment, and constructs of Black liberation, while nevertheless acknowledging it as symptomatic of the contested politics of emigration as settler colonialism. Therefore, by foregrounding *Plea*'s implicit rebuttal to the masculinist form, content, and project of emigrationism espoused in Black settler guides, we situate Shadd as theorist of Black community-building at the intersection of Black feminism and Black nationalism.

The Gendered Politics of Emigrationism

Though travel writing became more accessible to women writers in the mid-nineteenth century—including Black women like Nancy Prince and Mary Seacole—men still dominated the genre.[4] This was especially true of settler guides, which were almost always written by and for men. Ironically though, the opposite was true in Canada, where two of Shadd's white contemporaries also authored guides for prospective immigrants: Susanna Moodie's *Roughing It in the Bush* (1852) and Catharine Parr Traill's *The Female Emigrant's Guide* (1854). Considering this cluster of women-authored guides together, Rinaldo Walcott argues, prompts not only "a rethinking of how we understand [Canadian] national formation," but also an attention to situating "matters of gender, or rather of womanhood, as a central problematic of nation building."[5] But despite an existing discourse on the role of women in colonizing Canada West, a focus on guides for and by African Americans reveals a different story. "In contrast to what was widely available for male refugees,"

Ikuko Asaka notes, "there was no widely circulated textual resource useful for the fashioning of formerly enslaved women's political subjectivities."[6]

In what follows, we extend Asaka's contention about Canadian literature and Walcott's provocation about womanhood's centrality to nation-/community-building to the broader Black emigrationist discourse in North America at this time. A multifarious movement among nineteenth-century Black nationalists, emigrationism arose both as a critique of abolitionists who believed systemic racism could be expurgated from the United States once slavery was abolished and as a Black-led alternative to the colonization movement—a white-led philanthropic mission to resettle free African Americans from the United States in West Africa. Support for organized emigration was intermittent throughout the early nineteenth century until the passage of the 1850 Fugitive Slave Act renewed interest and consolidated the movement, as seen at the 1854 National Emigration Convention in Cleveland. Consolidation, however, did not mean consensus and delegates fundamentally disagreed about where emigrants should settle, what their ultimate goals were, and how they should proceed. Martin Delany, for instance, proclaimed that "the West Indies, Central and South America, are the countries of our choice," while arguing that Canada was merely a convenient way station that promised "temporary relief" for those fleeing from slavery in the United States, but ultimately not "permanent places upon which to fix our destiny."[7] He made this claim even as thousands of refugees from slavery were fleeing north to Canada after 1850 and even as his colleague Israel Campbell—one of four delegates from Canada—"made a speech in behalf of his country" and the convention voted to "recommend to the colored people throughout the 'States,' as the surest investment in social as well as political economy, to possess themselves with as much land as possible in the Canadas."[8] Thus, although the most proximate and arguably most practical site for Black relocation and settlement, Canada occupied an ambivalent status at best among the emigrationist movement.

We highlight the tensions and differences within the National Emigration Convention because even as Black leaders worked to perform solidarity and collectivity, differences of ideology, class, and gender percolate throughout the proceedings.[9] For example, despite being a close associate of Delany and a vocal advocate for emigrationism, despite advertising the convention in her newspaper, and the robust representation of women at this particular convention, Shadd did not attend, likely owing to her interpersonal feud with the Bibb family, the dedication of a significant portion of the conference to memorializing the recently deceased Henry Bibb, and the appointment of Mary Bibb as second vice president to the convention.[10] Had Shadd attended though, she would have found herself in the company of forty other women, nearly a third of the assembled delegation. Indeed, the National Emigration Convention seems to have prioritized gender inclusivity by nominating a majority of women to the finance committee and adopting an amendment that enabled women delegates to "contribute whatever they be disposed" to the proceedings. The convention also included overtly feminist messaging in its "Declaration of Sentiments": "the potency and respectability of a nation or people, depends entirely upon the position of their women; therefore, it is essential to our elevation that the female portion of our children be instructed in all the arts and sciences pertaining to the highest civilization."[11] This representation, however, equated with neither power nor control over messaging for women delegates. Not only were women fully excluded from the Board of National Commissioners and the Committee on Publication, but almost all of their substantive contributions were downplayed, anonymized, and erased in the published proceedings, while the full text of Delany's "Political Destiny of the Colored Race on the American Continent" was reprinted in full.[12]

These gestures toward inclusion notwithstanding, Carla Peterson rightly characterizes Black emigrationism as a movement beholden to "a masculinist ideology of Negro nationality" that ultimately "replicate[s] the values of Western, Christian, capitalist patriarchy."[13] Indeed, the 1854 convention is exceptional in its efforts toward gender equity. A decade before Shadd published her *Plea*, for example, a Black convention in Baltimore sponsored Nathaniel Peck and Thomas Price's fact-finding mission to the British colonies of Guyana and Trinidad "to ascertain the character of the climate, soil, natural productions, and the political and social condition of the coloured inhabitants."[14] A short twenty-five-page pamphlet published in both Baltimore and London, *Report of Messrs. Peck and Price* (1840) describes their travels and meetings with local officials about inducements for Black migrants and a dire labor shortage that threatened to stifle an agricultural economy with potential for unbounded growth: "Every plantation that we were upon (which were many)," they reported, "wanted from forty to fifty hands to carry on the cultivation already in operation."[15] This impression likely formed so clearly because Peck and Price met primarily with plantation owners/managers (i.e., former enslavers) and the local Emigration Society, all of whom were deeply invested in luring Black workers to the colonies and all of whom were men.[16] Consequently, the discourse around the prospects of emigration assumes an undeniably masculinist perspective, focusing on the various economic and political opportunities for Black men relocating to these locales. As Peck and Price traveled from estate to estate, they interviewed dozens of "gentlemen" and "proprietors" of plantations, but only included the testimony of a single laborer—an unnamed Black woman whose experience they offer as evidence of the tolerable work conditions and opportunities for diligent entrepreneurs to thrive: "We saw a young woman at an estate called 'Success,' on the island of Lagaun, finish her second task by twelve o'clock, and did not appear to be fatigued. In answer to a question put to her by us, that she could do three tasks every day, said if she felt inclined after dinner, she would do another task."[17] Despite portraying her labor as dignified and even undemanding (she "did not *appear to be fatigued*"), the scene nevertheless illustrates the urgency of the labor shortage. After all, "washwomen, nurses, and sempstresses are in demand" also, implying that this woman *must* toil in the fields because there are insufficient men to do so.[18] Thus, while we might be tempted to count this "young woman" among the "industrious and enterprising capitalists" the pamphlet entices, the scene also indexes the incomplete project of racial uplift—women must still work for wages because there are insufficient men to work the fields and provide for them, thereby continuing to bar women's access to the performative cult of domesticity.[19] Even as the scene concludes by restoring the young woman to the domestic sphere ("besides, each family has a very comfortable cottage to live in, containing generally two rooms on the first floor, and one above, with as much ground attached as they can cultivate in vegetables"), thereby intimating the restoration of patriarchal order and separate gender spheres, readers understand that she must return to the fields tomorrow until a male immigrant can relieve her.[20]

Similarly, Delany's *Condition, Elevation, Emigration, and Destiny of the Colored People in the United States*—published just months apart from Shadd's *Plea*—also betrays investments in a masculinist ideology through the erasure of women. While Delany's section on African American cultural achievements offers adulatory sketches of Ann Maria Johnson, Eliza(beth) Taylor Greenfield, Lucy Stanton, Mary Miles Bibb, and Shadd, his discussion of emigration remains strictly in the masculinist realm of geopolitics. In considering Canada, for instance, Delany is less concerned with living conditions than the likelihood that the United States would eventually annex Canada.[21] Even when Delany eventually recommends Central and South America as preferred sites for colonizing, he concludes by imploring readers, "Go not with an anxiety of political aspirations; but go with the fixed intention . . . of cultivating the soil, entering into the mechanical operations, keeping of shops, carrying on merchandise, trading on land and water, improving property—in a word to become the producers of the country, instead of the consumers."[22] This catalog of professions largely restricted to men categorically proscribes women from the "producers" who would contribute to the development of a Black nationality and communities in the proposed settlements.

While *Condition* was contemporary with Shadd's *Plea*, Delany's later *Official Report of the Niger Valley Exploring Party* (1861) more closely resembles its settler guide form. Describing Delany's travels with Robert Campbell in Liberia and Yoruba (modern Nigeria), the pamphlet offers a near exhaustive portrait of the regions' climates, soils, agriculture, diseases, civic organization, political culture, social customs, and potential for development through Black immigration. Here, Delany is preoccupied with the need for Christian missionaries and the promise of cultivating a thriving cotton market to compete with the U.S. American South. Women's contributions to this growing sector, however, were limited to the domestic sphere: "coloring and dy[e]ing is carried on very generally, every woman seeming to understand it as almost a domestic necessity" and adding that the refinement of red dye from camwood is "another domestic employment of the women."[23] Not only does Delany overlook the vital importance of dyed cloth to Yoruba religious and cultural ceremonies (including *adire*, for which Abeokuta is famous), but in the very next section, he marvels at "the manufactory of cotton cloth" and the "one hundred and fifty-seven looms in operation" throughout Yoruba without mentioning that the weaving of cotton was almost exclusively performed by women.[24]

Though the patriarchal character of emigrationism is perhaps unsurprising, we rehearse these representative examples to stress two aspects of Shadd's intervention. First, although the movement frequently discussed women and women even helped organize, their investments in patriarchy limited their imagination for women's roles in the new societies they were envisioning outside the United States. Second, the fact that these texts *did* discuss the role of women makes Shadd's apparent elision of women's issues in *A Plea for Emigration* all the more noteworthy. Indeed, Solomon argues that Shadd "missed ample opportunity to specifically address her female 'brethren'" and that *Plea* "failed to speak directly to Black women with regards to articulating or acknowledging their roles in the creation of a Black Canadian community."[25] While Solomon's criticisms are justified, we will argue in the next section that Shadd's adherence to the rhetorical situation of the settler guide explains her apparent failure here. More than simply avoiding women's issues altogether,

Shadd uses coded references to the labor women routinely perform and positions that work centrally to developing Black communities in Canada West. Therefore, if we view Shadd's seeming concessions to patriarchal forms not strictly as a missed opportunity, but rather as a savvy navigation of genre conventions, we can begin to trace the subtle ways that her *Plea* addresses, expands, and even centers women's contributions to community-building in Canada West. Shadd's centering of traditional domestic labor emphasizes Black women's intellectual, moral, and physical work as inherently valuable to the economic and social foundations to cultivate a thriving community, and crucial to the shaping of Black life in new settlements.

Black Feminism, Labor, and Community

Although readers of settler guides were presumed to be men weighing relocation (whether single or heads of household), the flow of migrants that the 1850 Fugitive Slave Law set in motion reveals another audience. According to Asaka, "substantial numbers of enslaved women acted on their desire for freedom and overcame adversaries without male assistance," fleeing to Canada "in all-female groups or alone" and sometimes leaving behind "their husbands and even their children in bondage."[26] Whether or not these women read Shadd's *Plea*, their journeys to and experiences in Canada trouble the phallogocentric presumptions regarding its audience and emigrationism's masculinist ideologies. How do we read *Plea* differently if we examine it as a text that addresses—at least in part—women who were considering migration to Canada West or had already migrated?[27]

The focus on Black women's roles in community-building and maintenance make clear the underlying Black feminist thought throughout Shadd's settler guide, a focus that we argue contributes to the theorizations of gardening, land cultivation, and ecology more broadly, critical analytics that were (and still are) important to the traditions of Black women's intellectual and political activism.[28] Across Black diasporas, community is a place both literal and metaphorical when thinking about the perseverance of Blackness, and practical and poetic given the precarity to life and livelihoods that Black communities face. As Angela Davis notes in her reflections on enslaved Black women's role in civil society, many were "thrust by the force of circumstances into the center of the slave community." This made Black women "essential to the *survival* of the community," and their labor thereby afforded at least a modicum of autonomy.[29] Community-building and collective welfare have always been a central concern of Black women's activism, ranging from nineteenth-century vigilance committees to Stacey Abrams and LaTosha Brown launching grassroots voting rights campaigns in the modern South. Community, therefore, is not only a goal advanced by Black women's organizing, but also a practice maintained by their labor, whether it is through basic homesteading or advocating for the rights and liberties of the collective. While their labor and ideas were often undervalued, this work remained indispensable to Black organizing.

As a number of scholars have shown, Black women's commitments to centering their experiences in society and community-building define the intellectual labor of "theorizing" (in Barbara Christian's sense of the word). Black feminist geography, for example, theorizes how Black women's experiences of land, space, and mobility reconfigure and reimagine space in ways that challenge heteropatriarchy and anti-Blackness. Black women's traversing land and space against cartographies of colonialism and (the afterlives of) slavery constructs an alternative logic and relationship to the land, producing what Katherine McKittrick describes as "spatial boundaries and subject knowledges that can subvert the perimeters of bondage."[30] In practice, this is exemplified in the potentials of Black feminist and decolonial praxis, which transform space into a "plot" where "the actual growth of narratives, food, and cultural practices . . . materialize the deep connections between blackness and the earth and foster values that challenge systemic violence."[31]

Though Black relationships to farming are necessarily encumbered by the extent to which plantation slavery's literal and figurative architecture structured Black experiences of anticultural labor and space, throughout history Black men and especially women have used gardening as a site of creativity, resistance, survival, and spiritual/nutritional sustenance. Most salient for our purposes is Walker's "In Search of Our Mothers' Gardens," which discusses the relationship between the physically, emotionally, and spiritually overwhelming labor expected of Black women throughout U.S. American history, labor that was essential yet largely invisible. These demands would have been especially onerous on Black women in Canada West, many of whom were settler colonists participating in the grueling labor of homesteading on "uncleared" land in addition to the domestic and moral responsibilities to their families that society imposed on them.[32] For Walker though, these exceptional demands did not annihilate Black women's artistic and aesthetic production, but merely redirected it into unexpected places, like her mother's garden: "I notice that it is only when my mother is working in her flowers that she is radiant, almost to the point of being invisible—except as Creator: hand and eye. She is involved in work her soul must have. Ordering the universe in the image of her personal conception of Beauty. Her face, as she prepares the Art that is her gift, is a legacy of respect she leaves to me, for all that illuminates and cherishes life. She has handed down respect for the possibilities—and the will to grasp them."[33] The point, for Walker, is that finding Black women's creative expression sometimes requires an examination of spaces outside those traditionally recognized as arenas for such work.

As a corollary to these arguments, we find in Shadd's work a contention that women's horticultural labors were not only sites of artistry and innovation that exemplify a Black feminist ethos that properly values these contributions to Black communities in Canada; they were also entry points into entrepreneurship, community-building, and public life otherwise restricted to them. Much like the emigrationist treatises and settler guides discussed above, Shadd foregrounds soil quality and agriculture in her discussion of the region's potential for Black settlements, reassuring readers at the outset that the climate is more salubrious and the land more fecund than the United States.[34] Formerly enslaved settlers reported that "the soil is unsurpassed by that of Kentucky and States farther south, and naturally superior to the adjoining northern States," and staple grains were produced at a much higher yield than in the United States "except on the application of fertilizing materials—a mode not much practiced in Canada hitherto, the land not having been exhausted sufficiently to require such appliances to further its productiveness."[35] Unlike the emphasis placed on large-scale plantation agriculture as in Peck and Price's guide or Delany's pamphlet, Shadd is more focused on family farms, gardens, and garden plants. Because staple and cash crops like wheat, buckwheat, oats, barley, rye, corn, "potatoes (white or Irish and sweet), carrots, turnips, pumpkins . . . squashes, and tobacco" grow so well, Shadd argues that family gardens might include a much more diverse variety of fruits and vegetables, including "tomatoes, cucumbers, onions, beets, cabbage and cauliflower, egg-plants, beans, peas, leeks, celery, lettuce, cantaloupes and spinach," all of which grow with "as great success, at least, as in the United States, and the specimens generally seen in the gardens and market-places are decidedly superior."[36] Similarly, Shadd dedicates an adjacent section to "Domestic Animals—Fowls—Game," wherein she discusses how the clearing of Canadian land opened space and opportunities for the husbandry of horses, sheep, and cattle, as well as eggs, cheese, and butter for consumption or sale.[37]

In emphasizing the roles of horticulture and family farms in the economic development of Canada West, Shadd privileges the contributions of women, whose domestic occupations included "keeping livestock and growing vegetables."[38] Family gardens were largely the purview of women. and while they were primarily used for the cultivation of fruits and vegetables for the family's consumption, Shadd's analysis underscores opportunities for enterprising women not only to create better domestic life for their families by expanding their culinary repertoires, but also to participate in economic and civic growth by bringing their garden yields to market. Indeed, because most farming in Canada at this time was "more as a means of present subsistence," openings for market expansion and enrichment were myriad, with "garden plants" presenting one of the ripest growth sectors. Shadd, for instance, celebrates the Toronto market as "one of the best markets in America," but then also indicates that Canadian produce has received acclaim and awards at state fairs in Michigan and New York.[39] The implication here is that the variety, quality, and abundance of fruits and vegetables produced from high-yield family gardens could collectively sustain a regional and even international market, and that women, as the proprietors of family gardens, would therefore play a prominent role in the economic development of the region.[40]

If we consider Shadd's foregrounding of horticulture as an entry point into the masculine-coded space of economy, we can situate her thinking within a longer genealogy of Black theorizing of gardening as resistance, liberation, and spiritual/nutritional sustenance. In Kimberly K. Smith's classic study of Black environmental thought, for instance, she notes that leading Black men like W. E. B. Du Bois, Booker T. Washington, and George Washington Carver all espoused gardening as integral to the racial uplift project of the late nineteenth and early twentieth centuries. The cultivation of natural beauty around the home, they argued, offered practical education, fostered self-sufficiency, and "provided an alternative to agricultural labor as a basis of black selfhood."[41] These masculinist genealogies of theorizing Black gardening finds their corollary in Black feminist thought and praxis, beginning with captive African women secreting seeds in their hair prior to the Middle Passage and enslaved women using gardens to supplement the paltry food allowances of enslavers to feed their families. More contemporary examples include Fannie Lou Hamer's Freedom Farming Collective, Black urban gardening in Detroit—right across the river from where Shadd settled in Canada West—and a revitalized interest in horticulture among Black women during the height of the COVID-19 pandemic.[42]

As these later examples illustrate, Black feminists understand gardening as central to the organizing and care work that not only builds but sustains Black communities. In particular, Shadd rightly understood the broader project of Black emigration to Canada after the Fugitive Slave Law as a moment of cultural transition and upheaval. In "The Status of Women in America" (1892), for example, Anna Julia Cooper examines the marginalization of women's labor during the "accumulative period" that followed the colonization of North America. "When the times of physical hardship and danger were past, when the work of clearing and opening up was over and the struggle for accumulation began," she writes, "again woman's inspiration and help were needed and still was she loyally at hand," even as women's physical and emotional labor remained unvalued and overlooked, and "time would fail to tell of the noble army of women who shine like beacon lights in the otherwise sordid wilderness of this accumulative period."[43] Cooper's arguments about the late nineteenth century contextualize Shadd's ideas of building a better community (for Black women especially) by elevating women's labor. The steady migration into Canada West during Shadd's time, and in particular after the passing of the Fugitive Slave Law, also created a period of swift changes. Aside from escaping the institution of slavery, emigrating and the guides that promoted it operated on prospects for economic growth, while still privileging of male-dominated enterprises. Canada West offered new opportunities for experiencing freedom and redefining Black life outside the shadow of slavery—a parallel accumulative period in which women's physical, intellectual, and emotional labor might be central rather than invisible.

Though Cooper's essay was written forty years after Shadd's pamphlet, her critical analysis on a social and cultural climate defined by rapid change within a capitalist context nevertheless illuminated the suppression of value in women's labor—and the potential for Black feminist liberation that such a culture of change might catalyze. Moreover, positioning Shadd's efforts to elevate women's work in this longer Black feminist intellectual genealogy helps us to understand both its potential and limitations. Like Cooper and Shadd, for instance, the Combahee River Collective were similarly motivated by the "shared belief that Black women are inherently valuable."[44] Their manifesto, "The Combahee River Collective Statement" (1977), shares *Plea*'s attention not only to the unique forms of oppression Black women have historically experienced, but that of all marginalized people in colonized societies: they are "concerned with any situation that impinges upon the lives of women, Third World and working people," emphasizing how Black feminism's antiracist critique is necessarily intersectional and consciously sensitive to how systems of oppression overlap.[45] Whereas the Bibbs' Refugee Home Society narrowly focused on the needs of impoverished single men and families fleeing slavery to settle in Canada West, for example, Shadd's community-building efforts attended to the experiences of families, single women, and middle-class emigrants from the United States, including those who wished to settle in Black communities and those who wished to integrate into white communities.

At the same time though, Shadd's conceptualization of gardening as a means of accumulating economic power cuts against the Combahee River Collective's anticapitalist ethos, even as both efforts "argue for the reorganization of society based on the collective needs of the most oppressed."[46] Similarly, while *Plea* largely conceives its Black feminist arguments as modes of expanding access to opportunities that capitalism and settler colonialism afforded Black emigrants in Canada West, more recent Black feminist theories and practices of gardening are invested in "critiques of patriarchy and capitalism, the development of relational leadership, responsible stewardship of the earth, and reciprocal caregiving."[47] Thus, even as *Plea*'s promotion of horticultural entrepreneurship identifies strategies for Black women to contribute to a burgeoning capitalist economy and even as its elevation of undervalued Black women's labor enabled the accelerating deracination of Indigenous peoples from North America during this era, its argumentation regarding Black women's centrality to community-building in Canada West laid the groundwork for more progressive efforts in future generations of Black women intellectuals.

Conclusion

The soil of Black feminist thought is an intellectual foundation that fosters new and innovative ideas, nourished by Black women's experiences and the worlds they inhabit. By drawing on contemporary and canonical Black feminist thinkers, we have situated *A Plea for Emigration* within a long intellectual tradition of Black women theorizing both their experiences and the worlds they (wish to) live in. Shadd's generative conception of community prioritizes Black women's labor as necessary to the community's cultivation and thriving, locating their creative expressions and material contributions to Canada West's economic and community development within the broader masculinist ideologies of Black emigrationism, Black nationalism, and Black Canada. By subtly centering women in these endeavors throughout *Plea*, Shadd commits to the Black feminist ethos of elevating and improving the conditions of a society's most vulnerable and/or oppressed members not only to frustrate established, regressive norms but also to envision a better community for everyone.

Despite these investments in empowering Black women and cultivating a strong community in *Plea*—which laid groundwork for Shadd's later involvement with the women's suffrage movement upon her eventual return to the United States—her proposals regarding Canada West, are ultimately fraught by their investments in capitalist enterprise and settler colonialism.[48] Consequently, we want to echo Shirley Yee's characterization of Shadd as "a complicated heroine who reminds us that activists are not unidimensional individuals who lead linear or simple lives, nor are they unencumbered by the ideological currents of their generation."[49] While Shadd's defaulting to these logics is more or less expected within the broader contexts of nineteenth-century Black nationalism and emigration, reading her work as both a contribution to and critique of these movements allows us to spotlight her writing's Black feminist potentialities while nevertheless holding it accountable. Shadd's attention to women's homesteading and horticultural practices as essential labor to Black settlements' survival, for example, advances a Black feminist argument within a masculinist genre (the settler guide) and a masculinist movement (emigrationism). While we recognize Shadd's understanding of these enterprises as entrepreneurial launchpads for Black women into economic and potentially political power, the more modern theorizations of Black feminist geography that her arguments eventually enable also complicate our understanding of her project. For example, even as McKittrick points out how "black geographic subjects differently produce space" through "the seeking out of alternative geographic options, and the coupling of geography with black matters, histories, knowledges, experiences, and resistances," these survivalist innovations are necessary precisely because they occur within "the white colonial and geographic contexts of Canada," including "geographic expansion and the profitable displacement of difference."[50] Those displacements entailed not only the geographic and historical obfuscation of Black people in Canada but also Black refugees from U.S. American slavery participating (however immediately or indirectly) in the ongoing dispossession of Indigenous people.

To recognize these implications is not to dismiss Shadd's emigration-ism as an irredeemable settler-colonial enterprise. Nor is it our intention to excuse her complicity as a pragmatic maneuvering within hegemonic discourses that her marginalized status as a Black woman necessitated. Rather, by situating her work within a longer intellectual genealogy of Black feminist thought, we can begin to see how the seeds she planted have been cultivated and tended by future generations of Black feminist thinkers, including Tiffany Lethabo King's groundbreaking thinking about Black and Indigenous coalitions/tensions throughout North America in *The Black Shoals* (2018). Whereas Shadd's thinking necessarily began *within* masculinist paradigms that were ultimately limiting for her, her Black feminist critiques have provided a starting point from which subsequent generations have envisioned more liberatory possibilities. Conceptualizing Shadd and her politics within these frameworks illustrates the possibilities that her work contained possibilities that, unfortunately, were not ready for harvest in her lifetime but were nonetheless rooting.

Notes

1. Phanuel Antwi, introduction to Mary Ann Shadd, *A Plea for Emigration; or, Notes of Canada West*, ed. Phanuel Antwi (Peterborough, ON: Broadview, 2016), 9. See also Richard Almonte, introduction to Mary Ann Shadd, *A Plea for Emigration; or, Notes of Canada West*, ed. Richard Almonte (Toronto: Mercury, 1998), 26.

2. Nassisse Solomon, "Calling to Her Brethren: An Examination of the Interactive Effects of Immigration, Race and Female Representation in the Life and Writings of Mary Ann Shadd Cary," in *Women in the "Promised Land": Essays in African Canadian History*, ed. Nina Reid-Maroney, Boulou Ebanda de B'beri, and Wanda Bernard Thomas (Toronto: Women's Press Canadian Scholars Press, 2018), 16.

3. Patricia Hill Collins, *Black Feminist Thought: Knowledge, Consciousness, and the Politics of Empowerment*, 2nd ed. (New York: Routledge, 2009), 34.

4. See *Narrative of the Life and Travels of Mrs. Nancy Prince, Written by Herself* (Boston: Nancy Prince, 1856); and Mary Seacole, *The Wonderful Adventures of Mrs. Seacole in Many Lands* (London: James Blackwood, 1857); as well as Elizabeth Stordeur Pryor, *Colored Travelers: Mobility and the Fight for Citizenship Before the Civil War* (Chapel Hill: University of North Carolina Press, 2016).

5. Rinaldo Walcott, "'Who Is She and What Is She to You?': Mary Ann Shadd Cary and the (Im)Possibility of Black/Canadian Studies," in *Rude: Contemporary Black Canadian Cultural Criticism*, ed. Rinaldo Walcott (Toronto: Insomniac Press, 2000), 36. Walcott highlights the ongoing erasure of Black writers and people from Canadian history, contributing to what Katherine McKittrick describes as the continually "surprising" presence of Blackness in Canada

(*Demonic Grounds: Black Women and the Geographies of Struggle* [Minneapolis: University of Minnesota Press, 2006], 91–120). Walcott's inclusion of Shadd becomes especially important given the racial politics of Moodie and Traill, whose guides advance Canada's settler colonial project and accelerate the construction of the Canadian colony/nation as white.

6. Ikuko Asaka, *Tropical Freedom: Climate, Settler Colonialism, and Black Exclusion in the Age of Emancipation* (Durham, NC: Duke University Press, 2017), 113.

7. *Proceedings of the National Emigration Convention of Colored People; Held at Cleveland, Ohio* (Pittsburgh: A. A. Anderson, 1854), 43, 37.

8. *Proceedings*, 11, 21.

9. On concerns about unity in the conventions movement, see Christopher James Bonner, *Remaking the Republic: Black Politics and the Creation of American Citizenship* (Philadelphia: University of Pennsylvania Press, 2020), 38–68.

10. Jane Rhodes, *Mary Ann Shadd Cary: The Black Press and Protest in the Nineteenth Century* (Bloomington: Indiana University Press, 1998), 25–50.

11. *Proceedings*, 26–27.

12. On women's contributions to this gathering, see "Women Inside (and Outside) of the 1854 Emigration Convention," *To Stay or to Go? The 1854 National Emigration Convention*, accessed August 16, 2021, https://coloredconventions.org/emigration-debate/women -involvement/. For methods of reading women's contributions to conventions even when the published proceedings tend to downplay them, see Eric Gardner, "A Word Fitly Spoken: Edmonia Highgate, Frances Ellen Watkins Harper, and the 1864 Syracuse Convention," in *The Colored Conventions Movement: Black Organizing in the Nineteenth Century*, ed. P. Gabrielle Foreman, Jim Casey, and Sarah Lynn Patterson (Chapel Hill: University of North Carolina Press, 2020), 72–85.

13. Carla L. Peterson, *"Doers of the Word": African-American Women Speakers and Writers in the North (1830–1880)* (New York: Oxford University Press, 1995), 112, 114.

14. *Report of Messrs. Peck and Price, Who Were Appointed at a Meeting of the Free Colored People of Baltimore, Held on the 25th of November, 1839, Delegates to Visit British Guiana, and the Island of Trinidad; for the Purpose of Ascertaining the Advantages to be Derived by Colored People Migrating to Those Places* (Baltimore: Woods and Crane, 1840), 3.

15. *Report of Messrs. Peck and Price*, 14.

16. Although some African Americans relocated to Trinidad and Guyana following Peck and Price's report (with the help of British sponsors), the Black press remained deeply skeptical ("Mssrs. Peck and Price," *Colored American*, November 7, 1840). See also Dexter J. Gabriel, "The British Emigration Scheme and the African American Emigration Movement to the Caribbean," in *In Search of Liberty: African American Internationalism in the Nineteenth Century Atlantic World*, ed. Ronald Angelo Johnson and Ousmane K. Power-Greene (Athens: University of Georgia Press, 2021), 165–96.

17. *Report of Messrs. Peck and Price*, 14.

18. *Report of Messrs. Peck and Price*, 18.

19. *Report of Messrs. Peck and Price*, 14.

20. *Report of Messrs. Peck and Price*, 14, 15.

21. Although the annexation of Canada to the United States never gained much political traction, Shadd's collaborator at the *Provincial Freeman*, Samuel Ringgold Ward, shared Delany's concerns about white nationalism in Canada fusing with its U.S. American counterpart. "In various parts of Canada Yankees have settled," he observes, and "some of them do not scruple to

make known their desire to see Canada a part of the Union, and thus brought under the control of the slave power, and made a park for slaveholders to hunt human deer in" (*Autobiography of a Fugitive Negro: His Anti-Slavery Labours in the United States, Canada & England* [London, 1855], 138). Though Ward understandably attributes such sentiments to U.S. American agitation, many white Canadian colonists were primed to support the extradition of Black fugitives from slavery back to the United States in order to reify Canada's whiteness (Asaka, *Tropical Freedom*, 111–38).

22. Martin Robison Delany, *The Condition, Elevation, Emigration, and Destiny of the Colored People of the United States* (Philadelphia: Published by the author, 1852), 187.

23. M[artin] R. Delany, *Official Report of the Niger Valley Exploring Party* (New York: Thomas Hamilton, 1861), 60–61.

24. Delany, *Official Report*, 61; Toyin Falola and Ann Genova, *Historical Dictionary of Nigeria* (Lanham, MD: Scarecrow Press, 2009), 85, 4.

25. Solomon, "Calling to Her Brethren," 26, 16.

26. Asaka, *Tropical Freedom*, 126. See also Adrienne Shadd, "'The Lord Seemed to Say, "Go"': Women and the Underground Railroad Movement," in *"We're Rooted Here and They Can't Pull Us Up": Essays in African Canadian Women's History*, coord. Peggy Bristow (Toronto: University of Toronto Press, 1994), 41–68.

27. *Plea*'s Black feminist ethos extended into her editorial management of her newspaper. As Benjamin Fagan notes, the *Provincial Freeman* (1854–57) "saw black settlers as a primary engine of Canadian progress" and "repeatedly located the Canadian spirit of improvement in the economic successes of the province's black inhabitants" (*The Black Newspaper and the Chosen Nation* [Athens: University of Georgia Press, 2016], 105).

28. As Chelsea Mikael Frazier notes, the genealogy of Black feminist ecological thought has been erased due to the prioritization of white (and often male) perspectives in ecocriticism, largely ignoring theories of land and environment in Black women's prose and cultural production ("Black Feminist Ecological Thought: A Manifesto," *Atmos*, October 1, 2020, https://atmos .earth/black-feminist-ecological-thought-essay/). She further suggests that such conceptions of land are "rooted in an ecological world-sense completely alternative to what readily comes to mind when we think about the environment." We can thus think of gardening's prioritization over the more popular cash-crop agriculture model in *Plea* as an alternative "world-sense" that analogizes Black women's essential participation in community to that of cultivating a flourishing garden bed.

29. Angela Davis, "Reflections on Black Women's Role in the Community of Slaves," *Black Scholar* 3, no. 4 (1971): 7; italics added.

30. McKittrick, *Demonic Grounds*, 40.

31. Katherine McKittrick, "Plantation Futures," *Small Axe* 17, no. 3 (2013): 10.

32. Peggy Bristow, "'Whatever You Raise in the Ground You Can Sell It in Chatham': Black Women in Buxton and Chatham, 1850–65," in *"We're Rooted Here and They Can't Pull Us Up*," 83–90.

33. Alice Walker, "In Search of Our Mother's Gardens," in *Within the Circle: An Anthology of African-American Literary Criticism from the Harlem Renaissance to the Present*, ed. Angelyn Mitchell (Durham, NC: Duke University Press, 1994), 408.

34. As Eunice Toh contends in her contribution to this volume, Shadd was highlighting "an affinity with the land that is pragmatic while also signaling a form of Black belonging," informing our own arguments about horticultural theory and practice in Black feminist thought.

35. Shadd, *A Plea for Emigration*, ed. Antwi, 25; subsequent citations are to this edition.

36. Shadd, *A Plea for Emigration*, 27–28.

37. Shadd, *A Plea for Emigration*, 30.

38. Bristow, "'Whatever You Raise,'" 101.

39. Shadd, *A Plea for Emigration*, 27–28.

40. While we have specifically circumscribed the scope of our chapter around Shadd's writing and thinking in *Plea*, her *Provincial Freeman* abounds with evidence of these ideas in practice, including regular articles offering practical horticultural advice, novel techniques for food storage, and recipes that women could prepare from gardens.

41. Kimberly K. Smith, *African American Environmental Thought: Foundations* (Lawrence: University Press of Kansas, 2007), 92; see also Monica M. White, *Freedom Farmers: Agricultural Resistance and the Black Freedom Movement* (Chapel Hill: University of North Carolina Press, 2018), 26–64.

42. White, *Freedom Farmers*, 65–87. Throughout the COVID-19 pandemic, Black U.S. Americans have continued and expanded gardening initiatives across the country as forms of self-care, ways of exploring natural medicine, and reconnecting to ancestral practices in growing, cultivating. and healing (Tracey Michae'l Lewis-Giggetts, "Just Bees and Things and Flowers: How Black Women Gardeners Will Survive in the COVID-19 Crisis," *Essence*, December 6, 2020; "Black Gardeners Find Refuge in the Soil," *New York Times*, October 26, 2021.

43. Anna Julia Cooper, *A Voice from the South* (Mineola, NY: Dover, 2016), 59, 60.

44. "Combahee River Collective Statement," in *How We Get Free: Black Feminism and the Combahee River Collective*, ed. Keeanga-Yamahtta Taylor (Chicago: Haymarket, 2017), 18.

45. "Combahee River Collective Statement," 26.

46. Taylor, *How We Get Free*, 5.

47. Ashanté M. Reese, "Making Spaces Something Like Freedom: Black Feminist Praxis in the Re/Imagining of a Just Food System," *ACME: An International Journal for Critical Geography* 20, no. 4 (2021): 452.

48. A member of the National Women's Suffrage Association, which primarily centered on white women's interests, Shadd used her involvement to "lobby for the inclusion of black women in the suffrage agenda" and would "assert their rights at the same time that they worked in other areas of reform" (Rhodes, *Mary Ann Shadd Cary*, 194).

49. Shirley J. Yee, "Finding a Place: Mary Ann Shadd Cary and the Dilemmas of Black Migration to Canada, 1850–1870," *Frontiers* 18, no. 3 (1997): 2.

50. McKittrick, *Demonic Grounds*, 92.

CHAPTER 8

"They Would Agitate for Independence of Thought and Action"

Mary Ann Shadd Cary's Black Feminist
Organizing in Washington, D.C., 1867–93

BRANDI LOCKE

By and large, scholarly and public acknowledgments of Mary Ann Shadd Cary's stances on Black women's rights and gender roles center on her pamphlets and editorials for the *Provincial Freeman* prior to 1860, while she lived in Canada.[1] Perhaps her early writings and speeches are centered on because her formative years illustrate important political and discursive challenges in an era marked by the fight for abolition, colonization, and self-definition. She used her self-made platforms as a newspaper editor and traveling speaker for Canadian resettlement ventures to speak out on a wide range of topics, from emigration to women's place in Black political organizing. Shadd Cary proved to move across geographic and ideological boundaries in ways that, at best, inspired important debate across the diverse and complex landscape of early Black politics in North America and, at worst, revealed the proneness of her own neighbors and colleagues to deploy public gender-based violence in order to silence her. The challenges and accomplishments of her early life offer scholars a compelling place from which to mobilize their fields to lift Shadd Cary from relative obscurity. Although she continued to advocate for Black women's rights and community organizing for another three decades after leaving Canada, scholarship on her later years is far less robust than that about her life prior to returning to the United States in 1867.

To understand Mary Ann Shadd Cary's politics as it evolved later in her life I examine her public writing and speeches after she moved to Washington, D.C., in particular the records documenting her activism from 1867 to 1893. Through her writings I aim to recuperate the possibilities of proto–Black feminist politics in both the telling of her story and the larger histories of political movements that contended with the anxieties and failures of Reconstruction and the rise of Jim Crow. Shadd Cary's prominence around the issues of emigration and Canadian resettlement dissolved during the Civil War, and with it one of her most robust avenues for public engagement.[2] Her story seems to wane, ironically, when she moved to the political epicenter that is Washington, D.C., to pursue new professional and political heights. However, Mary Ann Shadd Cary and her contemporaries experienced major setbacks and barriers when white suffragist and Black male-led political movements used Black women's embodied discourse[3] and financial contributions, but excluded them from the intellectual labor and political gains.

Shadd Cary's mounting dissatisfaction with her own continued marginalization in movements and her continued precarity in society inspired a profound transformation of her political consciousness and organizing methods. Historian Martha Jones notes that the gains by leading Black women from the 1830s through the 1880s made the proliferation of their independent organizations by the 1890s possible, but those efforts were publicly challenged and intraracially undermined to abate heightened social anxieties.[4] As an intellectual leader who crafted the political and legal thought of African Americans, she conceptualized for her colleagues a politics and praxis for the inclusion of Black feminism in their agendas for suffrage and labor organizing. Shadd Cary married her individual experiences of gender discrimination and her own racial consciousness to articulate pro-Black and feminist interventions that revise the ostensibly inclusive policies of larger movements. Last, her records for forming an independent group provide a critical lens and a fuller articulation of the Black feminist politics her peers were unreceptive to and her vision for how, as Jones puts it, "if the nadir was the problem, the women's era was the solution."[5] Through the vista of her organizing archive we locate Shadd Cary trying to incite and steer sea changes to feminism, suffragism, and Black labor organizing, filling out the gaps to movement and intellectual histories that occur when her archive and presence is left out. In particular I posit the group she founded belongs to the long history of the Black clubwomen's movement, adding to scholar Brittney Cooper's evidence that these groups also functioned as schools of thought that would establish women among the race's intellectual leaders.[6]

The Turn to Focus on Mary Ann Shadd Cary's Later Years

To date Jane Rhodes's biography remains the most substantial examination of Mary Ann Shadd Cary's postbellum life, and in particular it appears to be the lone work that attempts to trace the trajectory of Shadd Cary's political thought and activism across her lifetime. Studies about her thoughts on emigration, abolitionism, and the Fourteenth Amendment conclude with Shadd Cary's choice to end her activism around Canadian resettlement and turn fully to the uplift of African Americans in Washington, D.C. These works produce groundbreaking interventions in Black Canadian studies with Shadd Cary's intellectual and embodied discourse supporting scholars' new theories of performance, class, mobility, and borders.[7] Scholarship has also grown to situate Shadd Cary's interventions in North American Black political thought, rhetorical and communications methodologies, print culture, and literary histories through methodological and theoretical frameworks that differ from and build on Rhodes's work; however, the focus remains on her work in these areas prior to 1867.[8] Elizabeth Cali's study of Shadd Cary's use of heteroglossic rhetorical strategies is an important accounting of her early Black feminist politics and literary tradition. Cali draws attention specifically to her practice through the *Provincial Freeman* of, "upholding . . . her respectability and femininity through the rhetorical screen of her male publishing partners . . . [deploying] a multivalent demand for public recognition of her dignity *and* her national leadership by underscoring her womanhood while still maintaining a public newspaper presence."[9] I find that her speeches and writing directly to her activist peers similarly reveal a careful negotiation of her positionality and how she figures herself alongside Black women in calls for inclusion, but that retrenched gender discrimination forced her to trade rhetorical male screens for a mobilized, embodied female collective.

I begin with an outline of Mary Ann Shadd Cary's personal strivings following her departure from Canada because gender discrimination seems to demarcate the possibilities of her continued success as an intellectual, writer, and activist. After two years in Detroit Shadd Cary moved to Washington, D.C., in 1869 and turned her attention to the work of labor organizing and education, which she aimed to do as a leading political thinker and practicing lawyer. Washington's function as a central node for supporting newly freed men, women, and children, and reconnecting them to networks of Black kin and community was naturally the place for Shadd Cary to continue her advocacy work for cultural and political conditions conducive to stabilizing displaced and migrating Black communities. Historian Kate Masur notes that in the ten years before Shadd Cary's arrival almost thirty thousand freedmen moved to Washington, D.C., making African Americans over a third of the district's population—a trend that sustained into the next century. These freed people found that independent Black institutions such as churches and aid societies made their survival, education, and reunification with family possible.[10] Agencies like the Freedmen's Bureau and Savings Bank were white-led and sympathetic to white residents insistent that Washington, D.C., not become hospitable to the growing population of impoverished freedmen who would consider staying and joining calls to integrate and secure citizenship rights for all Black communities in the district.

While Mary Ann Shadd Cary was professionally successful as a D.C. teacher and principal, she struggled as a law student and would ultimately engage her professional goals in the field of law as a thinker and an organizer and through civil disobedience—but not through practicing as a lawyer.[11] She enrolled in law school as a reflection of her desire to advance her work as a legal thinker, which she intended to bring to bear on Black labor organizing. Howard University's School of Law should have offered her a space to link her practice of law with her advocacy for Black labor rights and financial empowerment. The first dean of the law school, John Mercer Langston, was connected to her and her family through shared activist networks, such as the Colored Conventions. She wrote a thesis about the way the law had enabled corporations to empower "enterprises of national and individual interest," which she was primarily concerned about for Black communities facing limited access to labor, financing, and economic structures to sustain industries Black entrepreneurs sought to enter as leaders.[12] Unfortunately Shadd Cary would not graduate with her law degree until 1883, twelve years later than expected; court records suggest she never practiced law in court.[13] What is most revealing is scholarly speculation around why she did not graduate with her class in 1871, which I amend by underscoring the structural inequalities evident in the various theories.

Although scholars have not found conclusive evidence as to why Shadd Cary did or could not graduate from Howard Law until over a decade later than planned, I draw attention to the common presence of gendered and

racial inequality across their conjectures. In 1870 she failed to secure a clerical job in congressional offices or federal agencies, despite recommendations
from two well-known, white Republican attorneys in Detroit. Such a job
would have enabled Shadd Cary to launch into her legal career while meeting
her financial needs as a widow raising her children, Sarah and Linton. Some
scholars also suggest that John Mercer Langston and other administrators at
Howard Law purposefully blocked Shadd Cary from graduating in order to
prevent her from subsequently going up for admittance to the bar in 1871.
Though the D.C. bar had started allowing women to practice law beginning
that same year, scholars posit that the risk of reprisal from the bar would
have been substantial enough for the school to sacrifice Shadd Cary for their
larger interest of admitting Black men, even though racial segregation would
keep most Black lawyers from the resources to effectively practice law in
Washington, D.C., until 1918.

Mary Ann Shadd Cary's Reconstruction-era legal work and civic practices
could not be achieved with the male-assumed mask she previously deployed,
and, more important, her actions suggest that in this time she felt they should
not need to be. Perhaps her gender was weaponized, but this time to justify
her exclusion from clerical jobs and graduation by Black and white legal colleagues who knew she was well-trained, intelligent, and capable, but easily
marginalized to maintain a male-dominated status quo. For example, Shadd
Cary's failed attempt in April 1871 to register to vote in person at city hall when
she was dismissed by a board of registrars including two Black men who likely
knew of her. A report she wrote reflecting on the incident draws a narrative
and analytic throughline from onlooking men wishing to enact public violence on her for her civil disobedience to the Republican politicians whose
commitment to the status quo of women's disenfranchisement ultimately
undermined their own party's power. Three years later she notarized a statement recalling the incident; however, there is no record of a court case coming
from her initial filing.[14] This is an important departure from scholars' observa-
tions of Shadd Cary's earlier success in publication as rooted in heteroglossia
and writing strategies that often obscured her gender, at times protecting her
from gendered attacks and marginalization.[15] The sum total of her experiences
with gender discrimination while pursuing her law degree demonstrated to
Shadd Cary the urgency with which feminist politics needed to be theorized
and established in Black law practices and labor organizing. Her inability to
enter legal practice and influence the institution from within would likewise
happen in her career as a journalist and writer for Black newspapers.

Mary Ann Shadd Cary's continued journalistic and editorial writing after moving to Washington, D.C., has received little scholarly attention and possibly contains even more evidence of her evolving politics late in life. Rhodes traces a general shift in her articles for Frederick Douglass's *New National Era* (1870–74) as turning more fully toward mobilizing Black women to engage in racial uplift by working in local temperance and educational organizations.[16] Her increasingly feminist and temperance-focused work did not gain fanfare by the other major Black newspaper in Washington, D.C., the *People's Advocate*, and when the *New National Era* closed she lost the lone newspaper sympathetic to her politics and agendas. In particular Shadd Cary's activities in Black women's economic organizing were framed by the *Advocate* as inconsequential suffrage talk.[17] Similarly we find a single temperance song published in 1877 in the *Christian Recorder*, the organ of the AME Church,[18] suggesting a disjuncture between platforms open to her and the kind of political, socially critical writing she sought to write and publish generally. I hope to see scholars revisit Shadd Cary's writings for the *New National Era* and unpublished pieces to trace a fuller trajectory of her career in journalism and her ongoing critical reviews of reform movements, especially in light of her practice of circulating her legal and feminist thought through the press.

Transforming Her Advocacy: Shadd Cary's Relationship to Activist and Political Institutions

Mary Ann Shadd Cary's contributions to labor and suffragist movements convey her interventions in the theories and praxes directing the work of Black labor organizers and white suffragettes in ways that exclude Black women. In her own struggles she saw a series of structural barriers that Black women widely experienced, as gender and racial discrimination erased their contributions to the histories and theories that her activist peers asserted in their organizational agendas and policies, and when taking legal actions or engaging in civil disobedience. Shadd Cary's records from participating in organizations from 1869 to 1876 suggest that she used speeches and existing procedures to introduce (or reintroduce) her interventions. I specifically look at her speeches and written contributions to the Colored National Labor Convention and the National Women's Suffrage Association. Shadd Cary revised the constitutional legal thought underpinning their claims to labor rights, protections, and suffrage to reverse the erasure of Black women who were embedded in those theories and histories. Her revisions enabled her to outline the specific ways Black women's inclusion in these movements involved more than a rhetorical or additive model of inclusion, but instead acknowledged and addressed the barriers and needs Black women faced that differed from Black men and white women. I contend that over this period Shadd Cary ultimately determined that depending on leadership to shift the fundamental vision and operations of their groups to meaningfully include Black women was not imminent or effective. She would take her theories and policy recommendations to craft her own praxis for organizing Black women's intellectual and economic labor upon founding her own group in the interstices between these major movements and before the formation of the national club movement.

The proceedings of the Colored National Labor Convention in 1869 document Mary Ann Shadd Cary's attempt to shape prevailing thought and discourse about Black labor to recognize Black women and to probe the limits of this organization's practices of inclusion. Scholar Pier Gabrielle Foreman describes the procedural and literary operations of the conventions as enacting a space to debate and disseminate emerging Black legal thought and "a collective (and also masculinist) articulation of Black subjectivity,"[19] both animating proposals for reform action and lobbying for their execution. Delegates met in Washington, D.C., to offer their theories about Black labor history and labor law precedent to argue for specific initiatives to develop and improve Black apprenticeships, labor unions, banking, land purchases for Black farmers, inclusive hiring, and campaigning for policies and politicians that support Black workers. According to the proceedings of the convention, Shadd Cary was instead met with resistance and marginalization, which she critiqued on the basis of the body's failure to meaningfully address the distinct economic and political barriers women face that impede the race's uplift.

The convention speakers' perfunctory acknowledgments of women's labor inequalities announced their shared conceptualization of labor reform as primarily for the benefit of male workers and entrepreneurs, to which Mary Ann Shadd Cary responded by infusing feminist political thought into their agenda. For the first two days of the convention, gender received four mentions in speeches and resolutions strictly in lip service to an agreed philosophical stance around not excluding or discriminating against workers and students on the basis of sex. The proceedings note that the near-closing remark on the second day by southern politician James Thomas Rapier (who would later become a U.S. congressman for Alabama) was that, "as to women's rights, he hoped it would be confined north of the Ohio River."[20] Her response to his dismissive rejection of Black women's enfranchisement is only noted on the record as, "Mrs. Mary Carey [sic], of Canada, made a few remarks, and the convention adjourned."[21] Again we find her silenced by the official record, as she had been when she delivered a bold and eloquent speech on emigration at the 1855 national convention in Philadelphia, of which no record exists. It is not until the next day's evening session that Shadd Cary unequivocally centers women in the official agenda through her role chairing the female labor committee and delivering its report for adoption to the record.

Shadd Cary delivered a retort that was not recorded in the proceedings, but she used the practice of convention resolutions to inscribe her feminist intervention and praxis into the official goals the body would commit to pursuing. Her committee's report began with the recognition of her renaming her role and group as "Chairman of the Committee on Female Suffrage," their resolution on women's labor protections, and an accounting of the status of women workers.[22] Shadd Cary utilizes the politics of naming to revise the official record in ways that prevent any refusal of her political framework that defines gender inclusion as securing the intertwined political and economic rights of women. The resolution acknowledges that labor organizing among African Americans was in its infancy; however, it takes aim at dominant gender norms and white labor models when it proposes that Black organizers "[profit] by the mistakes heretofore made by our white fellow citizens in omitting women as co-workers in such societies, that colored women be cordially included in the invitation to further and organize cooperative societies."[23] Not only is women's exclusion from worker's protections a fatal model to adopt from white politics, but the resolution also does not leave the option open for women to fall under the labor organizing efforts of male activists. Instead women are to be welcomed as co-organizers in unionizing and empowering Black workers. Rather than deploy her previous approach of calling attention to the successes of other societies to encourage a different line of political action, Shadd Cary calls out white American society and posits that Black organizers should break through the barriers of both race and gender rather than seek racial inclusion and parity by sacrificing women's rights.

The report on women's labor reframed working women's experiences, positions, and prospects in ways that align with existing convention resolutions for men's labor organizing, *except* without the vagaries that stymied women's empowerment under Victorian patriarchal norms. Although choosing to be vague about what exactly is meant in resolutions that call for the end of discrimination based on race and sex may have avoided controversial debates in sessions, the report exposes that such consensus is gained at the cost of ignoring and perpetuating women's oppression—a price too high for the race. The report outlines the multitude of industries Black women labor in with no organizing or protections from "monopoly or arresting extortion and oppression," identifying that women are not covered by patriarchy and so are vulnerable to the same structures of the political economy that Black men fall prey to. Shadd Cary's calls for women's labor organizers to "bring to the pursuits of freedom the knowledge of husbandry learned when in bondage" amounted to a demand for expanding the industries open to them since slavery to also include cooperatives, entrepreneurial ventures, and other agencies.[24] She reframes the stigmatized, enslaved past of Black womanhood as instead a body of economically relevant expertise and skills. She names sculptor Edmonia Lewis and physician Sarah Mapps Douglass as examples of the success that comes when Black men support them, framing women's individual success as a net gain in social and intellectual capital for the race despite perceived risks from gender norm transgression as educated, professional women engaging in public work.

Twenty-three years before Anna Julia Cooper would write, "Only the BLACK WOMAN can say 'when and where I enter, in the quiet, undisputed dignity of my womanhood, without violence and without suing or special patronage, then and there the whole *Negro race enters with me,*'"[25] Shadd Cary addressed the institutional underpinnings of women's position as the lynchpin for racial uplift. She wrote, "The formation, therefore, of associations . . . could not fail to impress upon the sterner sex the importance of removing all barriers to the full recognition and success of women as an important industrial and moral agent in the great field of human activities and responsibilities."[26] Shadd Cary presciently identifies institutional empowerment through labor organizing that overtly names women and dismantles their racial and gendered oppression as the means for the race to enter the great field of humanity with dignity. The race fails to achieve this if leading men continue to depend on the false cover of patriarchal power to protect Black women laborers, and specifically when inadequately representing women in unions and practices that ignore, silence, or exclude them, as Shadd Cary's report seeks to disrupt. According to records of the Colored Conventions Movement assembled to date by the Colored Convention's Project, this was the last time Shadd Cary participated in the movement, instead turning her attention to interracial suffragist organizations and pursuing other methods to enfranchise Black women.

Mary Ann Shadd Cary's contributions to the National Women's Suffrage Association (NWSA) chronicle the development of her view that emergent white feminist thought held potential for supporting a praxis that could enfranchise Black women. When the Equal Rights Association's leadership asked Black women to support the Fifteenth Amendment on the grounds that their oppression was racial and not gendered, feminists left the organization. In 1869 Elizabeth Cady Stanton and Susan B. Anthony founded the NWSA, and when the white women of the organization campaigned for their voting rights by impugning the character of Black male voters, many activist women like poet Frances Ellen Watkins Harper chose sides in this zero-sum political game and sided with their Black male colleagues. Evidently Shadd Cary determined that the racist undercurrent of white suffragists did not disqualify their models and political action from being useful to her cause of empowering Black women.

Scholar Kirsten Lee's adaptation and application of Fred Moten's concept of apposition is useful here in understanding Shadd Cary's rhetorical maneuvers when managing her relationship to this controversial group. Rhodes observes that in her reporting on NWSA events Shadd Cary used an "editorial they" to create distance between her and the organization.[27] Here rhetorically, and in later instances physically through embodied discourse (an example of which I discuss shortly), Shadd Cary operated her feminist platform in apposition, not opposition, to her pro-Black politics by which she worked the boundaries of white feminist spaces insofar as those movements offered tactical advantages to the primary project of Black women–centered racial uplift. Lee traces her rhetorical strategies for advising African Americans in developing a repertoire of migratory "movements as speech acts" that use "a relation of adjacency rather than flight" toward the "hemispheric abolition" of slavery and Black non-citizenship.[28] In the post-emancipation project of racial uplift I argue that intersectionality within speech acts, embodied discourse, and epistemological frameworks for political organizing replaces migration as the repertoire Shadd Cary practices and advocates for, similarly imagining the soft power of adjacency as a potent force in securing political and economic empowerment for the race that begins with women's rights. Shadd Cary signals to Black audiences her qualified membership in the group did not support their racism, but left room for her to acknowledge their successes and political utility to Black women. Deftly aware of her positionality when addressing audiences in order to leverage their political capital toward her goals, Shadd Cary turned her attention to the platforms suffragism offered while continuing to firmly assert her rooted place in the Black community of Washington, D.C.

In 1874 Shadd Cary and members of the NWSA addressed the Judiciary Committee of the U.S. House of Representatives on behalf of D.C. women seeking the right to vote and her constitutional law interpretation that dismantled the premises upon which Black people and women were disenfranchised. While no published record of her speech exists, the Shadd Cary papers at Howard University include her handwritten draft of the speech. Shadd Cary began her presentation by saying her presence was significant in that she represents the "millions of colored women, today, [who] share with colored men the responsibilities of freedom from chattel slavery."[29] Standing in for the presence of Black women of her day, she positions herself as the embodiment of the vast population of Black women who carried the same burden as Black men of liberating freedmen and supporting the Union during the Civil War. Her words here engage in what scholar Brittney Cooper calls embodied discourse to reinscribe Black women in the intellectual and political labor of conceiving of Black civic life in freedom. Shadd Cary states, "The colored woman, though humble in sphere, and unendowed with worldly goods, yet led as by inspiration, not only fed and sheltered and guided in safety the prisoner soldiers of the Union when escaping from the enemy, or the soldier who was compelled to risk life itself in the struggle to break the backbone of rebellion"[30] Reminding the committee that Black women sacrificed and directly participated in the Civil War as an investment in their citizenship rights in Reconstruction, Shadd Cary revises the notion of whom Reconstruction serves and why—particularly as it became increasingly evident that politicians were failing African American communities and reconciling with "ex"-Confederates. And in response to suffragettes being barred from participation in the official commemoration of the one hundredth anniversary of the American Revolution in 1876, Shadd Cary added ninety-five D.C.-based Black women signers to the NWSA's "Women's Declaration of Rights," in protest of the exclusion. These early years in the NWSA trace her efforts to push for Black women to be considered in their agendas, but it is clear that the group is not a site where Black women's political consciousness would be crafted and organized around.

Shadd Cary's shifts in political consciousness and methods become more dramatic beginning in 1878 because she intensifies her questioning of her loyalty to, and the utility of, political parties and organizations that had failed to deliver practical means to empower Black women. In 1878 at a convention of the NWSA she announced, "colored women would support whatever party would allow them rights, be it Republican or Democratic."[31] Over the next decade a debate swelled about the race's loyalty to the Republican Party versus a growing openness to independent and Democratic party politics in response to disillusionment. Shadd Cary observed the disappearance of the party's active commitment to racial progress and Black civil rights in action and did not find the label of "race traitor" compelling enough to stay loyal to a party that was no longer vested in earning and keeping Black voters. Rhodes notes how rightful her suspicion was when in 1878 the Republican-majority Congress passed the Organic Act, which effectively disenfranchised D.C. citizens from federal elections, and then she continued to see Republican legislators block Black political appointees. Here Shadd Cary steps beyond her usual position at the margin to instead court the other political parties, certainly in order to secure publication with Democratic-leaning newspapers, but more importantly to insist African Americans act as a powerful voting bloc capable of changing parties to best pursue their full citizenship rights.[32]

Shadd Cary Founds a Black Proto-Feminist Organization in Washington, D.C.

Mary Ann Shadd Cary took up a new organizing practice when in 1880 she founded the Colored Women's Progressive Franchise Association (CWPFA) to address her unanswered calls to organize women around their financial, educational, economic, and civil rights. The series of resolutions defining the mission and stances of the association spell out an important shift in Shadd Cary's political consciousness: that for Black women to be adequately considered and empowered by political movements, those movements would need to be transformed from the ground up. Symbolic inclusion had forced Shadd Cary to invent or grab opportunities within existing agendas to then announce the particular needs of Black women, and that proved inadequate across the issues of suffrage, economics, and institutional access.

Here Shadd Cary most clearly announces her conclusion that labor rights are shaped by a web of intersecting institutions in which women were marginalized and disenfranchised, and so effective organizing needed to address those connections in an expansive agenda. The founding document states that "the Colored Women's Progressive Franchise Association proposes . . . [to] seek to obtain the ballot to look . . . after the welfare of both girls and boys in the training of the youth . . . and to work promptly for the establishment of industries and to extend the number of occupations for women."[33] Following this resolution is the proposal to "establish and support newspapers controlled by those not opposed to equal rights for the sexes and to support a paper in this country which, conducted by colored women, shall set forth the capability of their class." We can see how the resolutions echo Shadd Cary's experiences of institutional failures to address these compounded discriminations that had undermined her professional goals and her advocacy work, even as movements like the Colored Conventions explicitly organized around these issues but primarily for the benefit of men.

The mission statement continues to outline the civil rights and freedoms that needed to be included in the context of this women's group. Referring to freedom of movement through migration the association proposed that "as this is the new gospel of freedom we hail the exodus people as practical illustrations and must encourage the exodus in every way." And in referring to the right to self-defense they proposed to "enlighten the people and there will be no need of long sentences nor vigilance committees." Shadd Cary and her peers would have shared a private, perhaps unspoken knowledge or experience with the ways that racial and gender discrimination threatened their physical safety. In a moment when leading Black men tried to recuperate social authority and claims to masculinity to resist the rise of Jim Crow segregation and minstrelsy, women lived through the failures of patriarchal protection and provision that they were implicitly called to endure to stabilize Black manhood. Shadd Cary and her club members briefly gesture to the practical gains Black communities can gain if self-defense and freedom of movement become protected rights they can advance with their feminist politics. Here, the CWPFA members' point is not exercising these freedoms themselves, but rather that they delimit the scope of their authority and the epistemological difference from men they bring to conceptualizing these tenets of constitutionally protected rights.

The resolutions also outlined specific initiatives, such as founding "a banking institution, cooperative stores, another printing establishment for instruction of both sexes" and "a joint stock company," as well as a list of industries in which women should be encouraged to start their own businesses. The specificity of these initiatives articulate what Shadd Cary found critically absent from male-led labor organizing, which she had tried to give voice to from the margins but would have required a comprehensive revision of their agenda and reallocation of resources. Undergirding these initiatives is an explicit gender analysis that asserted that dismantling sexist attitudes and practices was necessary to transforming labor organizing methods if Black women were to be centered. The association proposed "to take an aggressive stand against the assumption that men alone may begin and conduct [industry]" and that "they would agitate for independence of thought and action. Interdependence among members of organized bodies or committees working in harmony with this guild and following of individual leaders." Finally, the group proposed a culture of "vigorous investigative freedom of thought and speech and prompt action, as against demagogues or against wardship." In these resolutions we see the clearest articulation of Shadd Cary and her group's understanding of the cultural and ideological work their association engaged in through organizing. In denouncing the gender discrimination embedded in conceptualizations of the public sphere, intellectual liberty, and coalition politics, the association opens up the possibility for women to lead a collective reimagining of Black communities' relationship to these formations. The problems of disharmony, corruption, and subjugation to state power is answered by the independent organizing of Black women like Shadd Cary.

Records suggest that a few meetings of the association were held in a local church, but ultimately the association never became an effective body for executing its stated goals.[34] Nevertheless, the project of this association is a major shift for Shadd Cary, not because she was unpracticed in the organizing work women did for themselves, but because she launched it as a unapologetic proto-feminist statement in response to the failures of mass movements. Shadd Cary calls for women to not only be included or tolerated across institutions and industries but to be given the power and authority over institutional functions and knowledge production. She casts a wide net in proposing Black women be enfranchised, financially independent, economically empowered, embraced by the press as authoritative contributors, and masters of their own education and training, as well as that of their communities. This proto-feminist approach to organizing understood that activism in a narrowly defined single field would not be effective because of the ways that the effects of racial and gender discrimination interlocked across institutions, necessitating rights and protections in all aspects of their lives. Likewise, there is a proto-womanist ethic that pervades the policies of including and centering the needs of women, children, and the poor, as their collective vulnerability to economic oppression affects one another.

I assert that the association's mission statement serves as a significant link between Shadd Cary and the Black clubwomen's movement, bridging the disjuncture between her vision and the unprecedented successes of a movement that encompassed and advanced the work of her defunct group. Working in the interstices between Black-male labor organizing and white women's suffrage, Shadd Cary embarked on developing Black women's leadership and political thought that centered their particular needs. In 1895 Black women from across the country who had been organizing locally for the same agenda as Shadd Cary came together in Washington, D.C., and formed the National Federation of Afro-American Women. Meeting again in Washington, D.C., the following year, the federation joined with another league of clubwomen to form the National Association of Colored Women (NACW), an organization that exists to this day. The first convention in 1895 was organized by Josephine St. Pierre Ruffin, editor of the *Woman's Era*, the newspaper organ of the movement since 1894 and composed of contributions from Black clubwomen across the country. That Mary Ann Shadd Cary voiced strong opinions and led cutting-edge ventures throughout her life has made it easy to frame her as exceptional and disconnected from more palatable or less radical movements.[35] However, the arc of Black clubwomen's organizing would come to align with her politics and methods just a few years after she passed in 1893, and the impact of her leadership and vision reverberates through the records of her association and her writings critiquing the apathy and resistance she faced as a suffragist. And as I reflect on the unorthodoxy of locating Shadd Cary manifestos in convention proceedings, NWSA archives in Shadd Cary's papers at Howard University, and Black clubwomen's archives in the founding sketches of Shadd Cary's failed club, I remain encouraged. The prospects of scholarship that seeks to bridge the gaps Black women's histories and intellectual contributions fall through will find them in surprising places and in turn transform the ways we remember the movements they labored in.

Notes

1. Mary Ann Shadd Cary is celebrated as the first Black woman newspaper editor in North America, for the Canadian newspaper she founded in 1853 called the *Provincial Freeman*. Apart from Shadd Cary's Canadian descendants' efforts to remember and honor her, scholars have contributed substantially to memorializing her contributions to Black cultural and political movements. That scholarship is largely indebted to comprehensive biographies of Mary Ann Shadd Cary's full life and legacy. See Jane Rhodes, *Mary Ann Shadd Cary: The Black Press and*

Protest in the Nineteenth Century (Bloomington: Indiana University Press, 1998); Jim Bearden and Linda Jean Butler, *Shadd: The Life and Times of Mary Shadd Cary* (Toronto: NC Press, 1977).

2. Rhodes, *Mary Ann Shadd Cary*, 163–65.

3. Here I use Brittney Cooper's concept of "embodied discourse" as a term to encompass the ways Black women in speech, writing, and action made their bodies and interior lives publicly visible to make them knowable subjects, having epistemological authority that shapes a clear set of politics. For more on embodied discourse, see Brittney C. Cooper, *Beyond Respectability: The Intellectual Thought of Race Women* (Urbana: University of Illinois Press, 2017), 40–41.

4. This proliferation is known as the Black clubwomen's movement, a national network of local clubs founded and run predominantly by educated Black women with financial means and political acumen. These clubs transformed the institutional landscape of Black America, building a safety net and culture of race-based collective self-improvement called "racial uplift." My work here and in other forthcoming manuscripts considers the archival, intellectual, and literary legacies of the club movements. For a description of the rise of and challenges to independent Black women's organizing, see Martha S. Jones, *All Bound Up Together: The Woman Question in African American Public Culture, 1830–1900* (Chapel Hill: University of North Carolina Press, 2007), 171, 176, 179–80; Rhodes, *Mary Ann Shadd Cary*, 191–92.

5. Jones, *All Bound Up Together*, 176.

6. Cooper, *Beyond Respectability*, 50.

7. For scholarship focused on Mary Ann Shadd Cary's place and effect on Canadian and Black Canadian studies (which also focus on her early life as a result), see Kristin Moriah, "'A Greater Compass of Voice': Elizabeth Taylor Greenfield and Mary Ann Shadd Cary Navigate Black Performance," *Theatre Research in Canada* 41, no. 1 (2020): 20–38; Christian Olbey, "Unfolded Hands: Class Suicide and the Insurgent Intellectual Praxis of Mary Ann Shadd," *Canadian Review of American Studies* 30, no. 2 (2000): 151–74; and Rinaldo Walcott, "'Who Is She and What Is She to You?': Mary Ann Shadd Cary and the (Im)Possibility of Black/Canadian Studies," *Atlantis* 24, no. 2 (2000): 137–46.

8. For scholarship on Mary Ann Shadd Cary that centers on her early life, see Elizabeth Cali, "'Why Does Not Somebody Speak Out?': Mary Ann Shadd Gary's Heteroglossic Black Protofeminist Nationalism," *Vitae Scholasticae* 32, no. 2 (2015): 32–48; Carolyn Calloway-Thomas, "Mary Ann Shadd Cary: Crafting Black Culture Through Empirical and Moral Arguments," *Howard Journal of Communications* 24, no. 3 (2013): 239–56; Jim Casey, "Parsing the Special Characters of African American Print Culture: Mary Ann Shadd and the * Limits of Search," in *Against a Sharp White Background: Infrastructures of African American Print*, ed. Brigitte Fielder and Jonathan Senchyne (Madison: University of Wisconsin Press, 2019) 109–28; Jennifer Bernhardt Steadman, "Traveling Uplift: Mary Ann Shadd Cary Creates and Connects Black Communities," in *Traveling Economies: American Women's Travel Writing* (Columbus: Ohio State University Press, 2007), 85–111; Carol B. Conaway, "Mary Ann Shadd Cary: A Visionary of the Black Press," in *Black Women's Intellectual Traditions: Speaking Their Minds*, ed. Kristin Waters and Carol B. Conaway (Burlington: University of Vermont Press, 2007), 216–54; and Shirley J. Yee, *Black Women Abolitionists: A Study in Activism, 1828–1860* (Knoxville: University of Tennessee Press, 1992).

9. Cali, "'Why Does Not Somebody Speak Out?,'" 40.

10. Kate Masur, *An Example for All the Land: Emancipation and the Struggle over Equality in Washington, D.C.* (Chapel Hill: University of North Carolina Press, 2010) 28, 31–33.

11. Shadd Cary taught at the Lincoln Mission School and later at the Second District Grammar School, positions she likely secured from her long relationship with the American

Missionary Association, which founded schools serving Black students across North America. Despite being at the forefront of controversy around building and funding Black schools in Washington, D.C., while racial segregation and animus attempted to make Black schooling inferior, Shadd Cary successfully fought for her schools to provide education for both genders on par with white students. As a field in which women's contributions were acceptable within Victorian gender norms, perhaps Shadd Cary's success here can be explained in part due to structural affordances that were not available in the other arenas of her work that are marked by marginalization and silencing. See Rhodes, *Mary Ann Shadd Cary*, 176–77.

12. Rhodes, *Mary Ann Shadd Cary*, 186–87.

13. Rhodes, *Mary Ann Shadd Cary*, 209–10.

14. Rhodes, *Mary Ann Shadd Cary*, 195–96.

15. See Cali, "'Why Does Not Somebody Speak Out?'"; Casey, "Parsing the Special Characters."

16. Rhodes, *Mary Ann Shadd Cary*, 193, 198.

17. Rhodes, *Mary Ann Shadd Cary*, 202.

18. Rhodes, *Mary Ann Shadd Cary*, 199.

19. P. Gabrielle Foreman, "Black Organizing, Print Advocacy, and Collective Authorship," in *The Colored Conventions Movement: Black Organizing in the Nineteenth Century*, ed. P. Gabrielle Foreman, Jim Casey, and Sarah Lynn Patterson (Chapel Hill: University of North Carolina Press, 2021), 24.

20. *Proceedings of the Colored National Labor Convention: Held in Washington, D.C., December 6th, 7th, 8th, 9th, and 10th, 1869* (Washington, D.C., 1869), 13, Colored Conventions Project Digital Records, https://omeka.coloredconventions.org/items/show/591.

21. *Proceedings*, 13.

22. *Proceedings*, 21.

23. *Proceedings*, 21.

24. *Proceedings*, 21.

25. Anna Julia Cooper, *A Voice from the South* (Xenia, OH: Aldine Printing House, 1892), 31.

26. *Proceedings of the Colored National Labor Convention*, 22.

27. Rhodes, *Mary Ann Shadd Cary*, 193.

28. See Kirsten Lee's chapter ("Mary Ann Shadd in Mexico") in this volume.

29. Mary Ann Shadd Cary, "Speech, to Judiciary Committee re the Right of Women" (draft), 3, Digital Howard (2020), https://dh.howard.edu/mscary_speeches/2. Mary Ann Shadd Cary, "Speech, to Judiciary Committee re the Right of Women" (draft, ca. 1874).

30. Shadd Cary, "Speech," 5–6.

31. Rhodes, *Mary Ann Shadd Cary*, 197.

32. Rhodes, *Mary Ann Shadd Cary*, 206.

33. "Colored Women's Progressive Franchise Assn [*sic*]," mission statement, ca. 1880, Digital Howard (2020), https://dh.howard.edu/mscary_org/1.

34. Rhodes, *Mary Ann Shadd Cary*, 202.

35. Cali, "'Why Does Not Somebody Speak Out?,'" 32.

PART IV

"Subjects Better Understood,
and Within Her Sphere"

Black Digital Humanities

CHAPTER 9

Dimensions of Scale

Invisible Labor, Editorial Work, and the Future of Quantitative Literary Studies

LAUREN KLEIN

This essay, which considers the current use and future potential of quantitative methods in literary studies, is set in an unexpected place: the Canadian town of Windsor, located just across the river from Detroit, at what was then—in the spring of 1853, when this account begins—the terminus of Canada's Great Western Railway.[1] Windsor was also, then, the adoptive home of the abolitionist and educator Mary Ann Shadd (1823–93), who had emigrated there eighteen months earlier, from Delaware via New York, with the intention of opening a school.[2] Shadd opened her school shortly after her arrival in Windsor, but near-constant financial strain, coupled with the complex politics that surrounded her educational vision—she insisted on teaching Black and white children together—proved too much to bear. And so on March 23, 1853, Shadd made the difficult decision to shutter the school. The very next day, she published the first issue of her newspaper, the *Provincial Freeman*. In so doing, she earned distinction—and, more recently, coverage in the *New York Times*—as the first Black woman to edit a newspaper in North America (Specia).

But Shadd herself did not take credit for this achievement—at least for several years.[3] The inaugural issue of the *Freeman* listed Samuel Ringgold Ward, a more prominent Black abolitionist, as well as an orator and a minister, as its editor. (Ward was also, crucially, a man.) Astute readers would have taken note of an anonymous apology also printed in the issue, likely authored by Shadd, that explained: "As Mr. Ward is obliged to perform other labors for a livelihood, it is impossible for him to give the attention to the paper that he would were his pecuniary interests connected to it" ("Apology"). But the only textual indication that Shadd was "the real power behind the newspaper," as her biographer Jane Rhodes explains, was a short sentence printed under the masthead: "Letters must be addressed, *Post-paid*, to Mary A. Shadd, Windsor, Canada West" (74).

In this way, Shadd's editorial work exemplifies what is often called "invisible labor," a term that has come to encompass the various forms of labor that are literally invisible because they take place out of sight, or economically invisible because they take place away from the marketplace.[4] As several generations of feminist labor studies scholars have observed, it is both a cause and an effect of this invisibility that these forms of labor are undervalued and undercredited (or uncredited altogether) in the end result. The project of infusing value and credit into invisible labor—of making this labor visible to the eyes and to the economy—is a feminist one because, among other reasons, the primary example of invisible labor is unpaid domestic work, which has historically been performed by women.[5] The example of another nineteenth-century woman newspaper editor, the white abolitionist Lydia Maria Child (1802–80), underscores this point. As Child wrote in a letter to a friend in November 1841, "In addition to what men editors have to perform, I am obliged to do my own washing and ironing, mending and making, besides manifold stitches for my husband's comfort" (qtd. in Karcher 271). Also invisible in these lines is Child's whiteness, which enabled her to work both in her home and at her paper without being required to contend with the "specificity of racial difference" that, as Xiomara Santamarina has shown, marked the experiences of Black working women in the nineteenth-century United States (11).[6] But in this prototypal feminist complaint, one thing comes clearly into view: editing, like "washing and ironing, mending and making," is, emphatically, work.[7]

This essay takes up the editorial work of Shadd and Child, two women separated by race but connected by their commitment to abolition, in order to explore the degrees of visibility of the labor documented in the print record of the nineteenth-century United States. In this regard, it offers an additional layer of evidence in support of the argument advanced by Carla L. Peterson, Pier Gabrielle Foreman, and more recently, Manisha Sinha, among others, that positions women, and Black women in particular, at abolition's vanguard. I show how both women employed editing as a method of community formation and, in the case of Shadd, of staging (in the sense of both preparing for and performing) an alternative, possible world.[8] By comparing the contents of Shadd's and Child's newspapers through quantitative means, I am able to more clearly describe the nature of Shadd's contributions to that world-building project, as well as to what Derrick R. Spires has recently described as the "new forms of living and of articulating life" that nineteenth-century Black periodical culture enabled (17).

The example of these two women's editorial work, together, also punctuates an argument about invisible labor as it relates to the application of quantitative methods in the field of literary studies today. Largely because of the appeal of distant reading, both as a concept and a phrase, those who make use of quantitative methods in their work tend to frame their interventions in terms of the novel perspective that is afforded by a distant view. For example, Ted Underwood, in *Distant Horizons*, in describing his interest in exploring "the sweep of long timelines," analogizes the insights prompted by this perspective to how "the curve of the horizon only becomes visible some distance above the earth" (xxi, xi). While Underwood acknowledges that a distant view is "not enough, by itself, to give linguistic details a literary meaning" and that his approach is only "one of several possible ways" to move forward under the rubric of distant reading, he leaves unchallenged the emphasis on broad contours and generalizable patterns that is encouraged by a perspective of distance (xi, xxi). And while Richard Jean So and Edwin Roland, in this same tradition, seek to develop a "critical distant reading" practice that can account for the outliers, and other meaningful differences, that are often elided in analyses of text at scale, they nonetheless leave the structuring axis of *distant* and *close* intact. But there are additional insights that quantitative methods can help bring to light once their capabilities are imagined beyond the boundaries of *distant* and *close*. These insights require contextual framing—and feminist thinking—in order to be revealed.[9]

It is not a coincidence that many of these insights have to do with issues relating to women, to Black people, and to other minoritized groups. As Donna Haraway has observed, the technology of distance often obscures nondominant perspectives. But by expanding the conceptual dimensions of quantitative literary studies to include additional axes of inquiry—such as the axis extending from the visible to the invisible, as the example of editorial work suggests—we might begin to conceive of additional approaches that, instead of emphasizing the totalizing perspective granted by a distant view, seek to refract multiple perspectives on a greater scale. These perspectives come into focus by considering the context that surrounds the production of a particular body of work, as well as the actual bodies of those who labored to produce it. These perspectives are also, importantly, rarely assimilable into a unified whole. But by placing them within a multidimensional space of inquiry, we can explore their tensions as well as their alignments. And by focusing on the relations among these perspectives, quantification can become a powerful technique indeed, one that works to enhance the legibility of key textual details, thereby amplifying their significance.

To be clear: by enlisting a comparison between Shadd's and Child's editorial work in the service of an argument about the uses of quantitative methods in literary studies, I do not intend to elide the complexities of gender and race that the comparison introduces; nor do I intend to efface the fact that both women could choose to labor at a time when others remained enslaved. On the contrary, it is in support of their shared effort to extract work from enslavement and to envision new forms of collectivity and citizenship that, as I will argue, quantitative methods can be more purposefully deployed. I also do not intend to suggest that these women understood their editorial work as invisible labor, or even in more general feminist terms.[10] Rather, it is for us in the present—and I speak to literary scholars, and to others in the humanities, who hope to employ quantitative methods in their work—that these ideas about invisible labor are most instructive, for they shape what questions we think to ask, and attempt to answer, about the knowledge work of the past.

In calling for a conceptual reorientation from the axis of *distant* and *close* to a space defined by multiple dimensions of scale, I seek to make the case that quantitative methods can be used to probe the research questions about gender, race, and their intersection with labor that have thus far proved difficult (although certainly not impossible) to explore.[11] In the discussion that follows, I employ one set of such methods—namely, topic modeling followed by a statistical analysis—in order to show how quantification can help to surface certain aspects of editorial labor that would otherwise be difficult to see directly. I also show how the newspapers that constitute my corpus record a range of forms of labor—physical and emotional as well as intellectual—that we might better value and describe. Extending the example of editorial work to the labor required to perform quantitative work today, I demonstrate how the field of quantitative literary studies demands a broader conceptual frame. This expanded frame—one defined by the dimensions of distance, visibility, and others that future scholars must name—is required lest we continue to render invisible the additional forms of labor in which Shadd and Child engaged.

Surfacing Invisible Editorial Work Through Topic Modeling

In 1841, eight years before Shadd authored her first publication—a letter to Frederick Douglass, which he printed in his own newspaper, the *North Star*—Child assumed the helm of the *National Anti-Slavery Standard*. As the first woman to be named the editor of an abolitionist newspaper—and the official newspaper of the American Anti-Slavery Society (AASS) at that—Child knew she was entering an ideological battleground. Less than a year earlier, at the 1840 AASS annual meeting, the organization had split over several key issues, including the relation of women's rights to civil rights, the value (or lack thereof) of abiding by established political protocols, and the eroding moral authority of white religious leaders. But those who remained affiliated with the AASS were still not united. Was it better for the remaining AASS members to attempt to coalesce around the most basic goal, that of abolishing slavery? Or would it be a better strategy to shift the entire organization toward a more radical position? And regardless of any change to the AASS platform, how might the organization, which remained mostly white, work to establish more equal relationships between its white and Black members, and between itself and Black antislavery groups? Racial disparities had long been apparent to many of the movement's Black constituencies, of course, but they were becoming increasingly difficult for the white members of the AASS to ignore.

Despite these conflicts, Child committed herself to holding her personal course. As she later wrote in her farewell editorial, looking back on her two-year tenure as editor, "I am not aware that any of these whirling eddies have, at any time, made me swerve one hair's breadth from the course I had marked out for myself." That course, she goes on to explain, was guided by her own conscience and by a deliberate editorial strategy: to insert a "large proportion of literary and miscellaneous matter" into the paper as part of what she characterized as an "honest, open trick." Her gambit was that she might entice additional readers, primarily women and children, to "look candidly at [the] anti-slavery principles" that they might not have encountered otherwise ("Farewell" 190). Through the inclusion of less overtly political genres—news items, short stories, recipes, and even her own creative works—Child hoped to increase the numbers of those committed to the abolitionist cause.

It is important to emphasize that Child is speaking literally when she describes the process of inserting this literary and miscellaneous matter into her paper. Only one or two of Child's own editorials appeared in each issue.

The remainder of the material consisted of a handful of articles from other correspondents, both official and unofficial. In the mid-nineteenth century, few newspapers could claim large numbers of staff writers, if they could claim any at all. In most cases, it was the task of the editor to, quite literally, fill up the page. There was usually only one person—and sometimes two or three—who served as editor at any given time (although assistant editors, publishers, printers, and compositors often helped). The editor filled the issue primarily by selecting relevant content from elsewhere; this is the "culture of reprinting" that, as Meredith McGill has demonstrated, characterized much of the literary landscape of the antebellum United States. Editors either inserted borrowed content, as Child describes, often with a line or two of introduction, or they condensed or expanded it so that it would fit in a particular location on the page—at times working with the printer and compositor to rearrange the type itself. (In the smallest of operations, the editor and printer were often one and the same.) This work was therefore both physical and intellectual, in ways difficult to disentangle. It was also both visible and invisible, in ways that the technique of topic modeling can help unfold.

Topic modeling is a technique that derives from the field of machine learning, which employs an iterative, probabilistic method to identify groups of words, or "topics," that tend to appear together in the same document in statistically significant ways.[12] The technique was first developed in the 1990s through research funded by the Defense Advanced Research Projects Agency (DARPA). This work was aimed at automatically detecting changes in newswire text, so that governmental and military institutions could be alerted to emerging geopolitical events.[13] Early in the first decade of the twenty-first century, with the release of MALLET, a software toolkit for generating topic models (among other document classification and clustering models), the technique began to see more mainstream use. And in the 2010s topic modeling began to be deployed in digital humanities research—for example, by Lisa Rhody to probe the gendered language of ekphrastic poetry ("Topic Modeling"), by Rachel Buurma to explore Anthony Trollope's six-volume Barsetshire series, and by Jo Guldi to model the history of infrastructure in England.[14]

Topic modeling is a method that is described as unsupervised, because, while the scholar is responsible for assembling the set of documents to analyze and for writing the code that runs the topic model, the scholar does not specify which particular topics to look for in advance. Rather, the scholar specifies the number of topics to look for, and through a process of sampling—that is, by repeatedly selecting a topic for each word at random, on the basis of a probability distribution that is refined as the model becomes fitted to the data—the topics themselves become more refined and coherent over time.[15] Because the sampling process relies on random selection, the model yields a slightly different set of topics each time the code is run. This aspect of topic modeling inference is important to acknowledge, as Nan Z. Da also emphasizes in her criticism of how topic modeling has been applied in literary contexts. But unlike Da, who dismisses the technique because of the variability that the sampling process necessarily produces, as well as her belief that it lacks "meaningful applications" in the field of literary studies (625), I align myself with others across the humanities who employ topic modeling in their work in maintaining that the technique can lead to powerful insights when purposefully deployed and properly interpreted. I maintain, moreover, that we might find yet more meaningful applications of topic modeling when considering its uses within an expanded conceptual frame.

As an example of how the deployment of a topic model can be informed by ideas about invisibility as well as of distance, and of how context can be brought to bear on the interpretation of its output, consider how a topic model of a set of abolitionist newspapers can be used to better understand Child's strategy of editorial *copia*. How might we surface the invisible editorial work that went into her purposeful selection of the "miscellaneous matter" she introduced into the *Standard*, to phrase the question in more precise terms? And what of Shadd's similarly invisible editorial work, which we know she performed but, because of personal preference, social pressure, archival politics, or some combination of the three, is not documented for us in the present in as much detail? Framed in this way, topic modeling becomes a meaningful analytical tool indeed: it not only enables a view from a distance but also helps bring to light certain invisible aspects of knowledge production.

In the set of topics in Table 9.1—the ten most prevalent topics, of one hundred topics total, among the abolitionist newspapers in a corpus of nineteenth-century newspapers—the broader context into which Shadd and Child inserted their editorial efforts begins to cohere.[16] I constructed this list by performing some simple math on the output of a topic model that I ran on the newspaper corpus. I added up the proportion of each topic in each article in each paper identified as abolitionist in focus. (Among the outputs of a topic model is a breakdown of the proportion of each topic in each article.) I then sorted those sums from most to least prevalent and converted the proportions to percentages. Table 9.1 displays the ten most prevalent topics in

Table 9.1. The Ten Most Prevalent Topics in the Abolitionist Newspapers in the Corpus

Topic	Label	Percentage	Keywords
T65	U.S. politics	1.47%	party, democratic, whig, free, vote, political, election, parties, convention, democracy
T16	Abolition	1.43%	slavery, anti, abolitionists, american, society, abolition, pro, slave, liberty, garrison
T84	Rhetoric of action	1.36%	question, subject, opinion, public, duty, views, action, matter, regard, opinions
T89	Slavery and freedom	1.35%	freedom, liberty, free, god, land, slave, human, slavery, humanity, rights
T42	Formal	1.35%	society, meeting, friends, held, annual, county, organizing, anti, present, members
T10	Emotion	1.29%	heart, life, love, death, soul, heaven, earth, hope, grave, tears
T69	Political power	1.28%	political, great, power, public, influence, present, system, interests, progress, men
T11	Nature and summer	1.27%	bright, flowers, light, sweet, beauty, sun, summer, beautiful, fair, green
T93	Christianity	1.27%	god, christ, lord, bible, day, jesus, holy, christian, faith, spirit
T87	Religion and morality	1.26%	christian, moral, men, man, human, god, principles, evil, sin, religion

abolitionist newspapers, with the topic that makes up the largest proportion of those titles at the top of the list.

Each topic is identified by the letter "T" followed by a number between zero and ninety-nine. The number in the column marked "Percentage" is the aggregate percentage of the contents of all articles in the abolitionist newspapers in the corpus (several hundred thousand articles total) that the model has determined to be composed of that topic. The final column, "Keywords," shows the ten words most strongly associated with the topic. For example, in the topic most prevalent in the set of all antislavery newspapers, T65, the word "party" most often appears together with the words "democratic," "whig," "free," "vote," and so on. From this set of words, one could make the assessment that this topic is about politics. From the second, T16, in which the word "slavery" appears with "anti," "abolitionists," "american," and so on, one might conclude that this topic tackles issues of abolition and, perhaps, the role of the various antislavery societies trying to achieve it.

Researchers usually give short names to the topics so as to be able to refer to them more clearly; these are in the column marked "Label" in Table 9.1. I am singling out this feature because it is important to underscore that while the words associated with each topic are algorithmically determined, the label for each topic is chosen by the scholar who interprets the results. Below, I have labeled T65, the most prevalent topic at 1.47% of all abolitionist papers, "U.S. politics." The next topic, T16, at 1.43%, I have labeled "abolition." The next most prevalent topic is one that includes rhetorical language, and so on. It is not surprising that most abolitionist newspapers contain articles that discuss politics and abolition and that they frequently use rhetorical calls to action. But this is solid evidence that a topic model of these newspapers can yield meaningful results.

The model becomes more intriguing when looking at the topics that characterize specific newspapers and editors, such as the papers edited by Child and Shadd. The next two sets of topics (Tables 9.2 and 9.3) show, first, the topics associated with the *National Anti-Slavery Standard* during its entire editorial run and, second, the topics associated with the *Standard* only during

Table 9.2. The Ten Most Significant Topics in the *National Anti-Slavery Standard*

Topic	Label	PMI	Keywords
T49	Places	1.54	ohio, philadelphia, mass, office, york, miller, penn, standard, thomas, free
T32	Miscellaneous	1.48	table, york, duty, free, street, fair, ad, cotton, good, ads
T91	Shopping	1.10	street, philadelphia, books, goods, hand, prices, store, cases, assortment, attention
T46	Ads for dry goods	0.87	cents, corn, flour, wheat, american, advance, made, paper, dry goods, white
T16	Abolition	0.87	slavery, anti, abolitionists, american, society, abolition, pro, slave, liberty, garrison
T7	Organizing	0.52	friends, aid, fair, money, work, make, means, committee, time, funds
T2	Time	0.38	time, made, found, left, place, day, return, received, immediately, told
T62	War and annexation	0.37	texas, mexico, war, states, united, expansion, california, mexican, government, country
T42	Formal	0.36	society, meeting, friends, held, annual, county, anti, organizing, present, members
T97	Slavery	0.24	slave, slaves, slavery, free, master, negroes, states, property, slaveholders, emancipation

Table 9.3. The Ten Most Significant Topics in the *National Anti-Slavery Standard* While Child Was Editor

Topic	Label	PMI	Keywords
T70	Cooking and recipes	0.88	water, put, half, sugar, pound, cold, milk, salt, add, butter
T26	Foreign relations	0.63	united, government, states, american, cuba, foreign, relations, british, treaty, trade
T49	Places	0.63	ohio, philadelphia, mass, office, york, miller, penn, standard, thomas, free
T40	Correspondence	0.53	letter, office, post, letters, received, written, send, addressed, department, general
T42	Formal	0.49	society, meeting, friends, held, annual, county, anti, organizing, present, members
T14	Massachusetts	0.45	boston, mass, rev, john, wm, george, salem, charles, samuel, esq
T25	Travel and accidents	0.44	fire, railroad, city, train, boston, cars, company, accidents, york, road
T35	Federal government	0.40	house, congress, district, petition, representatives, adams, legislature, petitions, people, columbia
T9	Violence and crime	0.39	house, man, shot, negro, murder, mob, night, city, arrested, men
T5	State government	0.38	state, law, laws, act, states, citizens, person, persons, united, legislature

the time that Child served as editor. Here, rather than rank the topics by raw percentage, I rank them in terms of a statistical measure called pointwise mutual information (PMI). PMI is used to quantify the degree of association between a specific feature and a particular category so that the feature can then be ranked. (The number itself is a unitless measure; unlike inches or pounds, it does not correspond to a fixed measure in the world, and it is used for ranking purposes only.) In terms of my analysis, the features consist of the one hundred topics generated by the model. I then consider those features in relation to two categories: all articles published in the *National Anti-Slavery Standard* over the course of the twenty-five years represented in the corpus (Table 9.2), and then only the articles published in the *Standard* while Child was the editor (Table 9.3).

Put more simply, PMI enables the topics to be ranked not by their overall prevalence in the corpus (or in a subset of the corpus, as in Table 9.1) but rather by the strength of their association with a particular subset of the corpus. This ranking scheme can yield significant insight, as a comparison between Table 9.1 and Tables 9.2 and 9.3 makes clear. Table 9.1 demonstrates that the abolitionist newspapers in the corpus discuss the topics related to abolition more than any other topics in the corpus; this is a known finding of the sort that Da criticizes in her essay. But when we can identify which topics uniquely mark one particular paper, as in Table 9.2, or one particular editor's oversight of a paper, as in Table 9.3, the topics generated by the model become meaningful indeed. For this editorial oversight—the decision to insert certain topics and de-emphasize others—is the result of the intellectual and physical labor that Child describes in her editorial and in which all nineteenth-century newspaper editors—Shadd also among them—invisibly engaged.

In the list of topics in Table 9.3, we see the invisible aspects of Child's editorial labor refracted through a new lens. Her personal correspondence—not to mention her name on the *Standard*'s masthead—attests to the fact that she performed this work. Scholars have been able to point to specific editorials she composed or to specific articles she chose to reprint, but until now they have lacked the ability to describe the contours of her editorial work at this level of scale. The ranking of the topics reveals a paper fairly evenly split between political topics (T26, T42, T35, and T5) and the "miscellaneous material" that Child deployed as an editorial ruse. The topic model helps give additional shape to the effort she expended to balance the material that directly engaged issues relating to slavery and its abolition with the other types of content that she believed would indirectly, albeit no less powerfully, advance the abolitionist cause.

Looking at the topic model with a more focused lens, we might consider the significance of the topic most strongly associated with Child's tenure as editor of the *Standard*: T70, which centers on cooking ingredients and instructions. Child had a reason to be interested in cooking: in the late 1820s, she had authored a best-selling cookbook. But the high ranking of T70 points to how Child also wielded her interest in cooking as part of her strategy to compel more women to ally themselves with the abolitionist cause. It has been documented that the readership of the *Standard* swelled to 16,000 less than a year after Child assumed its helm—a huge number for its day, when a successful subscriber list numbered in the low hundreds. In explaining this response, scholars have pointed to the inclusion of specific features, such as the personal essays that would later be collected as *Letters from New-York*, as well as to the evidence that Child herself offers, in her farewell editorial, about her desire to make the *Standard* a "family newspaper" ("Farewell" 190). But the high ranking of a topic that explicitly deals with family matters provides additional evidence on a scale that cannot be perceived by a single reader. It confirms, moreover, how the ranking of topics can be considered evidence of the specific themes Child used to achieve her editorial feat.

Considered as a conceptual whole, the ranked topics also stand in for the additional forms of editorial labor that we cannot—and can never—see. We know from other evidence, such as Child's personal correspondence during her time as editor of the *Standard*, that she was indeed performing this work. In a letter written in March 1842 (Figure 9.1), after a merger with the *Pennsylvania Freeman* (after which the *Provincial Freeman* was named) required her to republish large amounts of its content in her paper, she laments, "I cannot manage the paper at all as I would. Public documents of one kind or another crowd upon me, and since the union with the *Freeman*, I am flooded with communications, mostly of an ordinary character." In the letter, Child describes the work of rewriting almost all this "ordinary" content, but even

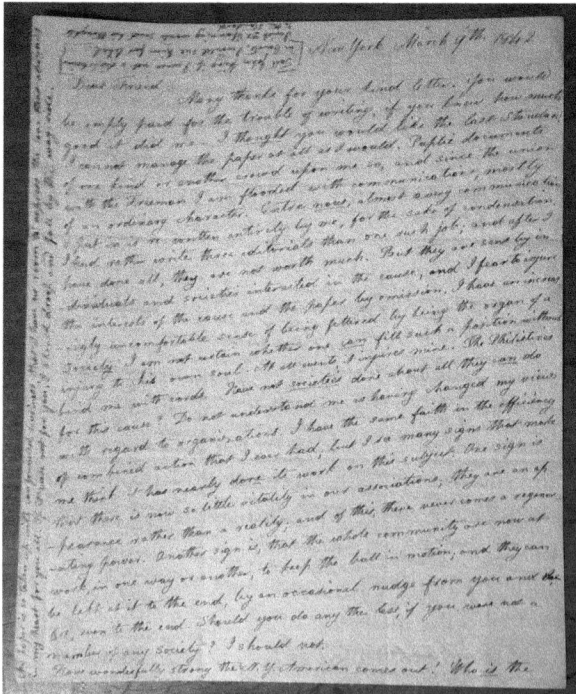

Figure 9.1. Lydia Maria Child's letter to Ellis Gray Loring, March 9, 1842. Courtesy of Manuscripts and Archives Division, Manuscript Collection 532, New York Public Library.

after that, she notes that "they are not worth much." She describes her desire to make more room for her own editorials, but with the "flood" of "communications," she cannot find enough space: "I fear to injure the interest of the cause and the paper by omission!" she exclaims (Letter to Ellis Gray Loring).

In Child's letter is found, on the one hand, an additional justification for a quantitative approach to analyzing the *Standard*. Her description of the "flood" of ordinary communications that has crowded out more important news suggests that even Child herself believes that her readers should be more selective in what they read. But on the other hand, the letter provides evidence of a form of intellectual labor that cannot be precisely located by any literary research method. Child's own arguments—the "three editorials" that she claims she would have written had she not been consumed by her editorial work—never made it out of her head. For this reason, we do not have the text of those editorials to analyze, nor do we have a clear indication of all the rewriting she claims to have done. Nevertheless, we can visit the Manuscripts and Archives Division of the New York Public Library, where this letter is housed, as I did while conducting my research, and contemplate the gaps in the printed record that are, paradoxically, documented on another page. Together with the editorials that Child was able to publish, and with the topics that point to her invisible editorial work, this letter brings us closer to acknowledging the full range of labor—the various forms it entailed and the degrees of effort it involved—that Child contributed to the abolitionist cause.

Invisible Editorial Labor and Its Physical Toll

In the section called "Communications" in the March 23, 1849, issue of the *North Star*, the newspaper edited by Frederick Douglass, readers encountered a letter that likely elicited a pause. "We should do more and talk less," the letter states, expressing no uncertain degree of frustration at the lack of progress from the abolitionist movement over the course of the previous several years and, in particular, at the organizing then taking place at the "colored conventions."[17] The letter goes on to excoriate the "corrupt clergy" for "inculcating ignorance as a duty, superstition as true religion," before concluding that the "possibility of final success" would hinge not on religious leaders but on teachers, who must convey to their students "the possibility of bringing about the desired end ourselves, and not waiting for the whites of the country to do so." The letter is signed "M. A. Shadd"—Mary Ann, of course, who was living in Wilmington, Delaware, and working as a teacher at the time (Shadd, "Wilmington").

Just two years later, in 1851, Shadd would heed her own advice to "do more and talk less" when she emigrated to Canada—and, just two years after that, launched her newspaper. A letter penned on the occasion of the paper's second anniversary, in 1854, attests to the range of effort that her commitment to action entailed: "That you have had formidable difficulties to contend with, in relation to your enterprise, none will doubt how much labor, activity, and ability that is required to fill the post of Editor, Publisher and Financier, all at the same time," wrote Shadd's friend and confidant, William Still (qtd. in Rhodes 97–98). As evidenced by this letter, and by those who had the opportunity to observe her at work, Shadd took on nearly all the roles required to keep the paper in print. And yet unlike Child, whose name was emblazoned on the masthead of the *Standard*, Shadd—who did not list herself as the editor of the paper until the final year of its run—could not claim formal credit for this broad scope of work.[18]

However, looking at the topics most associated with the *Freeman*, which were generated using the same method described above, we get a clearer sense of what was entailed by this "labor, activity, and ability" (Table 9.4). The top two topics, T57 and T8, offer a strong indication of the paper's international focus—a focus that Rhodes has also observed. Even the topic relating to U.S. politics, T26, farther down the list, has an international focus: "Cuba" and "British" are among its most significant terms.[19] (Recall that the political topics that dominated the abolitionist papers overall, listed in Table 9.1, had more to do with the internal workings of the federal legislature.) The topics that have to do with travel and transportation, T43 and T0, as well as T25, which also appears in Table 9.3 as a topic in the *Standard* during Child's tenure, suggest an additional emphasis on emigration, which is consistent with what scholars have argued about Shadd's personal politics. And T43 and T56, both of which have to do with animals and nature, reflect Shadd's attempt to engage with her rural setting. Also as in the topics associated with the *Standard* while Child served as editor, the recipe topic, T70, is featured quite prominently. And as they did in the analysis of Child's tenure at the *Standard*, these topics, taken together, represent the less visible but no less important aspects of editorial work—namely, the careful curation of content required for the paper to speak to a local and regional audience, as well as to advance larger social and political goals.

Table 9.4 The Ten Most Significant Topics in the *Provincial Freeman*

Topic	Label	PMI	Keywords
T57	Europe	0.97	french, france, russia, paris, england, emperor, austria, london, government, europe
T8	Britain and colonialism	0.90	england, british, lord, west, london, india, great, english, canada, colonies
T70	Cooking and recipes	0.71	water, put, half, sugar, pound, cold, milk, salt, add, butter
T25	Travel and accidents	0.57	fire, railroad, city, train, boston, cars, company, york, road, accident
T43	Nature and land	0.52	miles, land, river, country, great, west, indian, lake, mountains, indians
T0	Sea travel	0.46	board, captain, ship, vessel, boat, sea, port, steamer, vessels, capt
T56	Nature and animals	0.41	head, dog, tree, animal, long, bird, black, dogs, young, birds
T26	Foreign relations	0.35	united, government, states, american, cuba, foreign, british, treaty, trade, president
T29	Labor	0.33	labor, work, poor, people, land, condition, men, industry, laborers, wealth
T76	Family and work	0.32	man, house, boy, money, master, wife, father, young, children, years

Perhaps most significant for an argument about the ideological stakes of the abolitionist movement, however, is that the topics that best characterize the *Freeman* do not contain any of the topics centered on slavery and its abolition (unlike those in Table 9.1). The topics associated with the *Freeman* would thus seem to confirm the argument made by Spires, discussed at the outset of this essay, as well as those of other scholars of the Black press, such as Frances Smith Foster, who have established how "people of African descent used their print culture to help reinvent themselves as African Americans and to construct African America" (Foster 715). A thematic analysis of the *Freeman* contributes an additional layer of evidence to these arguments, offering a high-level perspective on the nature and scope of the African (North) America that Shadd sought to construct through her paper. And Shadd's vision was capacious indeed—a claim that holds true not only with respect to abolitionist newspapers in general, or with respect to the *Standard*,

Table 9.5. The Ten Most Significant Topics in *Frederick Douglass' Paper*

Topic	Label	PMI	Keywords
T80	Legal and courts	0.52	court, case, judge, law, trial, jury, fugitive, justice, decision, supreme
T1	Public speaking	0.46	meeting, audience, evening, douglass, people, speech, hall, made, lecture, present
T92	Race	0.43	colored, people, white, color, black, free, colonization, race, country, men
T30	Men's names	0.38	john, james, william, brown, thomas, henry, rev, george, esq, wm
T24	Temperance	0.34	temperance, smith, good, men, law, rum, great, reform, liquor, drink
T7	Organizing	0.30	friends, aid, fair, money, work, make, means, committee, time, funds
T65	Political parties	0.28	party, democratic, whig, free, vote, political, election, parties, convention, democracy
T97	Slavery	0.28	slave, slaves, slavery, free, master, negroes, states, property, slaveholders, emancipation
T96	Legal and laws	0.26	law, constitution, government, rights, power, laws, property, liberty, people, authority
T69	Political power	0.26	political, great, power, public, influence, present, system, interests, progress, men

but also with respect to other titles associated with the Black press, those that are more often held up as evidence of what the struggles for Black freedom in the nineteenth century entailed.

Consider a list of topics drawn from *Frederick Douglass' Paper*—the title that Douglass would adopt when the *North Star* merged with another abolitionist title (Table 9.5). *Frederick Douglass' Paper* was published over the same span of years as the *Freeman*, and for that reason is apt for comparison with Shadd's paper. It is also apt for at least two other reasons. First, its antecedent served as the venue for Shadd's authorial debut. And, second, in contrast to Shadd leaving her name off the masthead, Douglass used his name to title the paper itself. In other words, Black women might have been the abolitionist movement's vanguard, but they were not always able to claim the same credit as men for their forward-thinking work.[20]

A close examination of the topics associated with *Frederick Douglass' Paper* suggests that the paper moved beyond topics centered on abolitionism to address broader issues of politics and race, an emphasis that is not present in the topics associated with the abolitionist papers overall (table 1). But among the topics associated with *Frederick Douglass' Paper*, there is no evidence of the topics that have to do with daily life, or with nature, or with foreign affairs, all of which appeared in the *Freeman*. A triple comparison among the topics associated with *Frederick Douglass' Paper*, those associated with the *Standard* during Child's time as editor, and those associated with the *Freeman* crystallizes just how intent Shadd truly was on expanding her readers' sense of the possibilities for Black life—in Canada, after emancipation, and beyond.

In a recent issue of *Social Text*, Jessica Marie Johnson, a historian of Atlantic slavery and the Atlantic African diaspora who also creates digital projects of her own, argues for placing the field of digital humanities in closer dialogue with the Black freedom struggles that endure to this day. The "struggles engaged in by subjects racialized as Black to mark their humanity, make legible their legal and extralegal exclusion from societies built by their labor, and form new worlds by transforming and creating inclusive and equitable social conditions," Johnson argues, align with the transformative possibilities of digital scholarship, considered broadly (58). A thematic analysis of the *Provincial Freeman* provides evidence of Shadd's participation in that liberatory project of world building. After all, Shadd's activist credentials were sometimes questioned—because she advocated for expatriation rather than reform from within the United States, because she, unlike Child, was not always a consensus builder, and because she was a woman. But in the contents of her newspaper, refracted through the lens of a topic model, can be found compelling evidence that affirms the value of Shadd's forward-thinking activist work.

And this was emphatically work, to return to this essay's central theme. The one topic strongly associated with the *Freeman* that I have not yet discussed is T29 (Table 9.4), whose most significant keyword is "labor." Over the course of my research, I became increasingly intrigued by this topic, and so I wrote a short bit of code to rank all the articles published by the *Freeman* (slightly more than five thousand) according to the proportion of the labor topic that each article contained. What the ranking of articles revealed was that most of the articles at the top of the list had to do with the physical labor of farming. (The emphasis on farming also connects this topic more closely with the topics on animals and nature, which was not as clearly conveyed through the topic's keywords.) But reading through the top several hundred articles associated with this topic, I came across an article that I had already been alerted to by Rhodes's study: Shadd's farewell editorial, from June 30, 1855, in which she makes it clear that she was acutely aware of the multiple forms of labor that were required of her as a Black woman newspaper editor (Rhodes 70–99). These forms of labor were brought about by her editorial duties and magnified by both her gender and her race, as Shadd herself states. For even as she proudly declares to have "broken the Editorial ice" for "colored women everywhere," she does not hide the work that was required of her in order to do so: "Few, if any females had had to contend against the same business" that she had faced, she writes—referring to the criticism she had received as a result of her hard-hitting editorial style—with the exception of her sister-in-law, Amelia, who had "shared my labours for a while" ("Adieu").

These lines echo another editorial, published earlier in the month, which also appears high on the list of articles that contain the labor topic. In this editorial, Shadd characterizes the work required of "editors of the unfortunate sex" as "drudgery," done in the absence of others willing to "put their shoulder to the wheel" ("To Our Readers West"). Evident in this statement, as in her farewell editorial, is Shadd's sense of the significant affective and emotional labor involved in this work, as well as of its personal and at times physical toll. The topic model amplifies these claims, linking Shadd's own outlay of labor to a range of other forms of work. Shadd's characterization of her labor also anticipates the work of Vivian May, Grace Hong, Jennifer Nash, and other Black feminist scholars, who have long argued that the project of "feminist education" itself is a product of the "long intellectual and political labor of Black women," labor that exacts a very real physical cost (Nash 6).[21] For these reasons, we require additional methods that contribute to the project of naming and crediting this labor—some of which, like these two editorials, is directly documented in the printed record, and some of which, like Shadd's oversight of the paper, is far less easily perceived.

The History of Data and the Work to Come

In her landmark essay on the origins of Black print culture, Frances Smith Foster argues for the significance of another nineteenth-century periodical: the *Repository of Religion and Literature and of Science and Art*—a sister publication of the *Christian Recorder*, which is included in the newspaper corpus analyzed here. In her essay, Foster draws from the text printed on the back page of each issue of the *Repository*, in which the editors state that among their aims is to "furnish data for future comparison" (qtd. in Foster 730). Writing in 2005, Foster interprets this line as evidence that the *Repository* was published with the intention of being used, and used thoroughly, well into the future. But shifting the emphasis of the line from the word "future" to the word "data," we can see how the *Repository* might have also been intended by its editors to be used in a particular way: as a source of data that can shape the stories that we, as scholars in the present, can tell about the past.

More than 150 years later, we have the capacity to perform comparisons of precisely the form that the *Repository*'s editors envisioned. In fact, the topical comparisons among abolitionist newspapers that are described in this essay perform some of this very work. But the forms of labor that remain invisible, such as the labor that Shadd describes in her farewell editorial, suggest that an expanded conceptual frame is required if we are to honor the full range of work, and the full range of people, that have contributed to creating the cultural record that we rely on to conduct our quantitative analyses today. Shadd's account of her editorial labor also supports the arguments made by contemporary labor studies scholars, who remind us that discussions of labor far too often elide distinctions of gender and race, even as the labor performed by women, and by other minoritized groups, structures capitalism itself.[22]

These arguments, in turn, point to the similar co-construction of the concepts of gender and race and the concept of data—the very same concept on which quantitative methods are premised.[23] If we trace the concept of data back to its emergence, there can be found a clear link between the desire to count and classify information and the desire to count and classify people—specifically the desire to count and classify people according to gender and race.[24] The history of counting and classifying is inseparable from the larger colonial systems of domination and control.[25] And yet, as scholars who seek to use quantitative methods in our work, we are bound to our texts as data, which means we are also bound to the oppressive weight of the history of data. The burden of this history does not mean that quantitative methods should be rejected out of hand, however. Rather, the challenge is how best to wield the power of quantitative methods to contest these oppressive histories at the same time that we admit what we cannot and, at times, should not know. In the context of an ongoing, interdisciplinary, and increasingly urgent conversation about data and the methods employed to derive meaning from them, what literary scholars can contribute is an insistence on—and examples of—the value of context; the sustained attention to the gaps in both datasets and archives; and most crucial, an expanded set of models—both conceptual and computational—that enable us to acknowledge what remains out of reach, just as we push forward in our understanding of texts, cultures, and the people who labored to shape them.

Notes

This essay incorporates the knowledge and labor of many people, contributed over the course of many years. My early work with Jacob Eisenstein laid the groundwork for this essay, and his comments on numerous drafts have sharpened it significantly. Sari Altschuler, Sarah Blackwood, Natalia Cecire, Ryan Cordell, Nihad Farooq, Matthew K. Gold, Miriam Posner, Shawn Ramirez, Aaron Santesso, Kyla Schuller, Ted Underwood, Karen Weingarten, and Greg Zinman also contributed valuable feedback. I would also like to thank Molly O'Hagan Hardy and Thomas Augst, who organized the Digital Antiquarian conference at the American Antiquarian Society in 2015, which provided the impetus to begin writing this essay. Keynotes at the 2017 Keystone Digital Humanities conference and the 2018 Futures of American Studies Institute allowed me to refine it. Thomas Lannon, at the New York Public Library, provided crucial archival assistance. The work of the Colored Conventions Project has also significantly influenced the development of this piece.

1. The phrase "unexpected place" is a deliberate reference to Gardner's *Unexpected Places*, among the works responsible for establishing the importance of the Black press.

2. Shadd married Thomas F. Cary in 1856 and is sometimes referred to as Mary Ann Shadd Cary.

3. On Shadd and anonymity, see Casey.

4. Although Daniels was among the first to describe labor in terms of invisibility, the concept builds on the idea of reproductive labor articulated by Federici in her account of the movement Wages for Housework. In applying the concept to editorial work, I am indebted to Blackwood's theorization of editing as another form of reproductive labor: care work.

5. This is a simplification, of course; women have long employed—and, in the United States, enslaved—other women in order to perform this work as well. The racial and economic assumptions embedded in this assertion are addressed by, among others, Davis 222–44.

6. While Shadd was a member of what Rhodes calls the "northern black elite," her existence was nevertheless "shaped by discrimination and injustice, a constant struggle against poverty, and intergroup discord" (xv).

7. On the idea of the feminist complaint, see Ahmed.

8. Here I join Spires in building on the foundational work of Foster, as well as Peterson; and Foreman. Others who have contributed to this body of work on the Black press include Gardner; Fagan; Casey; Cohen and Stein; and Fielder and Senchyne.

9. For an in-depth account of how I understand the term "feminism" as multiple and intersectional, see D'Ignazio and Klein.

10. As Offen has established, the term "feminism" gained currency only in the 1890s, and even then only in France; it would take another two decades to cross the Atlantic.

11. As early as 2011, Bailey pointed out that "the ways in which identities inform both theory and practice in digital humanities have been largely overlooked." With respect to quantitative methods in particular, others have pointed out failures to engage with a range of conceptual issues relating to, among other things, gender, sexuality, race, class, and ability (see Posner; Nowviskie; Rhody ["Why I Dig"]; Clement; and Dinsman). Recently, others (Mandell; McGrath; and So et al.) have attempted to intervene in this area, but this work remains provisional.

12. For a discussion of topic modeling in a literary context, see Goldstone and Underwood.

13. For a history of topic modeling, see Binder.

14. See also Goldstone and Underwood.

15. It is important to note that most, but not all, topic modeling implementations rely on this process of sampling. To learn more about the specific method that I used for this analysis, Latent Dirichlet Allocation (LDA), see Underwood, "Topic Modeling."

16. These titles include: *Douglass' Monthly, Frank Leslie's Weekly, Frederick Douglass' Paper, Freedom's Journal, Godey's Lady's Book, National Anti-Slavery Standard,* the *Provincial Freeman,* the *Christian Recorder,* the *Colored American, The Liberator, The Lily,* the *National Era,* the *North Star,* and the *Weekly Advocate.* The corpus was created through a paid license agreement with the database provider Accessible Archives in November 2014, when I was permitted to scrape the HTML text of these newspaper titles (and associated metadata) from the Accessible Archives website. This initial corpus creation effort was performed as part of a research collaboration with Jacob Eisenstein on the project Interactive Topic Model and Metadata Visualization (TOME), supported by NEH Office of Digital Humanities Grant #HD-51705-13, which concluded in 2015. Between 2017 and 2018, I returned to the corpus, working with two undergraduate students, Nikita Bawa and Adam Hayward, to correct some of the most common transcription and encoding errors and to generate a set of exploratory topic models. In addition, these students, along with two graduate student interaction designers—Caroline Foster and Morgan Orangi— implemented the TOME browser that Eisenstein and I envisioned. On the basis of this exploratory work, I narrowed the corpus so that it contained only the articles that were published between 1827 and 1865. This resulted in 224,160 articles, most of which (83.5%) were explicitly focused on abolition. I then wrote new code to generate the topic model that is the basis of the analysis described in this essay. More specifically, I employed Gensim, the vector space and topic modeling library, making use of its wrapper for the MALLET implementation of LDA. I generated one hundred topics after one hundred iterations, filtering out the fifty most common words (out of just over a million words total). All notebooks for this project, including the code that generated the topic model and the calculations I refer to later in this essay, can be found at github.com/laurenfklein/dimensions-ofscale/. For more on the TOME project, see Klein and Eisenstein; Hayward et al.

17. Ironically, Frederick Douglass would soon be joined in his editorial efforts by a woman who went unnamed: Julia Griffiths, a white British abolitionist who arrived in Rochester in May of that year. For what is known of their relationship, see Douglas.

18. For more on the social dimensions of Shadd's invisible editorial labor, see McBrayer in this volume.

19. See McBrayer for an in-depth analysis of the *Freeman's* broad geographical scope.

20. Highlighting the role of Black women in abolishing slavery and in broader movements for Black liberation is a central goal of the Colored Conventions Project, which seeks to recognize how women were crucial to the conventions movement but who went unnamed in the official minutes of the convention meetings. See "Colored Convention."

21. On the protointersectional theories advanced by nineteenth-century Black women, such as Anna Julia Cooper, see May; Cooper. On Shadd's own "proto–Black feminist politics," see Locke in this volume. On the material effects of systemic violence, see Hong.

22. See Day, whose project builds on the Marxist critiques of Lowe; Roediger.

23. On the history of the concept of data, see Rosenberg.

24. For a powerful reckoning with this history, see Johnson. For a study that focuses on the legacy of eugenics, see Spade and Rohlfs. For a study of surveillance practices with a long historical sweep, see Browne. For a study of the history of self-tracking, see Wernimont.

25. On the association between colonialism and counting, see Farrell. On the tension between statistical measures and Indigenous populations, see Walter and Andersen.

Works Cited

Ahmed, Sara. "Feminist Complaint." *Feministkilljoys*, December 5, 2014. https://feministkilljoys .com/2014/12/05/complaint/.

"Apology." *Provincial Freeman*, March 24, 1854. Accessible Archives. http://www.accessible .com/.

Bailey, Moya Z. "All the Digital Humanists Are White, All the Nerds Are Men, but Some of Us Are Brave." *Journal of Digital Humanities* 1, no. 1 (Winter 2011). https://journalof digitalhumanities.org/1-1/all-the-digital -humanists-are-white-all-the-nerds-are-men-but -some-of-us-are-brave-by-moya-z-bailey/.

Binder, Jeffrey M. "Alien Reading: Text Mining, Language Standardization, and the Human- ities." In *Debates in the Digital Humanities 2016*, ed. Matthew K. Gold and Lauren F. Klein, 201–17. Minneapolis: University of Minnesota Press, 2016.

Blackwood, Sarah. "Editing as Carework: The Gendered Labor of Public Intellectuals." *Avidly*, June 6, 2014. https://avidly.lareviewofbooks.org/2014/06/06/editing-as-carework-the -gendered-labor-of-public-intellectuals/.

Browne, Simone. *Dark Matters: On the Surveillance of Blackness*. Durham, NC: Duke University Press, 2015.

Buurma, Rachel Sagner. "The Fictionality of Topic Modeling: Machine Reading Anthony Trol- lope's Barsetshire Series." *Big Data and Society*, July–December 2015, pp. 1–6.

Casey, Jim. "Parsing the Special Characters of African American Print Culture: Mary Ann Shadd and the * Limits of Search." In *Against a Sharp White Background: Infrastructures of African American Print*, ed. Brigitte Fielder and Jonathan Senchyne, 109–28. Madison: University of Wisconsin Press, 2019.

Child, Lydia Maria. "Farewell." *National Anti-Slavery Standard*, May 4, 1843, pp. 190–91. Acces- sible Archives. https://www.accessible-archives.com/.

———. Letter to Ellis Gray Loring. March 9, 1842. Manuscripts and Archives Division, Manu- script Collection 532, New York Public Library.

Clement, Tanya. "The Ground Truth of DH Text Mining." In *Debates in the Digital Humanities 2016*, ed. Matthew K. Gold and Lauren F. Klein, 534–36. Minneapolis: University of Min- nesota Press, 2016.

Cohen, Lara Langer, and Jordan Alexander Stein, eds. *Early African American Print Culture*. Philadelphia: University of Pennsylvania Press, 2012.

"Colored Convention Project Principles." Colored Conventions Project. https://colored conventions.org/ccp-principles.

Cooper, Brittney C. *Beyond Respectability: The Intellectual Thought of Race Women*. Urbana: University of Illinois Press, 2017.

Da, Nan Z. "The Computational Case Against Computational Literary Studies." *Critical Inquiry* 45, no. 3 (Spring 2019): 601–39.

Daniels, Arlene Kaplan. "Invisible Work." *Social Problems* 35, no. 5 (December 1987): 403–15.

Davis, Angela. *Women, Race, and Class*. New York: Random House, 1983.

Day, Iyko. *Alien Capital: Asian Racialization and the Logic of Settler Colonial Capitalism*. Durham, NC: Duke University Press, 2016.

D'Ignazio, Catherine, and Lauren F. Klein. *Data Feminism*. Cambridge, MA: MIT Press, 2020.

Dinsman, Melissa. "The Digital in the Humanities: An Interview with Jessica Marie Johnson." *Los Angeles Review of Books*, July 23, 2016. https://lareviewofbooks.org/article/digital -humanities-interview-jessica-marie-johnson/.

Douglas, Janet. "A Cherished Friendship: Julia Griffiths Crofts and Frederick Douglass." *Slavery and Abolition* 33, no. 2 (2012): 265–74.

Fagan, Benjamin. *The Black Newspaper and the Chosen Nation*. Athens: University of Georgia Press, 2016.

Farrell, Molly. *Counting Bodies: Population in Colonial American Writing*. New York: Oxford University Press, 2016.

Federici, Silvia. *Wages Against Housework*. Bristol, UK: Power of Women Collective and Falling Water Press, 1975.

Fielder, Brigitte, and Jonathan Senchyne, eds. *Against a Sharp White Background: Infrastructures of African American Print*. Madison: University of Wisconsin Press, 2019.

Foreman, P. Gabrielle. *Activist Sentiments: Reading Black Women in the Nineteenth Century*. Urbana: University of Illinois Press, 2009.

Foster, Frances Smith. "A Narrative of the Interesting Origins and (Somewhat) Surprising Developments of African-American Print Culture." *American Literary History* 17, no. 4 (Winter 2005): 714–40.

Gardner, Eric. *Unexpected Places: Relocating Nineteenth-Century African American Literature*. Jackson: University Press of Mississippi, 2009.

Goldstone, Andrew, and Ted Underwood. "The Quiet Transformations of Literary Studies: What Thirteen Thousand Scholars Could Tell Us." *New Literary History* 45, no. 3 (Summer 2014): 359–84.

Guldi, Jo. "Parliament's Debate About Infrastructure: An Exercise in Using Dynamic Topic Models to Synthesize Historical Change." *Technology and Culture* 60, no. 1 (2019): 1–33.

Haraway, Donna. "Situated Knowledges: The Science Question in Feminism and the Privilege of Partial Perspective." *Feminist Studies* 14, no. 3 (1988): 575–99.

Hayward, Adam, Nikita Bawa, Morgan Orangi, Caroline Foster, and Lauren F. Klein. "TOME: A Topic Modeling Tool for Document Discovery and Exploration." *DH2018*. Alliance of Digital Humanities Organizations, 2018. https://dh2018.adho.org/tome-a-topic-modeling -tool-for-document-discovery-and-exploration/.

Hong, Grace. "'The Future of Our Worlds': Black Feminism and the Politics of Knowledge in the University Under Globalization." *Meridians* 8, no. 2 (2008): 95–115.

Johnson, Jessica Marie. "Markup Bodies: Black [Life] Studies and Slavery [Death] Studies at the Digital Crossroads." *Social Text* 36, no. 4 (2018): 57–79.

Karcher, Carolyn L. *The First Woman of the Republic: A Cultural Biography of Lydia Maria Child.* Durham, NC: Duke University Press, 1994.

Klein, Lauren, and Jacob Eisenstein. "Exploratory Thematic Analysis for Historical Newspaper Archives." *Digital Scholarship in the Humanities* 30, no. 1 (2015): 130–41.

Lowe, Lisa. *Immigrant Acts: On Asian American Cultural Politics.* Durham, NC: Duke University Press, 1996.

Mandell, Laura. "Gender and Cultural Analytics: Finding or Making Stereotypes?" In *Debates in the Digital Humanities 2019*, ed. Matthew K. Gold and Lauren F. Klein, 3–26. Minneapolis: University of Minnesota Press, 2019.

May, Vivian. "Intellectual Genealogies, Intersectionality, and Anna Julia Cooper." In *Feminist Solidarity at the Crossroads: Intersectional Women's Studies for Transracial Alliance*, ed. Kim Marie Vaz and Gary L. Lemons, 59–71. New York: Routledge, 2012.

McGill, Meredith. *American Literature and the Culture of Reprinting, 1834–1853.* Philadelphia: University of Pennsylvania Press, 2003.

McGrath, Laura B. "Comping White." *Los Angeles Review of Books*, January 21, 2019. https://lareviewofbooks.org/article/comping-white/.

Nash, Jennifer. *Black Feminism Reimagined: After Intersectionality.* Durham, NC: Duke University Press, 2019.

Nowviskie, Bethany. "What Do Girls Dig?" *Debates in the Digital Humanities*, ed. Matthew K. Gold, 235–40. Minneapolis: University of Minnesota Press, 2012.

Offen, Karen. "Defining Feminism: A Comparative Historical Approach." *Signs* 14, no. 1 (1988): 119–57.

Peterson, Carla L. *"Doers of the Word": African-American Women Speakers and Writers in the North (1830–1880).* New York: Oxford University Press, 1995.

Posner, Miriam. "Some Things to Think About Before You Exhort Everyone to Code." *Miriam Posner's Blog*, February 2012. https://miriamposner.com/blog/some-things-to-think-about-before-you-exhort-everyone-to-code/.

Rhodes, Jane. *Mary Ann Shadd Cary: The Black Press and Protest in the Nineteenth Century.* Bloomington: Indiana University Press, 1998.

Rhody, Lisa. "Topic Modeling and Figurative Language." *Journal of Digital Humanities* 2, no. 1 (Winter 2012). https://journalofdigitalhumanities.org/2-1/topic-modeling-and-figurative-language-by-lisa-m-rhody/.

———. "Why I Dig: Feminist Approaches to Text Analysis." In *Debates in the Digital Humanities 2016*, ed. Matthew K. Gold and Lauren F. Klein, 536–40. Minneapolis: University of Minnesota Press, 2016.

Roediger, David R. *The Wages of Whiteness: Race and the Making of the American Working Class.* London: Verso, 1991.

Rosenberg, Daniel. "Data Before the Fact." In *Raw Data Is an Oxymoron*, ed. Lisa Gitelman, 15–40. New York: New York University Press, 2013.

Santamarina, Xiomara. *Belabored Professions: Narratives of African American Working Women.* Chapel Hill: University of North Carolina Press, 2005.

Shadd, Mary Ann. "Adieu." *Provincial Freeman*, June 30, 1855. Accessible Archives. https://www.accessible.com/.

———. "To Our Readers West." *Provincial Freeman*, June 9, 1855. Accessible Archives. https://www.accessible.com/.

———. "Wilmington, Jan. 25, 1849." *North Star*, March 23, 1849. Accessible Archives. https://www.accessible.com/.

Sinha, Manisha. *The Slave's Cause: A History of Abolition*. New Haven, CT: Yale University Press, 2016.

So, Richard Jean, Hoyt Long, and Yuancheng Zhu. "Race, Writing, and Computation: Racial Difference and the US Novel, 1880–2000." *Journal of Cultural Analytics*, January 11, 2019. https://culturalanalytics.org/article/11057/.

So, Richard Jean, and Edwin Roland. "Race and Distant Reading." *PMLA* 135, no. 1 (2020): 59–73. https://doi.org/10.1632/pmla.2020.135.1.59.

Spade, Dean, and Rori Rohlfs. "Legal Equality, Gay Numbers and the (After?)Math of Eugenics." *S&F Online* 13, no. 2 (Spring 2016). https://sfonline.barnard.edu/dean-spade-rori-rohlfs-legal-equality-gay-numbers-and-the-aftermath-of-eugenics/.

Specia, Megan. "Overlooked No More: How Mary Ann Shadd Cary Shook Up the Abolitionist Movement." *New York Times*, June 6, 2018. https://www.nytimes.com/2018/06/06/obituaries/mary-ann-shadd-cary-abolitionist-overlooked.html.

Spires, Derrick R. *The Practice of Citizenship: Black Politics and Print Culture in the Early United States*. Philadelphia: University of Pennsylvania Press, 2019.

Underwood, Ted. *Distant Horizons: Digital Evidence and Literary Change*. Chicago: University of Chicago Press, 2019.

———. "Topic Modeling Made Just Simple Enough." *The Stone and the Shell*, April 7, 2012. https://tedunderwood.com/2012/04/07/topic-modeling-made-just-simple-enough/.

Walter, Maggie, and Chris Andersen. *Indigenous Statistics: A Quantitative Research Methodology*. New York: Routledge, 2016.

Wernimont, Jacqueline. *Numbered Lives: Life and Death in Quantum Media*. Cambridge, MA: MIT Press, 2018.

CHAPTER 10

Parsing the Special Characters
of African American Print Culture

Mary Ann Shadd Cary and the * Limits of Search

JIM CASEY

The ongoing remediation of newspapers into digital surrogates is proving a remarkable, mixed boon. More than ever, scholars enjoy online access to a dizzying volume of rare and hard-to-find newspapers. Where previous generations required the time and money to travel the country scrounging for files of newspapers, today we may be just a click or two away from websites where we can run keyword searches on hundreds, millions, or even billions of words. In the process, a variety of subfields of periodicals studies have sprung up, all eager to mine these enormous repositories for new materials and new ways to understand our literary, cultural, and print histories.

Across these fields, digital repositories have become central, even crucial. Yet because the processes for creating and developing these digital resources are rarely transparent, a growing number of scholars have begun to scrutinize the politics of those processes. From the archives, as Benjamin Fagan and others have noted, the selection of newspapers for digitization often reflects racial and other social inequalities.[1] Once digitized, many commercial databases are prohibitively expensive, restricting access to those researchers at wealthy institutions. These vital conversations have only just begun to contend with the full breadth of necessary questions, already inspiring a wave of academic journal issues and projects focused on the distinct challenges of periodicals in digital environments.[2]

Those journals and projects join decades of work to create searchable digital resources. While many of these questions reach back to the rise of microfilm in the early twentieth century, today groups such as the Text Encoding Initiative (TEI) and the Text Creation Partnership (TCP) offer robust foundations for creating accurate digital editions of historical texts. At larger scales, it becomes necessary to rely on optical character recognition (OCR) tools that attempt to guess the words that appear on a digitized page. OCR tools have long struggled with the thin paper and faint inking on many historical newspapers, yet important strides are being made by groups such as the Early Modern OCR Project along with crowdsourcing platforms such as the National Library of Australia's Trove and the Zooniverse.[3] Poor-quality OCR may not be solved just yet, but those groups and platforms point to reliable long-term solutions for developing searchable historical newspapers.

Critiques of coverage and OCR, however, can account only partly for the impact on historical research of search engines. If conversations at the intersection of print culture and digital studies have tended to focus on the integrity of digital repositories, the modes of access enabled by search play a distinctly adjacent and still-invisible role. Databases of digital surrogates of historical newspapers are daisy chains of associated technologies. Each link in the chain introduces its own contours, its own affordances and limits, inviting us to interact with these digital artifacts in highly structured ways.[4] Faced with a range of ways to interact with a database, what is our first step to wade into a database that, like Chronicling America, holds more than twenty million pages? For most of us, research suggests, the first step in the research process is to "just Google it."[5] The volume of these databases, even as they afford the ability to read and browse widely, preserves the formidable challenge of what some call the "Great Unread."[6] A small number of scholars have employed computational methods to seek out larger patterns in these databases, exemplified by the rich essays by Lauren Klein and Demetra McBrayer in this volume.[7] Such studies, however, require the kinds of time, resources, and expertise that remain elusive for most scholars in the humanities. Instead, the primary response to the challenge of the great unread is a keyword search. If keyword searches are foundational for historical research in the early twenty-first century, it bears stressing that there is no such thing as a neutral search engine.

This essay is about the limits of search in research on early African American print cultures. Specifically, I present the case of Mary Ann Shadd, who, as one of the earliest-known African American women to edit a newspaper, signed her name to her columns with an asterisk. The asterisk was a way for Shadd to navigate the complex of racism and sexism that disrupted her editorship of her weekly newspaper, the *Provincial Freeman* (1853–57). In our current search engine technologies, that asterisk is forbidden from having any semantic meaning. The asterisk is a special character, prevented from having semantic meanings of its own, in order to help search engines operate more efficiently. The case of Mary Ann Shadd's asterisk is a cautionary tale not only against depending on keyword search in research but on the fault lines of race and gender that shaped historical print culture and infuse our information retrieval technologies.

This essay takes up those asterisks and the complex task of reading them in the nineteenth century and searching for them in the twenty-first. In the nineteenth century, Shadd's asterisks highlight an encoded form of editorial expression using punctuation that suggests the tensions between exposure in print and self-effacement. In the twenty-first century, asterisks take on new meanings within search engines that erase the typographical marks as meaningless—beyond what we can search, read, or locate.

An Unprecedented Editor: Mary Ann Shadd
and the *Provincial Freeman*, 1853–54

Mary Ann Shadd founded the *Provincial Freeman* in the spring of 1853 when, after her first few years as an emigrant in Canada, she had realized the need for a platform of her own. She emigrated to Canada in 1851 in the wake of the Fugitive Slave Act along with many other northern free and fugitive African Americans. Shadd was born in Wilmington, Delaware, to parents, Abraham and Harriet Shadd, who ran a successful small business and participated actively in the Philadelphia-area, middle-class community of activists, abolitionists, and Colored Conventions organizers. Shadd was one of many of her peers dedicated to building such institutions as schools, conventions, and the Black press. In Canada West, her first stop was in a small town called Windsor, across the border from Detroit, in what was then known as Canada West. Shadd had been trained as a teacher and had some experience as an educator, so she opened a school to teach the children of the many people arriving from the United States. Windsor was the end point for many on the Underground Railroad, but arriving into Canada West guaranteed little in the way of financial or other certainties. Very few of the recent emigrants could afford to pay Shadd much for their children's education. Instead, she began to rely on the American Missionary Association, a white-led philanthropic organization, for the $125 it cost her annually to keep the school open. Her funding from the AMA, however, did not last long, a break she long suspected the result of her increasingly bitter rivalry with Henry Bibb and his newspaper, the *Voice of the Fugitive*.[8] Initially on friendly terms, the two had found themselves on opposite sides of the acrimonious debates about the direction of the coalescing broader community of Canada West's Black population.[9]

That population included multiple, overlapping communities. Some people had already been living in Canada for years prior to the Fugitive Slave Act. Others came from northern American states where they had lived as free or fugitive citizens with deeply curtailed civil rights. Many others came from the South where they had lived as enslaved human beings.[10] Along with the poverty facing many of them upon their arrival into Canada, a signal struggle for early Black communities in Canada West was the challenge of social ties for so many whose previous and current living situations were sources of intense personal pain, loss, and trauma. Almost all of them were refugees from the United States, yet few of them shared much else in common. Bibb and Shadd's disputes in this view are less a contest between two large personalities than a set of collective debates within an emerging and heterogeneous population straining to build new lives in Canada West.

Within those collective debates, Shadd soon found herself the object of personal attacks. As rumors began to circulate in 1852–53 that Shadd and others were planning to start a paper to rival the *Voice of the Fugitive*, Bibb published a number of sexist articles attacking Shadd. One article referred to her as "a designing individual whose duplicity is sufficient to prove a genealogical descent from the serpent that beguiled mother Eve in the Garden of Eden."[11] The personal attacks only got worse. The need was clear: Shadd needed a space in print to refute these attacks. She had already tried to combat these attacks in public venues, but the physical performances before mixed-gender audiences exposed her to even harsher criticism. As Carla Peterson observes, Shadd's trials "dictated that Shadd Cary devise other modes of representation more suitable to her talents that would also draw the public gaze away from any 'blot or blemish' that it might imagine recorded on her body."[12]

Absent Editor, Invisible Editor: Shadd
Founds the *Provincial Freeman*

In March 1853, Shadd managed to publish a trial issue of a newspaper named the *Provincial Freeman*. She listed many men's names on the masthead of the first issue, including Samuel Ringgold Ward as the editor and Rev. Alexander McArthur as the corresponding editor. Given Ward's extensive experience in the press, his name on the masthead as the ostensible editor lent the *Freeman* instant credibility.[13] Another seven names appear as the Committee of Publication,[14] followed by instructions for correspondents that "letters must be addressed, *Post-paid*, to Mary A. Shadd, Windsor, Canada West; Rev. J. B. Smith and J. Baker, Travelling Agents." Shadd had omitted her name as the paper's editor. Instead, an editorial column titled "Introductory" by Samuel Ringgold Ward appeared on the front page, despite an article on the backside of that page noting that he was hundreds of miles away when the paper went to press. If that did not belie the actual editorship of the paper, Ward's "Introductory" column showed little enthusiasm for the new venture, declaring his reluctance to accept the editorial post and his plans to vacate soon. Ward was soon bound for England on a speaking tour where he remained for more than a year. He continued to travel widely in England, Canada, and the United States throughout the life of the *Freeman*.

A year after the trial issue, Shadd began issuing the *Freeman* regularly with a masthead nearly unchanged except for the addition of a white British printer named John Dick. Dick was a journeyman printer who had moved across the Atlantic to work for Frederick Douglass at the birth of the *North Star* in 1847. Along with his work on the *North Star*, Dick's politics are conveyed by a few of the other texts he printed, including the proceedings of the Seneca Falls women's rights convention and the 1848 Colored National Convention.[15] With his past work for women's rights, against slavery, and in newspaper publishing, John Dick was likely a welcome addition to the fledgling efforts led by Shadd to relaunch the *Provincial Freeman* in 1854.

A journeyman printer's experience would have contributed much to the day-to-day affairs of the *Provincial Freeman* in many areas, including the organization of collaborative editorial writing. In the 1840s and 1850s, the vast majority of editorial writing in the United States used the collective "we" and went unsigned. Most periodicals only had one or two editors, so readers could usually detect who had written what. There were a few rare and notable exceptions, and those usually came only on newspapers with large editorial departments. The *New York Tribune* began to have editors initial their columns in 1849. The *North Star* used a similar practice, as with the issue of April 7, 1848, which featured editorials by F. D. (Frederick Douglass), J. D. (John Dick), and M. R. D. (Martin R. Delany). The system of editorial initials was not always consistent, even on the *Tribune* or *North Star*, but served as a useful shorthand for readers to differentiate a host of contributing editors and writers.

The *Provincial Freeman* adapted that organizational system for its unusual situation of having both an absent editor and an invisible editor. When the printer John Dick contributed a column, he signed his writings with the letter D. For the first eight months of 1854, that letter was the paper's only overt editorial attribution, save for the several dozen columns marked at their conclusion with an asterisk. The *Provincial Freeman* published at least thirty-nine editorial columns with an asterisk. These columns have a distinctive prose style, rife with subjunctive clauses, and a running focus on emigration and women's rights. That combination of qualities corresponds to Mary Ann Shadd's previous writings and her many public speeches. I follow Jane Rhodes in concluding that these asterisks could only be the mark of Shadd's invisible editorship, a mark that Shadd would deploy to careful uses in 1854 for making quotidian announcements, for airing controversial opinions, and as a personal signifier within limited social circuits.[16] The asterisk was a complex usage of the affordances of nineteenth-century newspaper editorship (figure 10.1).

The irregularity of *other* papers, is of no benefit to ours, we have already had ample proof, and we do not wish to have an unfounded charge of neglect on our part, made against us also.   ✱

At the late anniversary of the American Anti-Slavery Society, held in New York, the following resolution was adopted. It shows, at least, that the members of that Society continue courageous and hopeful, and intend to persevere in their labors for the enfranchisement of the enslaved, through the regeneration of the moral sentiment of the American people. An arduous task, truly !   D.

Figure 10.1. Example of Mary Ann Shadd's asterisk signature in an untitled article in the *Provincial Freeman*, May 27, 1854, page 2. Courtesy of University of Pennsylvania Libraries.

Some of the articles signed with an asterisk were relatively quotidian. As in the snippet above, Shadd used the asterisks for a number of articles that did not ordinarily require any attribution. Along with the above lament about the late mails in the spring weather, she published others like the piece on July 7, 1854, that read, in its entirety: "Several frame buildings beginning at the corner of Queen and Yonge streets, were destroyed by fire on Tuesday last. *." This and other articles did not necessarily require any rhetorical protection afforded by the asterisk. For example, it is hard to imagine the possible negative consequences of publishing anonymous advertisements for traveling agents (April 22, 1854, and May 13, 1854), or to announce preparations for the First of August celebrations in Toronto and Hamilton, Canada West (June 24, 1854, and July 1, 1854). The use of it may have signified an implicit endorsement in notices about local revival meetings (April 22, 1854) or the receipt of the *American Phrenological Journal* (July 15, 1854), but such conclusions are difficult to support with so few examples. It is entirely possible that readers hardly noticed the small dots appended to some of the more ephemeral notes in the *Freeman*.

For wider audiences, other editorials used the veiled authority of the asterisk to treat much more controversial subjects. Throughout its publication the *Freeman* was staunchly pro-emigration, perhaps never more than in an editorial on June 3, 1854, in which Shadd declared opponents of emigration "as guilty, we verily believe, as Batchelder or any other slaveholder or slave-catcher in the land. *" Considering that the editorial was a commentary on the news that a brother of James W. C. Pennington had been kidnapped and taken south to be enslaved, Shadd's asterisk licensed a tone and topic that she might have hesitated to broach under her own name. That proved true a number of times. In that same issue in June 1854, Shadd penned an article attacking Julia Griffiths and some of the abolitionists for organizing a fundraiser in Toronto to benefit *Frederick Douglass' Paper* while ignoring the *Freeman*'s more local and immediate needs. "But will not Miss Griffith," the editorial asks, "leave a few coppers behind?"[17] The reply came—if only the *Freeman* had asked, the Toronto Anti-Slavery Society would have been happy to host an event. They were less inclined, however, after the attack in print. Impolitic or not, Shadd used the asterisk as a way to access the full authority of the editorial voice. As one of the earliest-known African American women to edit a newspaper, it was precisely the opaque quality of the asterisk, its very deficit of information, that enabled her to speak frankly without fear of direct personal reprisal. Self-effacement helped her move beyond the print and political spaces typically afforded to a person of her race and gender.

Whether Shadd deployed the asterisk for quotidian or controversial ends, readers could track them from week to week. The asterisks were at once unknown and recognizable, opening up the potential for readers to accumulate their own senses of the marks appearing underneath so many of the *Freeman's* editorials. By accruing meaning through their periodicity, their patterns and rhythms over time, Shadd's asterisks fit with a much larger body of semi-anonymous writing in the early Black press. That body of writing stretches across much of the nineteenth century, from Shadd to the use of pen names such as Ethiop (William J. Wilson) and Communipaw (James McCune Smith) in *Frederick Douglass' Paper* to later writing by Ida B. Wells under the name Iola. The use of such pseudonyms was not a neutral rhetorical gesture. For Shadd, the asterisk can help foreclose her exposure to any racist or sexist retaliation while simultaneously asserting the heft of her editorial presence.

As a typographical pseudonym, Shadd's asterisks likely signaled much more transparently within the circuits of her personal acquaintances. Along with her readers on fundraising trips, Shadd interacted frequently with activists, writers, editors, and religious leaders across Canada West and the northeastern United States. That William Still, of the prominent Still family, would serve as a regular correspondent for the *Freeman* attests to the reach of her personal networks as a woman who had lived and worked in Delaware, New York, Pennsylvania, and New Jersey before emigrating. More locally, Henry Bibb and his allies in Canada West had encountered Shadd in any number of public gatherings. They may have guessed at the identity of the person writing behind the asterisks. Shadd also traveled constantly throughout Canada West, gathering subscriptions, raising money, and writing travel reports for the *Freeman*. Reports published quickly after her visits gave clues to subscribers to the identity of the person using the asterisk.

In those fluid meanings, Shadd drew on a much wider array of expressive uses of asterisks in antebellum print culture. As her father, Abraham Shadd, had been an agent for *Freedom's Journal*, she may well have had opportunity to read *David Walker's Appeal*, which, as Marcy Dinius explains, used a variety of typographical symbols to powerful effect.[18] Along with the manicules (or pointing fist) in the *Appeal*, Walker unsettled the form of the pamphlet through asterisks that called the eyes of the reader, or the voice of the person reading aloud, back and forth between the primary texts and the many footnotes. Walker's asterisk was a transgressive character that bridged the main discussion and the marginal interjections. Shadd may have gleaned another use for her asterisks from Margaret Fuller in the *New York Tribune*. As the *Tribune* was the most frequently reprinted newspaper in the *Freeman* under Shadd's editorship, she was likely familiar with the hundreds of earlier columns in the mid-1840s that Fuller had signed with what she called her "star." Both Fuller and Shadd added the asterisk at the end of their editorial columns. Where Fuller used the asterisk to make herself more visible, as a budding celebrity in the *Tribune*, Shadd inverted that usage to make herself more invisible as the editor of the *Freeman*. Still others, including Frank Leslie and James Redpath, used the asterisks as placeholders for content deemed too odious or tantalizing for their audiences—as the mark of excised language. These examples are only a few of the conspicuous and expressive uses of the asterisk in the antebellum press. It was a potent single character, a character capable of sliding meanings while it circulated across different audiences.

Search Engines as Social Texts

Shadd's asterisks gesture to a much larger, possible literary history of editorial punctuation in the nineteenth century. I say "possible" because today those punctuation marks are being erased by the technologies employed to digitize the archives of early African American print culture. As an asterisk, Shadd's mark has become doubly invisible in search-assisted databases. No matter how Shadd's contemporaries may have deciphered her mark, today the asterisk (*) is parsed by search engines as a wildcard. The wildcard is one of a set of so-called special characters set aside by search engines as instruments for optimizing the speed and accuracy of information storage and retrieval. Owing to their need for these special characters, search engines disallow the asterisk as a result for any searches. Racial and gender fault lines that originated in print culture are perpetuated in the racial politics of search engines. It is, as Michel-Rolph Trouillot writes, a digital example of "formulas of erasure" that arise in the precise moments when historical facts are recorded, simultaneously excluding the unthinkable entities from the fields of power set up around recognized personal names.[19]

The case of Shadd and her asterisks shows that search engines are social texts. Search engines encode the priorities of their creators into their operations, as in the case of the Lucene search system that provides access to the repository of the *Provincial Freeman* in the Accessible Archives website. The name Lucene refers to search engines derived from a library of computer code written in the language Java by Doug Cutting in the late 1990s. In 2001, Lucene was taken over by the nonprofit Apache Software Foundation. Subsequent developers integrated it with web application software, such as Solr, Tomcat, and Elasticsearch.[20] The popularity of Lucene Apache is hard to overstate. It is used in thousands of the most highly trafficked websites today, from Twitter (now X) to Wikipedia and many more. Even those corporations that build their own search engines, such as Facebook and Google, share Lucene's basic principles for processing language. The broad impact of Lucene makes it an important technology to understand. A focus on Lucene is a reminder that every search engine contains its own set of ideas about language, even if those ideas are largely illegible without technical fluencies that remain uncommon in disciplines for the study of historical language, literature, and culture.

We do not need to be novelists to analyze novels; we do not need to be programmers to take a critical view of these technologies. We can approach them as users and ask valid questions. The following section explains the concepts and process of Lucene search engines. The intent is to provide a set of questions and vocabulary that humanists can use to critique our estranged dependence on search engines.

Digitization, or Adapting Archival Sources into Digital Texts

The process of creating a searchable database of archival sources begins with facsimiles. Figures 10.2 and 10.3 are facsimiles of two brief articles that Shadd published in the *Provincial Freeman*. The textual information in these facsimiles then needs to be converted into digital texts. Although many companies and organizations create digital texts by using OCR tools, Accessible Archives is unusual in that all documents have been transcribed in double-key entry. Double-key entry means that two individual transcriptions were created by hand and then merged. That process allows Accessible Archives to claim an accuracy rate of 98% based on a single dissertation study conducted by Wesley Raabe at the University of Virginia in 2006.[21] While those claims are more than a decade old, and merit reconsideration, the double-keyed transcriptions remove OCR tools as a relevant factor in the status of punctuation in the Accessible Archives databases. Once transcribed, all of

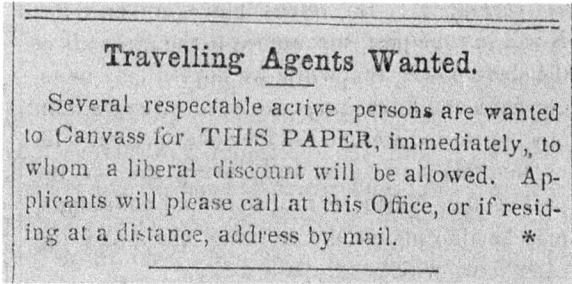

Figure 10.2. Sample snippet, "Travelling Agents Wanted," from the *Provincial Freeman*, April 22, 1854, page 2. Courtesy of University of Pennsylvania Libraries.

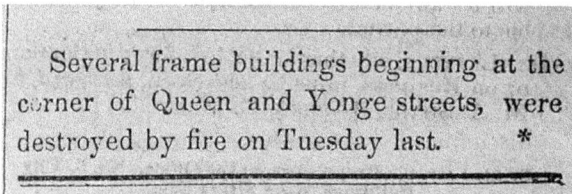

Figure 10.3. Sample snippet, untitled, the *Provincial Freeman*, July 1, 1854, page 2. Courtesy of University of Pennsylvania Libraries.

the characters and words should be search eligible. Any alphanumeric character can be entered as a search query to retrieve the two articles in Figures 10.2 and 10.3. The articles assuredly appear in the *Provincial Freeman* issues of April 22 and July 1, 1854, yet a search for the asterisks on those or any other dates returns only an error message: "Parsing error."

Lucene Indexing: From Text to Terms

The elaborate workflow of a Lucene search engine (Figure 10.4) begins with a process called tokenization. Tokenization breaks up the text and extracts single, independent tokens, or "terms." This process uses filters, called analyzers, to determine which combinations of letters and numbers can be extracted as distinct terms. There are many different kinds of analyzers. Each has its own settings and produces certain kinds of terms, but the most commonly used is the StandardAnalyzer. The Lucene StandardAnalyzer converts all words to lowercase and removes any punctuation or accent marks.[22] The result of running the StandardAnalyzer on the snippets in Figures 10.2 and 10.4 would be as indicated in Table 10.1.

In this filtering, Lucene interprets the texts on users' behalf. Users can still read or browse the full text, but tokenization extracts only the terms

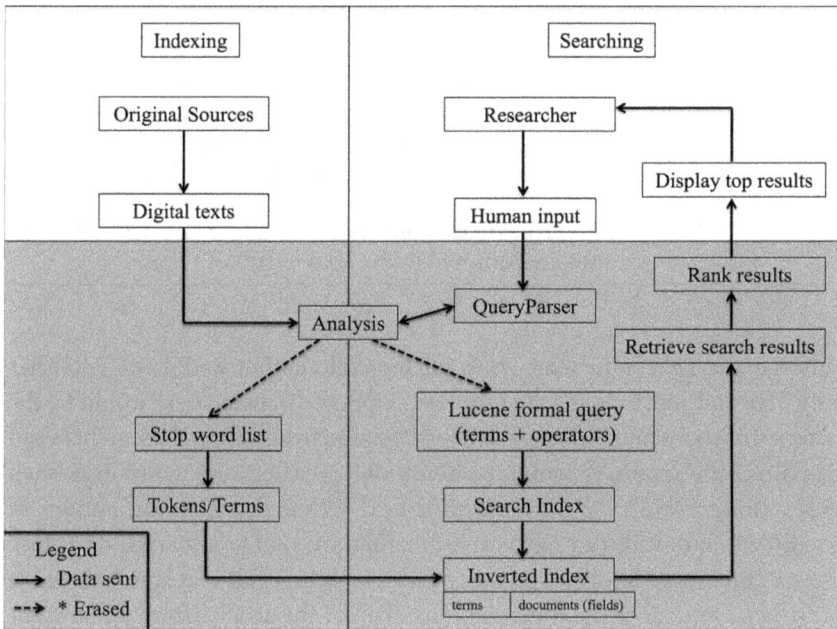

Figure 10.4. Workflow diagram of Lucene search. Created by Jim Casey.

that satisfy its rules. Those terms are filtered a second time in the process of tokenization against what is called a stop word list. The purpose of stop words is to filter out those terms that appear frequently in almost every single document, including around thirty terms in the StandardAnalyzer: "and," "are," "as," "but," "for," "the," "with," and more.[23] Removing some stop words can improve search results quite a bit, but selecting which words to include or exclude is an idiosyncratic decision akin to a set of principles that would guide a documentary editing project. With the *Freeman* a stop word list is unimportant, "because the documents in the Accessible Archives databases are unique and include language no longer in common usage."[24] The composition of the stop word list is one place where humanists can and should ask questions about what words are filtered out and why.

Once extracted and filtered, the terms are assembled by Lucene into a unit called "documents." "Documents" is a technical name that does not correspond to the vernacular sense of a document. Rather, a document is better understood as a collection of fields, or buckets of terms. A document may contain many fields. In Accessible Archives, the fields are named in a radio

Table 10.1. StandardAnalyzer

DocumentID	Text
1	several respectable active persons are wanted to canvass for this paper immediately to whom a liberal discount will be allowed applicants will please call at this office or if residing at a distance address by mail
2	several frame buildings beginning at the corner of queen and yonge streets were destroyed by fire on tuesday last

button to the right of the search box: full text, title, author, and "book publisher only." The full-text field for the *Freeman* snippets discussed here would be the same set of terms after being parsed by the StandardAnalyzer. Researchers can also direct the system to look for a query only in a certain kind of field, such as searching for "Shadd" in the author field. While the technical notions of documents and fields can seem arbitrary, they are vital to understand because they are the stored information that queries search. A full-text search does not actually go into all of the transcriptions of all of the articles from all newspapers. Rather, a full-text search scans all of these documents and their fields.

Once each article has been tokenized, filtered, and adapted into a document with multiple fields, the system needs to organize everything into an index. "Index" is here, again, a technically specific word. What Lucene calls an index may be more familiar to humanities scholars as a concordance. Like a concordance, a Lucene index provides a list of which terms appear in which documents. Lucene's inverted index maps terms to their appearances in any document. Table 10.2 shows a sample Lucene inverted index. Most Lucene instances also enrich the term listings with additional information, such as length, location on the page (to enable fuzzy searching), synonyms, and frequency of a term in a document. A Lucene index may remove the common suffixes of words to allow matching between queries and words with similar roots, such as for "heads," "headings," "headed," and so on.[25] As those types of information do not directly influence the handling of the asterisk, I omit them in this explanation. The advantage of this inverted index is that the system can store which words appear in multiple documents without having to store multiple copies of the text associated with each article. Then, inverted tables are aggregated further into a tree-like graph structure that ensures the information storage can be easily maintained and expanded with additional tables without creating a need to re-compute the entire index each time. Using those

Table 10.2. Inverted Index for Documents 1 and 2

Term	DocumentID
several	[1], [2]
persons	[1]
by	[1], [2]
yonge	[2]
street	[2]

structures, Lucene makes the storage of textual information more memory-efficient by avoiding the need to store copies of the full text of every article where the word "several" appears. Instead the system can use those references to pull up links to relevant documents in the list of search results.

Such a view of the Lucene inverted index as a concordance suggests some new ways to think about searchable repositories of historical newspapers. A Lucene index is not an archive, but a para-archive, a complex system for organizing, storing, and retrieving information abstracted from print or digital sources. Because an index is an abstraction of the texts, it is a threshold that structures our encounters with surrogates of historical print objects. A search does provide direct access to an archive. Searches engage a table of information abstracted from digital surrogates of printed objects. These layers underscore the role of faith implicit in these search acts—faith in the communities of computer scientists, programmers, and information professionals who contributed to the source code of Lucene and other search systems. Every technical development reflects the priorities set by a group of people about the balance of access, accuracy, and completeness. Their priorities become the practical structures, then, for these para-archives that determine what kinds of expressions are legible and may have value.

Lucene Parsing and Special Characters

Once the index has been built to adequately store the parsed tokens in all the right fields and documents, it is ready for researchers to access it through a search box on a user interface through queries. When a researcher enters a query, Lucene modifies the string of letters or numbers into a formal syntax structured to find hits in the index intuitively and accurately. This process helps users query a system without needing to memorize any arcane syntax for formal logical expressions. That systemic generosity is enforced by a set of operations known as a query parser. There are many different varieties of query parsers. Each parser enables a different kind of search query by interpreting the search string. The range of options for advanced searches provides clues about what kinds of parsers are active in a given search engine.[26] Accessible Archives appears to use the most common package that, in the latest release of Lucene 6.0.0 (at time of writing in 2016), is called QueryParser.[27]

QueryParser begins analyzing the string of characters by sorting them into terms and operators. QueryParsers deliberately replicate the process used to create the index. But where the initial analysis for the index looks only for terms, this round of analysis breaks a query into both terms and operators. On Accessible Archives, those operators can be expressed by clicking buttons or by entering special characters: + - & | ! ( ) { } [ ] ^ " ~ * ? : \ /. Because these operators give explicit and clear instructions to the system, the special characters can be powerful tools for adept users. That power, however, comes at the cost of the asterisk being able to have the status of a term, a status that would make it findable and therefore have meaning in the search act. Instead, the analysis performed by the QueryParser acts as a translator from human natural language into Lucene syntax. Helpfully, Accessible Archives supplies information about the results of this translation act at the top of most search pages. Thanks to this information, I can see the translation of a query for mentions of Mary Ann Shadd and the *Freeman* in other newspapers that do not mention her father Abraham as: ((((freeman)) AND ((shadd))) NOT ((abraham))). This is a basic example, but it demonstrates the conversion of a researcher's language into a formal expression. In contrast, the QueryParser rejects any queries that contain only a single asterisk. The system replies with the message: "Lucene Parsing Error." The translating function of the Query-Parser, then, is directly responsible for erasing Mary Ann Shadd's asterisk. The bounds of allowable translations by the QueryParser is one more place where researchers can and should ask critical questions: how does a system parse my questions into formal expressions?

Ranking Search Hits

The QueryParser rejects the asterisk in part because Lucene uses the special characters to organize the search results into a ranked list. A search for a common term can bring up millions of hits. Search engines depend on the logic of special operators to handle such large volumes efficiently. Access to thousands of articles in a digital repository may seem thrilling, but most researchers can meaningfully use only a few hundred search results. The need for efficiency is why Accessible Archives often supplies only the first two hundred results for a search and limits the total number of hits to fifty thousand.[28] Search engine developers have to balance the volume of documents recalled with the precision of the documents in a list of results[29]—even at the cost of excluding those who could only express their voices through asterisks.

Costly Searches: The Politics of Parsing African American Print Culture

The erasure of asterisks in search engines is not inevitable. In the jargon of information retrieval, allowing a user to search for a lone asterisk is "costly." Forbidding such costly searches makes sense for a few reasons. Searching for a lone asterisk not only brings up far more hits but also consumes significant amounts of computer memory. Memory used for a single search may be trivial, but that encumbers a system scaled up for hundreds, thousands, or millions of users. These searches also run on physical computers. Even leaving aside the energy efficiencies and fossil fuels involved in the physical computers, these searches will slow down the system for other users. A system bogged down by a lone wildcard search starts to lag, cascading the distributed rhythms of search-assisted research. Finally, along with the material concerns of memory and lags, search technology today is overwhelmingly led by profit-seeking companies who make staggering fortunes by selling intelligence about what appears in their indexes to advertisers. Information about how and what users find in Google's index is lucrative, spawning an entire industry of search engine optimization for exactly that purpose. Given that a wildcard search effectively requests all of the information stored in a given index, a wildcard search theoretically would provide access to silicon bonanzas. Even though Google and Facebook, among others, use different indexing and searching tools than Lucene, they still share Lucene's distaste for the lone asterisk.

Parsing away the asterisk is an unintended result of resource allocation and neglect of marginalized voices in historical print. Companies and groups that erase the asterisk control most of the culture industry in the early twenty-first century: Google, Twitter (now X), Netflix, iTunes, Facebook, and

Amazon. The same is true for many of the central resources for American literary history: Accessible Archives, JSTOR, the MLA International Bibliography on EBSCOhost,[30] and Gale Cengage's Nineteenth Century U.S. Newspapers. Gale Cengage at least offers an error message for the lone asterisk that speaks as a comment on Mary Ann Shadd's own difficulties: "Your search term has too few leading characters." While all of those sites deny the validity of Shadd's asterisk, some do parse the single character as a synonym for the term "asterisk." This synonym parsing is active on Wikipedia, Yahoo, and Bing, among others. Still others generously allow the lone asterisk to serve as a wildcard search, pulling up every document in the index on such sites as Chronicling America, the Digital Public Library of America, Umbra, Readex, and the Text Creation Partnership's release of the Early English Books Online, Eighteenth Century Collections Online, and Evans Early American Imprint Collection. While the synonyms or full access wildcard are not exactly the same as the QueryParser's erasure of Mary Ann Shadd's asterisk, they still encode the * as an operator and not a term. The asterisk remains unsearchable. No one is going to abandon search tomorrow. But the erasure of Shadd's asterisks may point to a broader project. Just as African American emigrants deliberated the terms of their culture in Canada West in the 1850s through the *Provincial Freeman*, so might we too learn a great deal from Mary Ann Shadd in this the adolescence of our digitized print.

Notes

1. See, for example, critical attention to the construction of digital periodical resources by Benjamin Fagan, "Chronicling White America," *American Periodicals* 26, no. 1 (2016): 10–13; James Mussell, *The Nineteenth-Century Press in the Digital Age* (New York: Palgrave Macmillan, 2012); Paul Fyfe, "An Archaeology of Victorian Newspapers," *Victorian Periodicals Review* 49, no. 4 (2016): 546–77; and Ryan Cordell, "Q i-jtb the Raven: Taking Dirty OCR Seriously," *Book History* 20 (2017): 188–225; along with efforts to develop countervailing digital projects such as the Recovering the U.S. Hispanic Literary Heritage Project, led by Nicolás Kanellos and Carolina Villarroel, and the Digital Colored American project, directed by Eurie Dahn and Brian Sweeney.

2. Ryan Cordell et al., "Forum: Digital Approaches to Periodical Studies," *American Periodicals* 26, no. 1 (2016): 1–24; Editing Modernism in Canada, accessed April 1, 2016, https://editingmodernism.ca; Modernist Journals Project, accessed April 1, 2016, https://www.modjourn.org/.

3. Early Modern OCR Project, accessed April 15, 2016, http://emop.tamu.edu; Trove, National Library of Australia, accessed April 15, 2016, http://trove.nla.gov.au/; Text Creation Partnership, accessed April 15, 2016, https://textcreationpartnership.org/.

4. Lisa Gitelman, *Paper Knowledge: Toward a Media History of Documents* (Durham, NC: Duke University Press, 2014).

5. Max Kemman, Martijn Kleppe, and Stef Scagliola, "Just Google It—Digital Research Practices of Humanities Scholars," ArXiv e-print, September 10, 2013, http://arxiv.org/abs/1309 .2434.

6. Margaret Cohen, *The Sentimental Education of the Novel* (Princeton, NJ: Princeton University Press, 1999), 23.

7. See, in this volume, Demetra McBrayer, "Mapping Mary Ann Shadd Cary," and Lauren Klein, "Dimensions of Scale."

8. The *Voice of the Fugitive* is available online through OurOntario's *Our Digital World Newspaper Collection* at http://ink.ourdigitalworld.org/vf. The *Voice* is another title in the antebellum Black press that deserves much greater attention.

9. My accounts of Mary Ann Shadd's life, work, and importance draw heavily throughout this essay on the excellent biography by Jane Rhodes, *Mary Ann Shadd Cary: The Black Press and Protest in the Nineteenth Century* (Bloomington: Indiana University Press, 1998).

10. Robin W. Winks, *The Blacks in Canada a History* (Montreal: McGill-Queen's University Press, 1997).

11. Rhodes, *Mary Ann Shadd Cary*, 73.

12. Carla L. Peterson, *"Doers of the Word": African-American Women Speakers and Writers in the North (1830–1880)* (New Brunswick, NJ: Rutgers University Press, 1998), 103.

13. In 1853, few African American editors had more experience or stature than Samuel Ringgold Ward. As Ward wrote in his editorial for the sole issue of the *Aliened American* in 1853, "I am requested to edit one paper, to act as corresponding editor of another, and, I am a regular contributor to a third" (April 9, 1853, p. 2). Along with the *Freeman* and the *American*, both started in 1853, Ward had helped edit the *True American* (1846–48); the *Northern Star* and *Colored Farmer* (ca. 1846–49); and the *Impartial Citizen* (1849–53).

14. In the copies that I examined though Accessible Archives and OurOntario, the digital reproduction from microfilm made this section impossible to read.

15. *Report of the Proceedings of the Colored National Convention Held at Cleveland, Ohio, on Wednesday, September 6, 1848* (Rochester, NY: Printed by John Dick, at the North Star Office, 1848), Colored Conventions Project Digital Records, https://omeka.coloredconventions.org /items/show/280; *Report of the Woman's Rights Convention, Held at Seneca Falls, N.Y., July 19th & 20th, 1848* (Rochester, NY: Printed by John Dick, at the North Star Office, 1848), https://www .nps.gov/wori/learn/historyculture/report-of-the-womans-rights-convention.htm.

16. See Rhodes, *Mary Ann Shadd Cary*, chap. 4 ("We Have 'Broken the Editorial Ice'") and 240n27.

17. Mary Ann Shadd, "A Bazaar in Toronto for 'Frederick Douglass' Paper,' &c," *Provincial Freeman* (Toronto), June 3, 1854. Accessible Archives.

18. Marcy J. Dinius, "'Look!! Look!!! At This!!!!': The Radical Typography of David Walker's *Appeal*," *PMLA* 126, no. 1 (2011): 55–72.

19. Michel-Rolph Trouillot, *Silencing the Past: Power and the Production of History* (Boston: Beacon Press, 2012), 96 and 115.

20. Richard Lawrence, "Lucene Frequently Asked Questions," Jakarta Project, February 4, 2002, https://web.archive.org/web/20020204075100/http://www.lucene.com:80/cgi-bin/faq /faqmanager.cgi?file=chapter.general&toc=faq#q1.

21. J. D. Thomas, "The Double-Keyed Full Text Difference," Accessible Archives blog, December 2, 2012; Wesley Raabe, "Harriet Beecher Stowe's *Uncle Tom's Cabin*: An Electronic Edition of the *National Era* Version" (PhD diss., University of Virginia, 2006).

22. Note that the StandardAnalyzer works for English-language terms. The documentation for Lucene 6.0.0 (released April 2016) lists thirty-five language-specific analyzers (http://lucene .apache.org/core/6_0_0/analyzers-common/index.html).

23. Manu Konchady, *Building Search Applications: Lucene, LingPipe, and Gate* (Oakton, VA: Mustru Publishing, 2008), 29.

24. *Accessible Archives User Manual 4.0*, Accessible Archives, accessed February 26, 2024, https://coherentdigital.net/s/AAI-User-Manual-40.pdf.

25. The foundational expression of this idea is in Martin F. Porter, "An Algorithm for Suffix Stripping," *Program* 14, no. 3 (1980): 130–37.

26. One of the notable contributions of the Google search engine is the use of a single box for all operations. Compare the single Google box to the user interface on Accessible Archives that allows at least a handful of boxes, buttons, and menus. There is no perfect design, as developers must balance adding advanced features with the burden of learning how to use those features.

27. Although Lucene is a self-contained Java library, it needs to be integrated with a server platform for users to be able to access it. Accessible Archives currently uses Apache Tomcat, an open source web server. The web server does not have any direct bearing on the status of asterisks, so I omit any discussion of it here.

28. *Accessible Archives User Manual 4.0*.

29. Amit Singhal, "Modern Information Retrieval: A Brief Overview," *Bulletin of the IEEE Computer Society Technical Committee on Data Engineering* 24, no. 4 (2001): 35–42.

30. Because the MLA International Bibliography disregards the asterisk, the character * in the title of this essay will be unsearchable.

CHAPTER 11

Mapping Mary Ann Shadd Cary

Using Bibliographic Analysis to Uncover Labor

DEMETRA MCBRAYER

In the April 22, 1854, issue of the *Provincial Freeman* (1853–57) Mary Ann Shadd Cary responds to correspondence from "Benjamin," who wishes the newspaper would remain within a small, select group of "friends": she writes that their "'friends' can hardly stand farther off than they do."[1] Shadd Cary would again assuage readers' concerns that the newspaper was not becoming more foreign, whether by contribution or support, fiscal or otherwise. In an October 28, 1854, issue she responds to accusations that the *Freeman* receives too much foreign money and content. These concerns belie a tension between what information is made accessible within the *Freeman* and to whom. It also speaks to Shadd Cary's ideological approach for the newspaper: anything benefiting Black life and hastening the end of slavery is necessary information. Shadd Cary's idea of what content is required by the newspaper conventions of the time as well as the content her audiences expected is equally diasporic and immediate. She envisions a far-reaching Black community whose experience is informed by an equally diverse range of countries and events. The newspaper then consistently addresses the needs of this vast community: it charts the prices of markets in prominently Black Canadian towns, announces land sales, and explains conversion rates for dollars into silver, underscoring how she considers the newspaper's most important function to be disseminating integral information to those emigrating or escaping to Canada from the United States.[2]

As an activist and editor, Shadd Cary educates, informs, creates, and elevates this shifting Black community, as defined by her and the *Freeman*'s devotion to "Anti-Slavery, Temperance, and General Liberation."[3] To do so, she began publishing the *Freeman* with detailed information on agriculture, anti-slavery organizations, activities, and debates, anti-Black violence, legislation, and slavery in the United States, the successes of the Underground Railroad, and information about the international campaigns and politics of Britain.[4] The newspaper is a bricolage of information for the diasporic Black community Shadd Cary addresses, one similarly vast in its array of source material. In a time when Black lives were threatened by anti-Black violence and legislation that delineated where they could and could not be, Shadd Cary envisions a borderless Black community, one to whom her paper offers guidance and safety.[5] While syndication and correspondences are typical for newspapers of the time, the geographic breadth represented in the *Freeman* underscores Shadd Cary's interest in geography both as a means of community creation and safety. The inclusion of materials from the Dominican Republic model international Black communities and their struggles for equity, and other pieces from China imagine Black investment in international affairs.[6] Likewise, materials on growing anti-Black violence and laws, as well as the potential expansion of slavery westward in the United States, delineate where Black readers were safe or not.[7] By reprinting this vast array of materials across the United States and, indeed, material from the paper's "friends," Shadd Cary documents the geographies of anti-Blackness within the United States and offers pathways of emigration or escape to her African American readers.

Shadd Cary's editorship is inextricably tied with her multifaceted identity—antislavery activist, lecturer, teacher, and more—and it is necessary to acknowledge her complexity to understand her labor as an editor, as none of those titles are truly separated. Shadd Cary's lectures, tours, and community activism necessitated her travel throughout North America for the antislavery effort and to promote the *Freeman*. Likewise, her position in the community provided the support that helped her circulate the newspaper within Black Canadian communities for three years. This essay explores how descriptive bibliography and mapping technology help us capture and understand Shadd Cary's labor by facilitating the understanding and acknowledgment of labor, particularly of Black women.[8] To do so, I build off previous research into Shadd Cary's invisibility, divisiveness, and work on and about Black nationalism, temperance, and emigration.[9] I then utilize this as a guiding framework for the methodology behind the metadata creation for the descriptive bibliography, which, in turn, shapes the data that forms the maps. In this project, I inquire how the methodologies of digital humanities and book history can push against the inherent aspects of those fields that obscure or overlook Black life to center and celebrate it.

This project, therefore, examines the entirety of the *Provincial Freeman* with a slightly augmented principle: examining contents as a means of attributing labor as correctly as possible to the editor, often Mary Ann Shadd Cary, whenever feasible throughout the newspaper. This work was done in a simple form by logging every piece, when possible, in an issue of the *Freeman* (from information on the printing to advertisements to main text pieces). The information details: the author of the piece, the name or opening line of the piece, the section heading, the geographic information of the piece (city, state/province, country), whether it is a disclosed reprint, and where that reprint is from. In consideration of the vast amount of editorial labor, this project operates in a somewhat gray area. We can never totally recapture Shadd Cary's labor, as much of an editor's work remains invisible despite its pervasive nature, and like much African American archival work, a complete, detailed record rarely exists.

To best explain this, I briefly overview descriptive bibliography and why I use this method for examining the *Provincial Freeman*. I follow with what mapping technology encompasses and why I am using maps rather than solely quantitative data on Mary Ann Shadd Cary's labor. Last, I take a closer look at what these geographies remind us of: the realities of shifting geographies of the early and mid-nineteenth-century United States in a time of increasingly anti-Black violence and legislation that made the country an ever-changing geography for African Americans. In doing so, I argue that Mary Ann Shadd Cary's labor, though largely recognized as editorial, is akin to that of a cartographer, in that she utilizes the *Provincial Freeman* to delineate legal and fugitive boundaries of safety and danger for escaping or emigrating African Americans. Doing so not only quantifies the labor that Shadd Cary completes as editor of her newspaper but also reminds us of the numerous ways that her labor is not solely within and behind the *Freeman* but also within her community.

Descriptive Bibliography

Descriptive bibliography concerns itself with the materiality of texts and explores any unique aspects of a text's creation.[10] To do so, bibliographers describe a book either through measurements or formulas and in turn examine where a text differs from its ideal copy—a version of the text that notes every aspect intended during the printing of a text.[11] Such divergences are determined by comparing, for example, differences in measurements of title pages or, more commonly, in the differences between one copy's collation formula and the ideal's. In doing so, bibliographers can identify where, say, a page was inserted or excised and as a result trended more toward hand-press materials, as they provided a variety of individualized texts that are equally and potentially divergent from a text's ideal. Discussions on bibliography require an acknowledgment that the availability of special collections materials reflect issues of accessibility and representation in collections. While there has been significant progress in balancing the exclusivity of collections, what has been collected, maintained, and studied speaks to long-held values, institutionally and scholarly.

Despite its somewhat limited beginnings, descriptive bibliography can adapt innately to an ever-expanding definition of "text," one that represents the necessities of nineteenth-century African American communities. Considering the vast amount of possible information about a text's material aspects, descriptive bibliographies can be exhaustive. Bibliographers must then determine, as Philip Gaskell notes, the intent and audience for whom the bibliography serves.[12] In this, descriptive bibliography is malleable. Projects like the Black Bibliography Project investigate how descriptive bibliography can be reshaped for Black texts.[13] Adapting and testing what aspects of descriptive bibliography can work for African American texts also asks that we consider what those texts are, as the African American print culture of the nineteenth century is as diverse as the community it represents. Material texts can range from books to pamphlets, conference proceedings to scrapbooks. Most evocative are the ephemeral texts less considered by descriptive bibliography but so integral to nineteenth-century African American life: newspapers.

The African American press in the nineteenth century involves debates on representation, uplift, equity, and antislavery, among numerous other issues concerning Black life. Reaching a large radius of readers with relevant content, African American newspapers create and maintain a community despite the attempts by prevailing white supremacist society to deny their existence and power.[14] Newspapers became a social activity, read aloud among crowds or families and the topics of daily exchanges, manifesting community through this shared experience. Everyone in a particular area could share and discuss the material they had all read or engaged in the day previous.[15] This social aspect also resembles how political and community-based engagements were overwhelmingly social activities for African American women, who were active political participants despite African American women's lengthy contemporaneous and historical elision.[16] The vast, diasporic community of nineteenth-century African American press imagines and represents a vibrant newspaper culture that reaches the community widely and quickly. The proceedings for the National Convention of Colored Citizens at Buffalo, New York, in 1843 demonstrate this understanding of both the need for and possibility of African American newspapers. Composed of key figures in abolitionist and Black print culture of the time, such as Charles B. Ray (1807–86)[17] and Henry Highland Garnet (1815–82), the Committee Upon the Press outlines how an African American newspaper could "unite us [African Americans] in a stronger bond, by teaching us that our cause and our interests are one and common," while also allowing African Americans to "learn about, as well as from each other."[18] Such a newspaper could also work against the prevailing anti-Blackness of the white print culture of the time, showing for readers what the committee referred to as the "correct views" of African American life, values, and beliefs.[19] Newspapers were vital to the next stage of African American activism, a coordinated effort to create, shape, and educate their community.

While an African American newspaper was seen as the logical next step in community building and activism, it required labor, time, and expense. Seen as the organizers and crafters of a cacophonous discourse, editors shape the community their paper envisions, and as such, they are involved in nearly every aspect of the planning, organization, support, and distribution of a newspaper.[20] Ranging from maintaining contact with correspondents, recruiting subscribers and agents (and retaining those networks), writing material, choosing material to reprint, securing advertisements, and organizing the entirety of the newspaper's materials—all of which does not account for how embedded in the print culture of the nineteenth century an editor had to be to find sufficient material to reprint—editors expended time, money, and energy in crafting a single issue of a newspaper. Every aspect of a newspaper, from its content to organization, bears traces of an editor's labor, both physical and intellectual.[21] Yet, despite the totality of the work necessary in creating and compiling an issue for the printer, editorial work is often invisible labor.

It is this very invisible labor of newspaper editors that descriptive bibliography's malleable nature helps recover. Focused on the materiality of the text, descriptive bibliography, as mentioned earlier, directs us behind the presses, centering those the text as object obscures. Jonathan Senchyne's analysis of how African American printer Primus Fowle is legible through the gradual breaking of an engraving within the *New-Hampshire Gazette*'s masthead, an exemplar of Fowle's labor in pulling the hand press, reminds us how African American bodies are often lost behind the material object.[22] Tending to the bodies involved in the circuits of production, particularly those of African Americans, adds to the growing work of rectifying the persistent bibliographical marginalization of African American bodies and materials.[23] Furthermore the recognition of labor, particularly in the *Provincial Freeman*, recenters the historically and contemporaneously erased labor of African American women. By utilizing descriptive bibliography with a focus on the labor of creating a newspaper, we can examine and recognize the enormous amount of work Mary Ann Shadd Cary carried out as editor of the *Freeman*.

To do so, the aforementioned gray area surrounding the matter of labor then operates as a windfall in this project: Due to the nebulous nature of editorial labor and the undefined nature of the work, I attribute as much as feasibly possible to Shadd Cary without rendering her work meaningless, using information available on when she edits the newspaper alone or in partnership with her brother Isaac D. Shadd.[24] Where Shadd Cary does not "sign" her contributions to the newspaper, the work is not attributed to anyone, or the work is not clearly from or attributed to another author or newspaper, I have given credit to Shadd Cary as an unlisted contribution. I also note pieces by Shadd Cary whether under her pseudonyms or alongside her brother.[25] Rather than assume she has written every single aspect of this paper—Shadd Cary's family contributed to the newspaper and editorial work throughout its run—this method attributes Shadd Cary with the labor of reading, and choosing the materials included in the newspaper. As such, descriptive bibliography lets us look past the material object, and making labor our focus allows us to look further, recovering and understanding Shadd Cary's work as an editor.

Mapping

Mapping is a growing aspect within the digital humanities, one that shows us new ways of envisioning texts or the work behind them. Mapping often involves using a geographic information system (GIS) program, such as ArcGIS or QGIS. One creates geographic data and from that creates a visualization that facilitates new insights into a text. As such, mapping has been used in digital humanities work to examine, for example, how space and intersectionality determine access.[26] There are, however, understandable concerns surrounding the use of geographic information in studying minoritized communities, particularly that geographic data can be static: Boundaries are more or less rigid depending on someone's race during the nineteenth century, particularly so after the Fugitive Slave Act of 1851. Likewise, boundaries and census data can overlook complex dynamics of race and even more complex stories of emigration. Yet this data can be dynamic with historical contextualization or with the addition of numerical data.[27] As descriptive bibliography reminds us of those who create and distribute texts, GIS allows us to look beyond simple location markers and understand the vastness of Mary Ann Shadd Cary's print culture and the integral part geography plays in both the *Provincial Freeman* and her activism.

To do so, this project utilizes a descriptive bibliography to log geographic information tied to labor as well as each location's number of contributions, showing the wide print culture of Shadd Cary and the newspaper. To correctly attribute the labor of a piece, I look to who wrote the piece. If it carried Shadd Cary's initials or her pseudonymous asterisk (*), then the work is attributed to her and the location of the *Freeman* at the time, aligning with Jane Rhodes's detailed biography of Shadd Cary's life.[28] A similar system is used in determining the location of a contribution: If a piece had a clear geographic location, as is often the case with correspondences, then I attribute that to where the author of the piece indicates their location. For pieces from another newspaper, I list that location as where that newspaper was printed. Finally, I list any unknown sites as "unclear" in the descriptive bibliography's data.[29] With this, computational functions produce quantitative data on the frequency at which a specific author, city, state/province, and country appear in the *Freeman*. In consideration of the project's scope and intent, I use Power BI, which utilizes aspects of ArcGIS, for mapping these networks, as it conveys geographic information and frequency in a reader-friendly way.[30] Doing this reveals what we may expect: Shadd Cary's nationalist and pro-British beliefs shape a significant amount of the *Freeman*'s information. There are 7,991 (72.8%) contributions from Canada West, 1,453 (13.24%) from the United States, and 1,210 (11.02%) from the United Kingdom. The fact that Shadd Cary's contributions are created in Canadian locations is unsurprising, as much of the *Freeman* is made up of her work, nearby companies and correspondents, and information for newly emigrated or escaped Black people to Canada West. The contributions also speak to immediate concerns: reporting on the United States attests to the life and dangers of African American life, and pieces on the British Empire address Black life in Canada West, document the actions of the British Empire, and entice those considering emigration.

While contributions from Canada West, the United States, and the United Kingdom speak to those immediate concerns, the geographic data from the *Freeman* pulls us back to acknowledge the expanse of influences on the newspaper. Large quantitative data draws us toward these mass occurrences and begs for analysis and conversion to information, and the mapping of these data points offers a panoramic visual of that information, as contributions range from China to the Dominican Republic, from Austria to Nicaragua. Though contributions from some countries are not many, they are nonetheless necessary in acknowledging the wide range of Shadd Cary's diasporic community (Figures 11.1 and 11.2). For example, articles from China detail British and Chinese fighting as well as the poisoning of a British correspondent, while the article concerning the Dominican Republic speaks of the

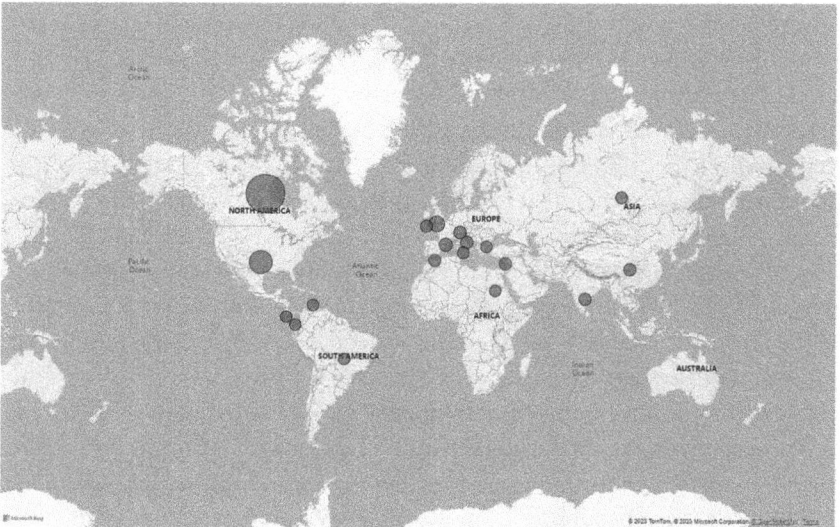

Figure 11.1. A map of the world with gray circles indicating what countries are present within *The Provincial Freeman*. This map was produced in PowerBi with data created by Demetra McBrayer, using OpenStreetMap's baselayer with attributions by Microsoft Bing and TomTom.

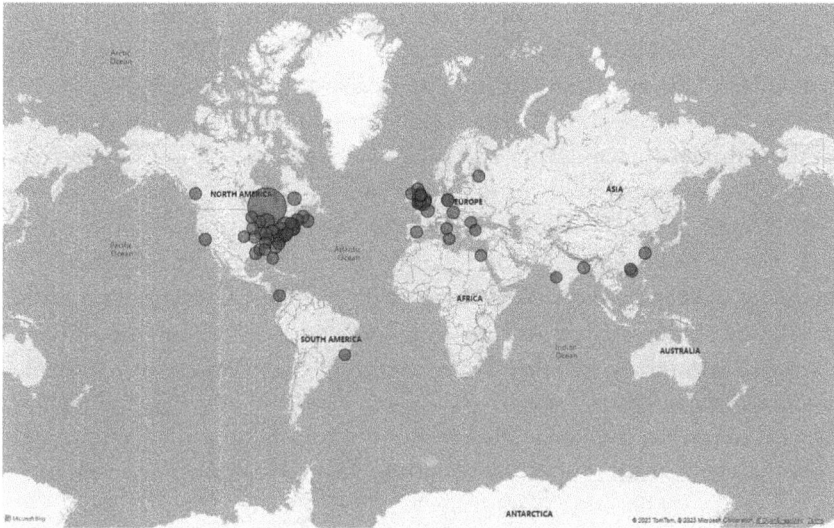

Figure 11.2. A map of the world with gray circles indicating what cities are present within *The Provincial Freeman*. This map was produced in PowerBi with data created by Demetra McBrayer, using OpenStreetMap's baselayer with attributions by Microsoft Bing and TomTom.

access Black inhabitants of Santo Domingo have and the threat of revolution against a system that allows Black political representation.[31] Drawing our attention to all of these different world events and entanglements likewise indicates how these pieces exemplify Shadd Cary and the *Freeman*'s guiding ideology: to document and elevate Black life. Canada West was a British territory during Shadd Cary's life, and as such, concerns about British involvement in China speak to the status of the British Empire. Sharing information about the successes of and threats to Black life in Santo Domingo addresses Black revolution and independence throughout the diaspora. These pieces likewise underscore the tension of a burgeoning Black identity that seeks equity, rights, and prosperity at the time while embedded in various colonialist systems. The newspaper's pages, bulging with antislavery activism, details of American slavery's horrors, and coverage of Britain's empirical conquests and politics represent the complicated interstices of Shadd Cary's and the diasporic Black community's activism.

These tensions imbricate with Shadd Cary's work as editor. Pieces, such as "The English in China" from the April 4, 1857, issue come secondhand, a reprinting from what is only named as a "Scottish Paper." These pieces indicate the print culture that operates at the time, sharing information as widely as possible across organizations (such as antislavery) or countries (such as the United Kingdom). A Scottish paper then travels along British empirical trade routes and into the hands of a well-read Black woman within Canada West. Of 10,977 individual pieces in the available run of the *Provincial Freeman*, 1,308 of them are reprinted materials. While laboring as an activist and public speaker, Shadd Cary nonetheless reads and widely shares information in the hopes of shaping Black life and advancing the antislavery cause. Indeed, Shadd Cary acknowledges this labor in her June 30, 1855, column, "Adieu," her, albeit temporary, goodbye to the newspaper and her role as editor. She describes her work as editor of and advocate for the *Freeman*, traveling to elicit subscribers (and likely advertisers).[32] She maintains connections with correspondents from Canada West and the United States who contribute to the newspaper (Figures 11.3 and 11.4).

Her labors are both at and away from the editorial desk of the *Freeman*—what I believe is the most compelling aspect of this newspaper. For, though we

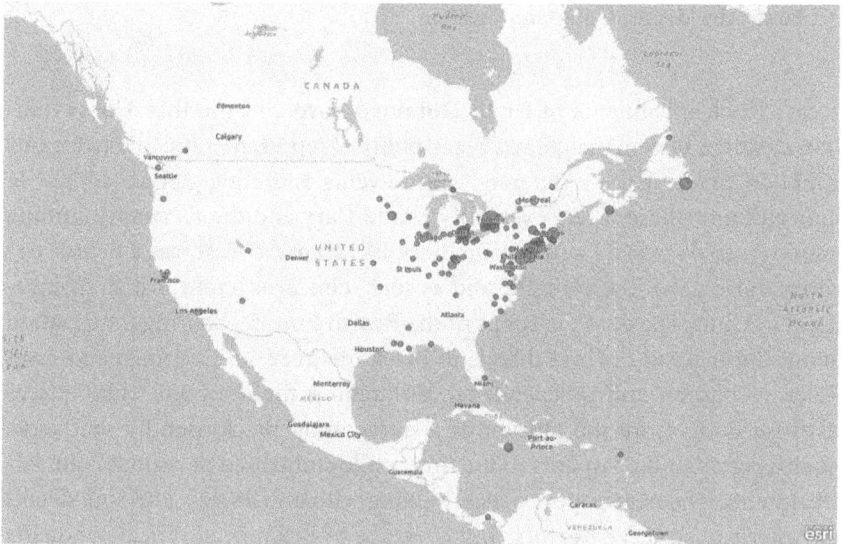

Figure 11.3. A map of the U.S. and lower Canada depicting contributions to The Provincial Freeman by number of contributions. This map was produced by Demetra McBrayer in ArcGIS for PowerBi, using the Light Gray Canvas baselayer by Esri with attributions from Esri, Garmin, FAO, NOAA, USGS, and EPA.

Figure 11.4. A map of lower Canada, specifically Ontario and its surroundings, and the upper east U.S. by number of articles contributed. This map was produced by Demetra McBrayer in ArcGIS for PowerBi, using the Light Gray Canvas baselayer by Esri with attributions from Esri, Garmin, FAO, NOAA, USGS, and EPA.

may note the vast geographies within the *Freeman*, we must attend to the ways that geography and boundaries interact within and outside of the newspaper. Shadd Cary imagines the role of editor as bound to the idea of community and family, of traveling in search of subscribers to keep the newspaper going. Once Shadd Cary returns to the newspaper, made explicit in its May 10, 1856, issue, the newspaper advertises lectures from her and coeditor H. F. Douglass, and other issues detail the work of traveling and speaking on both antislavery and the *Freeman*.[33] Shadd Cary's editorship, like the geographies and boundaries she engaged, was dynamic; it participates in the vast print culture of the time over a range of countries and navigates the shifting geographies of the nineteenth century, both in the United States and Canada West. As anti-Blackness grew in the United States, the country's topography itself was continually transient, ever shifting, and Shadd Cary herself navigated the complicated geography of Black activism within Canada West, initially settling in Chatham, Ontario, only to be pushed out by Henry Bibb, Mary E. Bibb, and supporters for Toronto. Jewon Woo's essay in this volume demonstrates how this fraught relationship helped craft a community of contemporary Black women activists for Shadd Cary, though their antagonism would lead to difficult times within her life. Despite forced relocation, Shadd Cary would remain embedded within the Black communities for which she worked. In fact, the *Freeman* never ventured far from Black communities in English-speaking Canada West during its printing. Jane Rhodes notes that Toronto and Chatham both had nearby Black settlements and large Black communities.[34] Black life and communities, no matter how far, were always kept near.

The Story Geography Tells

Geographic indicators give a sense of the vast labor of Mary Ann Shadd Cary, the communities she made, and the print culture she participated in, yet also remind us of geography's role in the *Provincial Freeman*. Indeed, Shadd Cary's reminder of Black presence and its occupation of and movement through Canada West is a radical act. As Katherine McKittrick notes, Canada's overtly white European identity requires the erasure of Blackness and its geographic presence.[35] Shadd Cary's continued documentation of a Black community then asserts the presence of a Black Canadian history and geography, of an alternate mapping of Canada West with space for Black Canadians. This alternate mapping and its testimony to Black life in Canada West is essential, as the erasure of Black Canadian geographies not only represses an integral history but displaces a community. This displacement refuses "their social, economic, and political commitment to places and spaces both within and beyond Canada," attempting to prevent Black Canadian movements, and any international Black movement, for equity.[36] Yet, as Brandi Locke shows within this collection, Shadd Cary's work simultaneously intervenes and revises exclusionary practices. By evidencing Black communities, their histories, and their geographies, Shadd Cary's works then undermine white Canada West's erasure of Black presence and history, refuting the idea that Black presences in Canada West are "non-Canadian, always other, always elsewhere, recent, unfamiliar, and impossible."[37] In doing so, Shadd Cary unmoors geographic boundaries from the laws of white Canada West to recognize how contingent geography and borders are on race, an aspect she parallels in her coverage on the United States.

While utilizing both descriptive bibliography and geographic data presents us quantitative understandings of Mary Ann Shadd Cary, and potentially

African American women largely, it is not the only story this information offers. Tending to the particulars of a newspaper and centering African American women's labor in those spaces unfurls the complicated nature of geography. Geography presents itself not only in the circulation of materials, both the reprinted and the newspaper itself, but also in revealing the way the *Freeman* itself encounters, dictates, and contests anti-Black geography in the nineteenth century. From this emerges an understanding of how Shadd Cary and the *Freeman* by extension guide the African American community among a continually shifting set of boundaries and borders as they emigrate to Canada West. As well, this draws us toward how Shadd Cary does so as part of her work as an activist and editor, neither labor ever truly uncoupled.

Examining the content of the *Freeman* further for geographic information reveals how she reported on and worked against the growing anti-Black geography of, particularly, the United States. While Shadd Cary's concerns over violence against African Americans and legislation align with her activism, they are dialogic texts as well, carrying multiple voices for their readers. Thus, materials within the *Freeman* utilize pieces on anti-Black violence or legislation as a way of warning its readers. Heavy reporting on the potential of slavery in western American territories and debates on slavery in states such as Kansas send a clear message: do not go here.[38] Shadd Cary then utilizes the newspaper as a way not only of informing but also of reforming boundaries. Anti-Black legislation and violence map themselves over the United States; in her own way, Shadd Cary acts as a cartographer for African American emigrants seeking freedom in Canada. Her reporting serves the practical purpose both of informing but also of mapping where those emigrating or escaping could not tread without immense danger, much like Victor Hugo Green would do with *The Green Book* (1936–66). The passage of the Fugitive Slave Act of 1850 had already remapped the United States into new anti-Black spaces and borders, but Shadd Cary's remapping continues to show how those borders and geographies were mercurial. For example, Shadd Cary reprinted an article from the *Norfolk Herald* in the June 30, 1855, issue, detailing the arrest of six fugitive enslaved African Americans and a man, Sales, who attempted to secure their travel for escape. Many warnings like this appear across the newspaper: only a column over is a reprint from the *Richmond Dispatch* of June 1855, advertising rewards for the capture and return of self-emancipated African Americans. Shadd Cary's reprintings are multivocal: they demonstrate the horrors of U.S. slavery; further the pro-Canadian emigration position; and clarify unsafe locations for African Americans to inhabit.

However, the *Freeman* not only delimits the geography of what is unsafe; it also advertises what is safe. Between the reprinting from the *Norfolk Herald* and the *Richmond Dispatch* is another posting: "Under Ground Rail Road" from the *Norfolk Beacon*, also of Norfolk, Virginia. This brief article details several African Americans, who are "induced to take through tickets" along the Underground Railroad—a stretch of which owes its success to its "legions of officers from Massachusetts at every station."[39] The inclusion of "Under Ground Rail Road," strategically placed by Shadd Cary, shows the complicated nature of nineteenth-century American geography for self-emancipated African Americans emigrating to Canada West. Though this is not surprising for those who study this period, it not only delineates the complexities of geography during the time but acknowledges two types of less-recognized labor on Shadd Cary's part that her editorship enables: communicator of borders and of the Underground Railroad.

Just as a newspaper editor carries many jobs hidden by the materiality of the final product, utilizing descriptive bibliography to understand Shadd Cary's labor reveals its multitudinous nature. And it is not surprising that an aspect of that labor carries forward what she was exposed to at a young age—Shadd Cary's parents were conductors on the West Chester route of the Underground Railroad, and Shadd Cary would remain within its proximity, most notably through her connection to one of its more famous workers, William Still.[40] William Still, known for his publication *The Underground Railroad: A Record of Facts, Authentic Narrative, Letters, &c.* (1872), is threaded throughout the work of the *Freeman*. A friend of Shadd Cary's, Still would become a subscriber and an agent for the newspaper and a correspondent,[41] and many of the newspapers digitized by the Ontario Community Newspapers Portal contain marginalia of William Still's name on the front page, a factor lost in transcribed versions of the paper available on, for example, Accessible Archives. Still's proximity and the included articles concerning the Underground Railroad remind us that Shadd Cary's labor for the *Freeman* as editor includes her labor as an activist in a more dynamic way. She maintained connections with networks of activists working on the Underground Railroad and detailed its work and successes for readers. Doing so required Shadd Cary to labor not only as an editor but as a community member and an activist—none of which can be separated.

Attending to the messy reality of studying nineteenth-century African American newspapers also opens new avenues for inquiry: How does the *Provincial Freeman* report on the Underground Railroad and how does the

Freeman itself map with the Underground Railroad? Does it reprint more frequently from newspapers in towns with a branch on the Underground Railroad? Also, considerations of Shadd Cary's political ideologies become apparent in the section headings and materials within the newspaper: agriculture, the costs at markets, advertisements for land sales, and conversion charts for turning dollars into sterling silver all speak to the way that Shadd Cary's Black nationalist ideology dictates the form of her newspaper. Exploring the form of contemporary newspapers that participated in the debate for Black emancipation and equity may be fruitful.

To fully understand the position of Mary Ann Shadd Cary, we must reconsider newspapers not only as material objects but also as sites of data for exploration. Doing so responsibly and respectfully requires that we acknowledge what life was for African American women of the time, in context with local and international print culture and histories. And we must attend to all aspects of a newspaper as worthy of study: advertisements, correspondences, words of wisdom—these sections speak to some aspect of Shadd Cary's ideology as well as what she viewed as necessary for her job as an activist and community builder. Looking at marginal spaces within newspapers helps us find revelations that recenter African American women in newspapers of the nineteenth century.

Notes

1. "Remarks," *Provincial Freeman*, April 22, 1854. This project utilizes scanned copies available through the Ontario Community Newspapers Portal, whose digitization work was supported by the University of Windsor. This collection is not the entirety of the Freeman, stopping in September 1857 and missing a few issues. There are portions of the newspaper missing, so those portions are omitted from the descriptive bibliography's data. The only intentional omission within the descriptive bibliography is of the time from August 22, 1855, to April 26, 1856, after Shadd Cary left the newspaper; however, explicitly attributed correspondences from her during this span are included.

2. The *Provincial Freeman* then operates like settlement homes of the time, such as Jane Addams's Hull-House Settlement.

3. Mary Ann Shadd, "The Prospectus of the Provincial Freeman," *Provincial Freeman*, April 22, 1854.

4. See also R. J. Boutelle and Marlas Yvonne Whitley's "Plotting New Gardens: The Black Feminist Roots of Community-Building in *A Plea for Emigration*" within this collection.

5. See also Kristin Moriah, "'A Greater Compass of Voice': Elizabeth Taylor Greenfield and Mary Ann Shadd Cary Navigate Black Performance," *Theatre Research in Canada* 41, no. 1 (2020): 20–38.

6. "The Dominican Republic," *Provincial Freeman*, May 13, 1854; Tyson Yates, "Origin of the Chinese Rebellion," *Provincial Freeman*, April 29, 1854.

7. "Lynch Law in Dona Ana County," *Provincial Freeman*, June 30, 1855; "Arrest of Fugitive Slaves," *Provincial Freeman*, June 30, 1855; "Slavery in California—Prospect of Establishment," *Provincial Freeman*, June 24, 1854.

8. Safiya Umoja Noble, "Toward a Critical Black Digital Humanities," in *Debates in the Digital Humanities 2019*, ed. Matthew K. Gold and Lauren F. Klein (Minneapolis: University of Minnesota Press, 2019), https://dhdebates.gc.cuny.edu/read/untitled-f2acf72c-a469-49d8-be35 -67f9ac1e3a60/section/5aafe7fe-db7e-4ec1-935f-09d8028a2687#ch02; "Colored Convention Project Principles," Colored Conventions Project, accessed August 1, 2021, https://colored conventions.org/about/principles/.

9. See Benjamin Fagan, *The Black Newspaper and the Chosen Nation* (Athens: University of Georgia Press, 2016); Jim Casey, "Parsing the Special Characters of African American Print Culture: Mary Ann Shadd Cary and the * Limits of Search," in *Against a Sharp White Background: Infrastructures of African American Print*, ed. Brigitte Fielder and Jonathan Senchyne (Madison: University of Wisconsin Press, 2019), 109–27; Carolyn Calloway-Thomas, "Mary Ann Shadd Cary: Crafting Black Culture Through Empirical and Moral Arguments," *Howard Journal of Communications* 24, no. 3 (2013): 239–56; Nneka D. Dennie, "'Leave That Slavery-Cursed Republic': Mary Ann Shadd Cary and Black Feminist Nationalism, 1852–1874," *Atlantic Studies* 18, no. 4 (2021): 478–93.

10. See Fredson Bowers, *Principles of Bibliographical Description* (Oak Knoll Press, 1995); Phillip Gaskell's *A New Introduction to Bibliography* (New Castle, DE: Oak Knoll Press, 1972); G. Thomas Tanselle, *Selected Studies in Bibliography* (Charlottesville: University Press of Virginia, 1979); Tanselle, *Bibliographic Analysis: A Historical Introduction* (Cambridge: Cambridge University Press, 2009); Tanselle, *Descriptive Bibliography* (Charlottesville: Bibliographical Society of the University of Virginia, 2020); W. W. Greg, *A Bibliography of the English Printed Drama to the Restoration* (London: Bibliographical Society, 1970); and David F. Foxon, *The Technique of Bibliography* (Cambridge: Cambridge University Press, 1955).

11. Philip Gaskell, *A New Introduction to Bibliography* (New Castle, DE: Oak Knoll Press, 1972), 315.

12. Gaskell, *New Introduction*, 322.

13. "About," Black Bibliography Project, accessed April 1, 2021, https://blackbibliog.org /about/; "Consortium," Black Bibliography Project, accessed April 1, 2021, https://blackbibliog .org/consortium/.

14. Eric Gardner, *Black Print Unbound: The "Christian Recorder," African American Literature, and Periodical Culture* (New York: Oxford University Press, 2015), 16.

15. As reading newspapers was social, they could also be read aloud on the street for any passersby or congregating groups of people to hear the latest. They were also read aloud at homes, as mentioned. So, regardless of literacy, someone could be an engaged participant in the culture that African American presses of the nineteenth century created.

16. See Elsa Barkley Brown, "To Catch the Vision of Freedom: Reconstructing Southern Black Women's Political History, 1865–1880," in *African American Women and the Vote, 1837–1965*, ed. Ann D. Gordon et al. (Amherst: University of Massachusetts Press, 1997), 66–99; and Tera W. Hunter, *To 'Joy My Freedom: Southern Black Women's Lives and Labors After the Civil War* (Cambridge, MA: Harvard University Press, 1998).

17. Charles B. Ray was a known abolitionist and co-owner of the *Colored American* (1837–42). Other members of the committee are listed within the minutes as R. Banks, William P. McIntire, N. M. Jones, T. Woodson, and S. H. Davis.

18. *Minutes of the National Convention of Colored Citizens; Held at Buffalo; on the 15th, 16th, 17th, 18th, and 19th of August, 1843; for the Purpose of Considering Their Moral and Political Condition as American Citizens* (New York: Pierce & Reed, 1843), 28, Colored Conventions Project Digital Records, accessed June 10, 2021, https://omeka.coloredconventions.org/items /show/278.

19. *Minutes*, 28.

20. Jared Gardner, *The Rise and Fall of Early Magazine Culture* (Urbana: University of Illinois Press, 2012), 65.

21. Cynthia Lee Patterson argues that Charlotte Perkins Gilman organized the contents of her magazine *The Forerunner* (1909–16) to support or convey the moral of the serial chapter included in that issue. Though there may arguably be formats in place, it cannot be ruled out that editors organize the material within their newspaper with intent. See Cynthia Lee Patterson, "Charlotte Perkins Gilman: A Living in Periodical," *American Periodicals* 30, no. 2 (2020): 126–48.

22. Jonathan Senchyne, "Under Pressure: Reading Material Textuality in the Recovery of Early African American Print Work," *Arizona Quarterly* 75, no. 3 (Fall 2019): 112, https://doi .org/10.1353/arq.2019.0013.

23. For more on circuits of production, see Robert Darnton, "What Is the History of Books," in *The Kiss of Lamourette: Reflections in Cultural History* (New York: Norton, 1990), 107–36; and Thomas R. Adams and Nicolas Barker, "A New Model for the Study of the Book," in *A Potencie of Life: Books in Society*, ed. Nicolas Barker (London: British Library, 1993), 5–43.

24. Shadd Cary initially lists Samuel Ward and Alexander McArthur as corresponding editors for the paper; however, neither was involved in the editing and production of the newspaper. The use of their names allowed Shadd Cary to edit a paper on her own. Likewise, we know she returns to the paper on May 10, 1856, as her name appears in the newspaper's masthead alongside her brother and H. Ford Douglass. According to other scholars, H. Ford Douglass participated more as a contributor, so the data logs the editorial contributions while he is listed as an editor as done by the Shadd siblings.

25. Mary Ann Shadd Cary contributions include those under her asterisk (*), and I have listed work with her brother Isaac as "Shadd Siblings" within the descriptive bibliography database.

26. Aimi Hamraie, "Mapping Access: Digital Humanities, Disability Justice, and Sociospatial Practice," *American Quarterly* 70, no. 3 (2018): 456, https://doi.org/10.1353/aq.2018.0031.

27. Richard Jean So and Edwin Roland, "Race and Distant Reading," *PMLA* 135, no. 1 (January 2020): 61, https://doi.org/10.1632/pmla.2020.135.1.59; David J. Bodenhamer, "The Potential of Spatial Humanities," in *The Spatial Humanities: GIS and the Future of Humanities Scholarship*, ed. John Corrigan, Trevor M. Harris, and David J. Bodenhamer (Bloomington: Indiana University Press, 2010), 16–17.

28. Jane Rhodes, *Mary Ann Shadd Cary: The Black Press and Protest in the Nineteenth Century* (Bloomington: Indiana University Press, 1998).

29. I corroborated the geographic information through the Library of Congress's information, searches through academic databases, and the general internet. When I felt even slight

uncertainty, I erred on the side of caution and did not include it within the data. One example is Toronto's *Globe* (1844–1936) and London's *Globe* (1803–1921). Both are reprinted in the *Provincial Freeman*; however, it is unclear sometimes which newspaper is being cited. The *Freeman* may only state "*The Globe*" for where the item originates and little more. Further searching may clarify this, but for now I chose not to include unverified geographic data so as not to misportray the newspaper's materials.

30. This project is envisioned as a long-life project that will one day have an interactive map and, as such, use a different GIS program, like the ArcGIS or QGIS.

31. "The English in China," *Provincial Freeman*, April 4, 1857; "The Dominican Republic," *Provincial Freeman*, May 13, 1854.

32. Eric Gardner discusses how a newspaper such as the African Methodist Episcopal Church's *Christian Recorder* was repeatedly faced with the issue of subscribers not paying for their newspapers. As such, advertisements began to proliferate in the newspaper as a substitute for the lost revenue from subscribers. See *Black Print Unbound: The* Christian Recorder, *African American Literature, and Periodical Culture* (Oxford University Press, 2015).

33. S., "Lectures!!!," *Provincial Freeman*, May 10, 1856.

34. Rhodes, *Mary Ann Shadd Cary*, 30–31. For more on Chatham and its importance as an early Black settlement in Canada West, see Howard Law, "'Self-Reliance Is the True Road to Independence': Ideology and the Ex-Slaves in Buxton and Chatham" in *A Nation of Immigrants: Women, Workers, and Communities in Canadian History, 1840s–1960s*, ed. Franca Iacovetta with Paula Draper, and Robert Ventresa (Toronto: University of Toronto Press, 1998), 82–100; Heike Paul, "Out of Chatham: Abolitionism on the Canadian Frontier," *Atlantic Studies* 8, no. 2 (2011): 165–88; and Boulou Ebanda de B'bèri, Nina Reid-Maroney, and Handel Kashope Wright, eds., *The Promised Land: History and Historiography of the Black Experience in Chatham-Kent's Settlements and Beyond* (Toronto: University of Toronto Press, 2014).

35. Katherine McKittrick, *Demonic Grounds: Black Women and the Cartographies of Struggle* (Minneapolis: University of Minnesota Press, 2006), 92, 96, https://www.jstor.org/stable/10.5749/j.ctttv711.1.

36. McKittrick, *Demonic Grounds*, 99.

37. McKittrick, *Demonic Grounds*, 99. See also Eunice Toh's "Mary Ann Shadd Cary's Black Soil Ecology" within this collection, as ties to land and geography are intertwined with belonging and citizenship.

38. "Slavery in California"; Richard Mendenhall, "Slavery Now Existing in Nebraska," *Provincial Freeman*, June 24, 1854; "Kansas a Slave State," *Provincial Freeman*, May 19, 1855.

39. "Under Ground Rail Road," *Provincial Freeman*, June 30, 1855.

40. Rhodes, *Mary Ann Shadd Cary*, 17.

41. William Still appears as the "Philadelphia Correspondent" with his initials, W.S., signed at the bottom. He increasingly becomes more visible over the course of the newspaper's publication, as he becomes an agent of the *Freeman* after several issues as only a correspondent. This does not, however, account for any work done that was acknowledged within the pages of the *Freeman*. Still may have advertised Shadd Cary's newspaper prior to taking on the official position of agent.

CONTRIBUTORS

R. J. BOUTELLE is an assistant professor of English and an affiliate faculty member in Africana studies and women's, gender, and sexuality studies at the University of Cincinnati. His articles have appeared in *Atlantic Studies*, *MELUS*, and *American Literature*, and he is the author of *The Race for America: Black Internationalism in the Age of Manifest Destiny* (UNC Press, 2023).

JIM CASEY is an assistant professor of African American studies, history, and English at Penn State University. He is the associate director of the Center for Black Digital Research. Casey specializes in nineteenth-century African American studies, periodicals, and print culture, with particular emphasis on the early Black press. He is currently completing a book project, "The Invention of Editors." He is coeditor, with P. Gabrielle Foreman, of *The Colored Convention Movement: Black Organizing in the Nineteenth Century* (UNC Press, 2021).

ROSALYN GREEN is a retired research chemist and teacher with a BA in chemistry from Hampton University and an MA in Secondary Teaching from Wilmington University. She is an avid researcher of African American history and genealogy who also enjoys applying her research skills to uncover her family's history and genealogy and teach others how to do theirs too. She has authored articles that have appeared in *AAHGS News*, the *Journal of the Afro-American Historical and Genealogical Society*, and the *Bulletin of the Northumberland County Historical Society* and was a collaborator on the Shadd's Daughters Oral History Project.

LAUREN KLEIN is an associate professor in the Departments of English and Quantitative Theory and Methods at Emory University, where she also directs the Digital Humanities Lab. She is the author of *An Archive of Taste: Race and Eating in the Early United States* (University of Minnesota Press, 2020) and coauthor, with Catherine D'Ignazio, of *Data Feminism* (MIT Press, 2020).

With Matthew K. Gold, Klein edits *Debates in the Digital Humanities*, a hybrid print/digital publishing stream from the University of Minnesota Press.

KIRSTEN LEE is a doctoral candidate in English at the University of Pennsylvania. Her research and teaching interests include early African American literature, class struggle, abolition, and gender and sexuality. She is currently completing a dissertation on the meaning and location of borders/borderlands in long nineteenth-century African American literature and political thought.

BRANDI LOCKE is a doctoral candidate at the University of Delaware. Her dissertation explored literary and visual experiments in the national publications of Black women's activist organizations. Her research interests include Black feminist thought, visual culture, Black women's literary traditions, and digital and public humanities.

DEMETRA MCBRAYER studies nineteenth-century American literature at the University of Delaware, focusing on women of color and the print culture and material cultures surrounding their lives, writings, and reception. This research seeks to recover and engage the roles these women play in long histories of intellectual theory.

A. T. MOFFETT is a dancer and dance educator whose creative work centers on arts-based research. Her writing is published in the *Journal of Dance Education, Research in Dance Education* and the book *Undergraduate Research in Dance*. She serves as a dance panelist for the National Endowment for the Arts and as the executive director of the Delaware Institute for the Arts in Education. Originally from Kentucky, A. T. earned a BA in Dance from Radford University in Virginia, an MFA in dance from the University of Oregon, and an MA in Urban Affairs and Public Policy from the University of Delaware Biden School of Public Policy and Administration in 2022. She is a recipient of a 2017 Individual Artist Fellowship in Choreography from the Delaware Division of the Arts.

KRISTIN MORIAH is an assistant professor of English at Queen's University. She was a 2022 visiting fellow at the Pennsylvania State University Center for Black Digital Research and the Pennsylvania State Humanities Institute. Her research interests include sound studies and Black feminist performance, particularly the circulation of African American performance within the Black diaspora and its influence on the formation of national identity. Her research has been supported by fellowships from the Social Sciences and Research Council of Canada, the Rare Book School at the University of Virginia, and the Harry Ransom Center.

DIANNA RUBERTO conducts critical community-engaged research about the experiences and agency of Black low-income populations in urban policy processes. Her research interests include racial politics, citizen participation, urban development, and arts and cultural policy. She earned her PhD in Urban Affairs and Public Policy from the Biden School at the University of Delaware in 2023 and is currently a National Poverty Fellow in the Institute for Research on Poverty at the University of Wisconsin–Madison doing a residency in the Office of the Assistant Secretary of Planning and Evaluation in the U.S. Department of Health and Human Services.

LYNNETTE YOUNG OVERBY is a professor of Theatre and Dance (retired) and was the former director of the Community Engagement Initiative at the University of Delaware. Overby is a Teachers College, Columbia University Fellow in the Arnhold Institute for Dance Education Research, Policy, and Leadership. She also serves as a satellite partner for the Center for Black Digital Research at Penn State University. Overby's leadership roles have included serving as president of the National Dance Association and the Delaware Dance Education Organization. She is the author or editor of over sixty publications including fourteen edited and authored books. In 2018 she received the Lifetime Achievement Award from the National Dance Education Organization, and in 2021 she was appointed to serve on the National Council on the Humanities.

EUNICE TOH is an advanced PhD candidate pursuing a dual title degree in English and African American and diaspora studies at Penn State University. Her dissertation "Black Cosmo-cologies: Rebirth and Renaissance in the Long Nineteenth Century," explores how terrestrial topographies illuminate the politics and aesthetics of Black ecologies. Her work has appeared in *African American Review*.

RINALDO WALCOTT is a professor and chair of the Department of Africana and American studies at the State University at Buffalo, where he holds the

Carl V. Granger Chair in Africana and American studies. He is a writer and critic. His research is in the area of Black diaspora cultural studies and gender and sexuality with interests in nations, nationalisms, multiculturalism, policy, and education broadly defined. As an interdisciplinary Black studies scholar, Walcott has published in a wide range of venues on everything from literature to film to theater to music to policy.

MARLAS YVONNE WHITLEY is a PhD student in English and American literature at New York University and a multidisciplinary writer. Her research encompasses Black feminisms, nineteenth- and twentieth-century hemispheric studies and global modern literature with interests in Black women's intellectual histories, poetics, affect theory, and Marxist theory. Her current work is on the critical uses of color theory across Black women's media and transcendentalisms in nineteenth-century Black feminist texts.

JEWON WOO is a professor of English at Lorain County Community College, Ohio. Her research focuses on Black print culture, performance, early Black newspapers, pedagogy for underrepresented students, and digital humanities. She recently published a digital humanities project, The Ohio Black Press in the 19th Century (ohioblackpress.org). She is currently working on a book project, "Newspaper Reading Home."

INDEX